SHAKESPEARE AND RACE

This volume draws together thirteen important essays on the concept of race in Shakespeare's drama. The authors, who themselves reflect racial and geographical diversity, explore issues of ethnography, politics, religion, identity, nationalism and the distribution of power in Shakespeare's plays.

The authors write from a variety of perspectives, drawing on Elizabethan and Jacobean historical studies and recent criticism and theory. They pay attention to performances of the plays in different ages and places, as well as to the text, and they consider the distinction between authorial intent and subsequent appropriation.

An introductory essay describes the Elizabethan understanding of race and sets the context for the ensuing chapters, which reflect shifts in scholarship over the last forty years. Most are reprinted from volumes of *Shakespeare Survey*; others have been specially commissioned. They tackle the ethnic implications of Shakespearian drama in South Africa, the Caribbean, Germany and the Arab world as well as England. A broad range of plays and poems is included, while particular essays focus on *Othello, The Merchant of Venice* and *The Tempest*.

CATHERINE ALEXANDER is a Lecturer at the Shakespeare Centre, Stratford-upon-Avon and Research Fellow at the University of Birmingham. She has written on eighteenth-century appropriations of Shakespeare.

STANLEY WELLS is Emeritus Professor and Director of the Shakespeare Institute, University of Birmingham. He is General Editor of the Oxford Shakespeare, editor of *The Cambridge Companion to Shakespeare Studies* (1986), co-author of *William Shakespeare: A Textual Companion* (1987) and author of *Shakespeare: A Dramatic Life* (1995).

SHAKESPEARE AND RACE

EDITED BY

CATHERINE M. S. ALEXANDER

AND

STANLEY WELLS

CAMBRIDGE
UNIVERSITY PRESS

PUBLISHED BY THE PRESS SYNDICATE OF THE UNIVERSITY OF CAMBRIDGE
The Pitt Building, Trumpington Street, Cambridge, United Kingdom

CAMBRIDGE UNIVERSITY PRESS
The Edinburgh Building, Cambridge CB2 2RU, UK   www.cup.cam.ac.uk
40 West 20th Street, New York, NY 10011–4211, USA   www.cup.org
10 Stamford Road, Oakleigh, Melbourne 3166, Australia
Ruiz de Alarcón 13, 28014 Madrid, Spain

First published 2000

Printed in the United Kingdom at the University Press, Cambridge

Set in 11/12.5pt Baskerville No. 2   [GC]

A catalogue record for this book is available from the British Library

Library of Congress Cataloguing in Publication data

Shakespeare and race / edited by Catherine M. S. Alexander and Stanley Wells.
p. cm.
ISBN 0 521 77046 7 (hardback) – ISBN 0 521 77938 3 (pbk)
1. Shakespeare, William, 1564–1616 – Views on race.   2. Literature and
society – England – History – 16th century.   3. Literature and
society – England – History – 17th century.   4. Shakespeare, William,
1564–1616 – Characters – Blacks.   5. Blacks in literature.   6. Race in literature.
I. Alexander, Catherine M. S.   II. Wells, Stanley W., 1930–
PR3069.R33 S5   2000
822.3′3–dc21   99-089004

ISBN 0 521 77046 7 hardback
ISBN 0 521 77938 3 paperback

Contents

Illustrations

Contributors

JONATHAN BATE, *University of Liverpool*

CELIA R. DAILEADER, *University of Alabama*

MICHAEL DOBSON, *University of Surrey, Roehampton*

BALZ ENGLER, *Universität Basel*

BARBARA EVERETT, *University of Oxford*

BERNARD HARRIS, formerly *University of York*

MARGO HENDRICKS, *University of California, Santa Cruz*

G. K. HUNTER, *Yale University*

LAURENCE LERNER, *Vanderbilt University*

ANIA LOOMBA, *University of Illinois, Urbana-Champaign*

MARTIN ORKIN, *University of Haifa*

JAMES SHAPIRO, *Columbia University*

WOLE SOYINKA, *Emory University*

Editorial note

In exploring Shakespeare and Race the essays in this volume consider a range of plays and are written from a variety of perspectives by authors who themselves represent racial and geographical diversity. The chapters by Margo Hendricks and Celia R. Daileader have been specially commissioned: the remainder are reprinted from volumes of *Shakespeare Survey*. All reflect changing perceptions of the understanding and interpretation of 'race', revealing, through their difference of style and approach, some of the complexity and breadth of the subject.

These essays draw on history, criticism, theory, reception and performance, to explore ethnography, politics, religion, the creation of identity, nationalism and the distribution of power, and to grapple with the distinction between authorial intent and subsequent appropriation. We believe that they provide an informative and sometimes provocative collection which will enhance the study and understanding of Shakespeare's text.

CATHERINE M. S. ALEXANDER
STANLEY WELLS

CHAPTER I

Surveying 'race' in Shakespeare

Margo Hendricks

Like a number of Shakespearians intrigued by the question of race and the works of William Shakespeare, my first critical engagement with the matter of race in early modern English literature occurred when, as an undergraduate, I read *Othello*, in particular Gerald Eades Bentley's 1958 introduction to the play. Bentley's commentary is striking in its near total inattention to Othello's skin colour: Bentley's only comment about the matter is to state, 'Othello is a man of action whose achievement was immediately obvious to an Elizabethan audience, in spite of his exotic colour and background, because of his position as the commanding general for the greatest commercial power of the preceding century.'[1] When so much has been made of Othello's hue, Bentley's lack of commentary on the place of colour and race in the play seemed singularly odd. Yet it was not until much later that I considered Bentley's omission to be an astute stratagem to redirect the reader's attention and gaze away from Othello's colour and to his stature as a warrior, and to the complex moral dimension that status entails in Shakespeare's tragedy.

Since then, I have taught Shakespeare's canon, written about a number of his texts, and, over the course, I have developed something of a deep interest in the concept of race in Shakespeare, Renaissance English literature and culture. This interest, however, is not solely linked to what I consider the obvious markers of race – *Othello*, *The Merchant of Venice*, *Titus Andronicus* and *Antony and Cleopatra*. Rather, my interest concerns the epistemology of race in the period. Thus when asked to write the introductory essay to this volume, I pondered what such an introduction might convey to its reader in keeping with the aim of the volume, namely to highlight the on-going relevance of the essays published in the volume for the study of Shakespeare and his canon. My introduction, thus, will follow a familiar format in that it offers an overview of the contents of the volume either newly published or reprinted in the order of their composition. My own reflections at the

end of this introduction are less an essay and more a personal commentary on the matter of Shakespeare and race.

With the advent of post-colonial theory, race studies and cultural
studies, it is quite easy to believe that practitioners of these techniques
are the first to interrogate 'Shakespeare and race' as an epistemological
query; yet what this volume demonstrates is that, in fact, we are only
the inheritors of an intellectual, critical and political tradition. The
publication of *Shakespeare and Race* acknowledges the continuing importance of the intellectual labours of a generation of scholars increasingly
ignored or dismissed in the rush to 'racialize' Shakespeare's canon
and/or Elizabethan England, and also reminds us of the work yet to be
done. With reference to this last point, I must own that I consider
myself culpable. I too have frequently overlooked the work of an 'older'
generation of Shakespeare scholarship on race. Now I have begun to
redress this oversight.

STILL SIGNIFICANT AFTER ALL THESE YEARS

In 1958 *Shakespeare Survey* published an essay entitled 'A Portrait of a
Moor' by Bernard Harris, which draws attention to the acquisition by
the Shakespeare Institute of a portrait of Morocco's Ambassador to
Elizabeth's court in 1600. As Harris notes, the 'portrait . . . is of considerable interest to students of history, of art and of the theatre' (p. 23).
For the historian (literary and social), the painting serves to put to rest
a long-standing debate as to whether there was a viable presence of
Moors and Africans in Elizabethan England. For Harris, the painting
provides visual, and thus irrefutable evidence, or 'ocular proof'. Harris
uses this portrait as a starting-point for a more detailed account of the
complex 'commercial and diplomatic' 'relations between England and
Barbary' (p. 23). This ambassadorial portrait reveals a geo-political
complexity that can, as Harris argues, 'assist a producer of *The Merchant
of Venice* when he comes to the stage direction, "Enter Morochus, a
tawny Moore all in white"' (p. 23).

In his efforts to link the English social history behind and alongside
the 1600 painting of the Ambassador from Morocco, Harris charts the
relations between these two geographic spaces: the role of the Barbary
Company (led by the Earls of Leicester and Warwick) in fostering an
alliance; the merchant adventurers Richard, George, Arnold and Jasper
Tomson; and the correspondence and financial details surrounding the
visit of Morocco's ambassador to England. As Harris shows, the Moorish

embassy created some havoc, politically and financially, for Elizabeth's subjects. For example, John Stow writes:

Notwithstanding all this kindness shown them together with their dyet and all other provisions for six moneths space wholly at the Queenes charges, yet such was their inveterate hate unto our Christian religion and estate as they could not endure to give any manner of alms, charitie, or relief, either in money or broken meat, unto any English poore. (p. 32)

In the writings of the day, the Moors were described as subtle, 'stubborn', 'bestial' and intolerant. This imagery and commentary, Harris argues, suggest that 'To Elizabethan Londoners the appearance and conduct of the Moors was a spectacle and an outrage, emphasizing the nature of the deep difference between themselves and their visitors, between their Queen and this "erring Barbarian"' (p. 35). Thus, Harris concludes, 'When Shakespeare chose, for this audience, to present a Moor as his hero, he was not perhaps confused in his racial knowledge, simply more aware than his contemporaries of the complex pattern made by white and black' (p. 35).

Despite this final comment, and his earlier allusion to *The Merchant of Venice*, Harris largely ignores Shakespeare's plays. It is left to the readers of 'A Portrait of a Moor' intuitively to make the interpretative links with Shakespeare's drama. Even so, Harris effectively sketches a historical landscape that makes sense of both *Othello* and *The Merchant of Venice* as textually formed and framed by the changing racial landscape of Early Modern England. As Harris himself notes, 'To recount the story of the embassy in some detail is to take us nearer to Shakespeare's England, perhaps even, in a sense, to Shakespeare's Moor' (p. 24). I would add that the portrait of the ambassador from Morocco and Harris' essay serve to remind us of the political forces that frame a society's 'racial imagination' just as effectively as the literary ones.

G. K. Hunter's 'Elizabethans and Foreigners' similarly maps the 'impact of foreigners on' Elizabethan society (p. 37). Yet Hunter's account is strikingly different from 'A Portrait of a Moor' in two ways. First, Hunter is much more intrigued by the impact of this contact in terms of Elizabethan literature, and second, he is much less interested in the actual presence of these foreigners in Elizabethan society than in the 'framework of assumptions concerning foreigners' (p. 37) who enter England during the sixteenth century. As a result, 'Elizabethans and Foreigners' becomes a model for a literary analysis that bridges the presumed divide between 'social' and 'literary' history; in essence, Hunter's essay cogently demonstrates the importance of links between context and interpretation. Hunter begins by asking a crucial question: 'What was the framework of assumptions concerning foreigners' in Elizabethan England? Drawing upon a wide range of texts – travel accounts, romances, plays, and poetry – Hunter reminds us that the Elizabethan (and by extension Shakespeare's) vision of foreignness had a complex and evolving material and philosophical history.

Beginning in the middle ages, the English engagement with 'foreigners' often functioned on two levels: spiritual and material. In the early travel narratives, Mandeville's *Travels* for example, places such as Jerusalem, Africa and India were frequently idealized in terms of their spiritual significance as sites of biblical history and theological relevance. As new knowledge about the world, acquired through voyages to Africa, India and the Americas, supplanted old, the Elizabethan imagination had to be refitted. In essence, the 'framework of assumptions' about foreigners had to be expanded. What is significant, however, is that the impact of these voyages on the literary imagination in the sixteenth century may be less dramatic than we have come to believe. As Hunter argues, 'we should beware of supposing that a pattern of races emerged readily from the Europe that Christendom had become, a pattern capable of supplying moral discriminations rich and complex enough for literary use' (p. 45).

What apparently occurred, according to Hunter, was the emergence of 'material for caricature,' not 'for character' (p. 45). Within Elizabethan culture and literature, the foreigner serves to inaugurate a 'process of *vulgarization*' (p. 47) based upon the intimate knowledge of the foreigner. Thus, in Hunter's view, the more deeply racialized stereotypes and characterizations are those most familiar to the English – Dutch, German, Italian, Irish and Spanish nationals. And importantly, the Elizabethan's 'awareness of foreigners was closely conditioned by a traditional religious outlook on the world' (p. 51). This 'religious outlook', of course, situated Jews and followers of Islam as the antithesis to all Christians. Even so, the Elizabethan imagination could sustain the racialization of the Italian as a deeply held belief alongside the traditional racializing of the Jew and the emerging racialization of the American Indian.

Despite their dates, these two essays easily reflect the type of scholarship typical of New Historicism. Both 'A Portrait of a Moor' and 'Elizabethans and Foreigners' offer 'thick descriptions' of Elizabethan culture and society that have come to mark the type of inter-textual analyses generated by New Historicists. Even more significant is the way these two essays cogently adumbrate a Renaissance English discourse of race without recourse to contemporary (i.e. twentieth-century) theoretical discussions. In other words, both Harris and Hunter manage to convey the relationship between cultural interaction and the emergence of racial ideologies as acts of history. For both Harris and Hunter, though in differing ways, the literary text encapsulates the assumptions, expectations and representations that define the Elizabethan notion of race and, as a consequence, provides the idea with its historical and thus empirical meaning. Only in their subtle avoidance of the more vexing issue dancing liminally on the periphery of their analyses – is Shakespeare 'racist'? – do these essays appear 'dated'. That is, neither author directly engages the implications of his findings for questions about authorial subjectivity and its texts.

In quite different ways, Barbara Everett's '"Spanish" Othello: the Making of Shakespeare's Moor' and Wole Soyinka's 'Shakespeare and the Living Dramatist' entertain the problematic that Harris and Hunter astutely avoid: is there a link between the politics of Shakespeare and race studies and the politics of race inherent in his canon? The argument of Everett's '"Spanish" Othello' is that '"Moorishness" was a condition that had a meaning, for Shakespeare and his audiences, once casually familiar though long lost to us' (p. 66). Everett bases her argument not on Venice and/or Shakespeare's source, Cinthio, as one might expect but rather on the Spanish genealogy behind three of Shakespeare's characters in *Othello*. Everett traces the Spanish context for the names of Iago, Roderigo and by extension the Moor. According to her, Shakespeare's audience would most likely have recognized that the anglicized version of Iago was James, that St James was the patron saint of Spain, and hence have been aware of the general history of St James as 'Santiago Matamoros, St James the Moor-killer' (p. 67). Thus, Everett contends, 'Every time the name "Iago" drops with helpless unconsciousness from the Moor's lips, Shakespeare's audience remembered what we have long forgotten: that Santiago's great role in Spain was as enemy to the invading Moor, who was figurehead there of the Muslim kingdom' (p. 68).

Everett acknowledges that there are limits to this type of reading, but the 'imaginative resonance possessed by mere names' often reflects 'certain harsh facts in the world outside the plays' (p. 68). Like Harris and Hunter, Everett draws upon social and political events of the day to frame her interpretation; she cites Elizabeth's proclamation expelling 'negars and blackamoors' from England, papal commentary on Moors and Jews, and Spanish history. What is significant in Everett's essay, however, is her observation on Othello's colour:

If Shakespeare himself had been asked what colour his Moor was, I think he would have answered that few actors in his experience would permit a shade dark enough to hide the play of expression. Othello is, in short, the colour the fiction dictates. And it is in order to make this point that I have hoped to suggest that the Moor may be quite as much 'Spanish' as 'African'. (pp. 72–3)

This suggestion is intended as a 'challenge [to] our perhaps too simple "African" sense of Othello' (pp. 78–9). Ultimately, Everett concludes that Othello's links to the Moorish figure Rogero in Ariosto's *Orlando Furioso* may provide a better sense of Othello's racial and social identity than any other source, especially a source that dwells on his colour (as Cinthio's text does). In the end, for Everett, Othello 'is almost any "colour" one pleases, so long as it permits his easier isolation and destruction by his enemies and by himself' (p. 72).

Wole Soyinka's 'Shakespeare and the Living Dramatist' also explores the 'ethnicity' of Shakespeare and his characters through the politics of culture. In what might be viewed as a precursor to post-colonialist readings of Shakespeare's drama, Soyinka balances his deep admiration for what he terms 'the paradox of timelessness and history' that infuses Shakespeare's poetics and the politics of race and culture that surround this most complex Elizabethan writer and dramatist. In 'Shakespeare and the Living Dramatist,' Soyinka elegantly and imaginatively demonstrates the fluidity of racial identity in a world shaped by colonialism and its politics. In the Arab world, William Shakespeare has nearly the same acclaim that he possesses in Europe. In fact, as Soyinka states, 'the Arab world was not content to adopt or "reclaim" Shakespeare's works' but to claim him as one of their own (p. 84). That is, Arab writers and dramatists have argued that Shakespeare 'was in fact an Arab. His real name, cleansed of its anglicized corruption, was Shayk al-Subair, which everyone knows of course is as dune-bred an Arabic name as any English poet can hope for' (p. 84). As a consequence, the translations and adaptations of Shakespeare's plays by Arab writers and dramatists serve only to 'return' Shakespeare's canon to its rightful language.

Soyinka's ironic piece about the Arabization of Shakespeare only partially conceals his astute yet ambivalent reading of the politics of the Shakespeare industry and its implications for post-colonial societies. Soyinka begins with a comment on his own experience at an RSC production:

Some years ago, I watched a production of *Antony and Cleopatra* at the Aldwych, by the Royal Shakespeare Company – and winced throughout the entire night. We all have our prejudices of course, but some of these prejudices are the result of experience. Perhaps the RSC knew that it had a problem in persuading even an English audience to accept any interpretation of Cleopatra by an English actress – so the actress sent up the whole thing. . . . (pp. 85–6)

His reaction, as Soyinka posits, is balanced by 'the near-unanimous opinion of the Arabic critics themselves on the translations and adaptations of their "compatriot" Shayk al-Subair's masterpieces in that they were, in the main, the work of "scald rhymers" who "ballad him out of tune"' (p. 86).

Soyinka notes that, among Arab writers,

it is claimed – as one of the reasons for endowing Shakespeare with Arab paternity – that only an Arab could have understood or depicted a Jew so 'convincingly' as in *The Merchant of Venice*. Similarly, the focus is sometimes placed on *Othello* – the Moor's dignity even in folly has been held up as convincing proof that no European could have fleshed out this specific psychology of a jealousy complicated by racial insecurity but a man from beneath the skin – an Arab at the very least. (p. 87)

To substantiate this argument, Soyinka writes, one need only look closely at Shakespeare's works where his use of non-English locales further distances him from any English roots. In the end, Soyinka observes, 'one acknowledges with gratitude the subjective relation of other poets and dramatists to the phenomenon of Shakespeare, for even the most esoteric of their claims lead one, invariably, to the productive source itself, and to the gratification of celebrating dramatic poetry anew' (p. 99).

In his ironic discussion of the uses to which post-colonial Africa and Arab nations put Shakespeare, Soyinka only hints at a traditional notion of race in relation to Shakespeare's works. As a novelist and dramatist, Soyinka clearly is less interested in the politics of race in Shakespeare's poetry than he is in the poetry of politics. His 'Shakespeare and the Living Dramatist' thus distances itself from the other essays in this volume. Yet Soyinka's discussion serves as an important segue to those concerned with 'race', nation and Shakespeare. As Soyinka highlights, importing Shakespeare requires a 'naturalization' and assimilation of his characters, themes and poetics. And, as Soyinka contends, Shakespeare's use of 'foreign' locales makes this naturalization process quite simple. As Shakespeare's 'racial identity' disappears, what is left is the power and the 'timelessness' of his poetic voice.

Balz Engler's 'Shakespeare in the Trenches' engages the competing 'racial' claims that two nations, England and Germany, make on the person and canon of William Shakespeare and his poetic voice. Engler's essay looks at a particular moment in Shakespearian history, the tercentenary of Shakespeare's death, April 1916, a time when England and Germany were at war. Both nations prepared celebrations in honour of Shakespeare but, as Engler illustrates, these celebrations were strikingly different yet had the same political and ideological purpose. In England, the celebration was an elaborate week-long patriotic affair. Productions, publications, even a 'Shakespeare prayer', were devised to recognize not only Shakespeare's 'genius' but more importantly his significance as a 'patriot.'

The German celebration, while much more subdued, was no less firm in its claim to Shakespeare – though some Germans questioned the propriety of the continued performance of his plays. Despite this minority voice, and although he was born an Englishman, Shakespeare's 'opinions, as expressed in his plays, were in accordance with the German position in the war', according to Rudolf Brotanek (p. 103). In fact, Shakespeare became an ideological object fought over by both nations; in a prologue to a German production of *Twelfth Night*, Feste delivered a 'message from Shakespeare' whereby Shakespeare declares himself a fugitive who seeks and finds a 'second home' in Germany. As Engler notes, 'In Germany the claim that Shakespeare was *unser*, ours, presented a problem, of course' (p. 105). German response to this dilemma was to remind the German people that Germany 'had naturalized Shakespeare in a long effort of appropriation. . . . As such Shakespeare could come to be considered one of the three greatest German authors, along with Goethe and Schiller' (p. 106). Ultimately, Engler's essay reminds us that 'Shakespeare' is always a contextual matter: 'the context in which we perceive Shakespeare and his works, *how we use them*, [is what] determines their meaning' (p. 107).

This dictum might very well be the motto of 'the Shakespeare industry' and is the central concern in Michael Dobson's essay, 'Bowdler and Britannia: Shakespeare and the National Libido.' Since the late seventeenth century, editions of Shakespeare's plays and poetry have spawned what has become trivialized as 'the Bard Biz', especially in the publishing industry. For Dobson, the Bowdler edition reflects the complex intersection of the veneration of William Shakespeare and 'the construction of modern sexuality and the construction of English national identity' (p. 112). In a cogent reading, Dobson brings to light the policing of Shakespeare's text as part of the deployment of Shakespeare as national poet and his works as moral exempla. For example, George Granville's production of *The Merchant of Venice* in 1701 included an appearance by Shakespeare, or at least his ghost, on stage. Informed by the ghost of John Dryden of the tendency to present homoeroticism on the stage, Shakespeare's ghost 'promises to do what he can to remedy the situation, offering his play (now properly *"Adorn'd and rescu'd by a faultless hand"*) as a contribution to the internal discipline which is the proper and unique function of literature' (p. 114).

Productions and editions of Shakespeare's plays were purged of potential or real eroticism and, as Dobson argues, became part of a national trend to 'discipline and promote British manhood' (p. 116). Furthermore, as an icon of English masculinity Shakespeare himself had to be represented as 'disciplined'. That is, for Shakespeare to function as a national icon 'his body [must be] left out of the picture entirely' (p. 117). Or, if his body remains it is a decidedly heterosexual one (the insistence that the sonnets are addressed solely to a woman for example). What is at stake, Dobson contends, is the nation's own identity, and that identity perforce must be masculine, British, and a virile heterosexual. The mandate for 'the lopping away of his [Shakespeare's] particular textual and sexual lapses' permits eighteenth-century editors and producers of Shakespearian plays to link Shakespeare's 'transcendence' of both his 'own body' and his 'corpus' (p. 121) to his stature as patriot *par excellence*. Nowhere is this better exemplified than in the 1769 Stratford Jubilee.

As Dobson notes, this celebration 'did not seem to require the performance or even the quotation of any of Shakespeare's plays' (p. 121). One reviewer observed, in the *Middlesex Journal*: 'It has been generally believed, that the institution of the Stratford jubilee was only a matter of taste and amusement; but the more sagacious see a great political view carried on at the bottom of it' (p. 121). In citing this review, Dobson points out that Shakespeare is not only to be idealized as an example of British ingenuity and productivity but also as an aid to populating 'the Midlands in the cause of England's industrial future' (p. 121). With the 1769 Stratford Jubilee Shakespeare's role as national icon of masculinity and creativity is solidified. In essence, as Dobson playfully puns, what the Stratford Jubilee bore witness to was 'Shakespeare's triumphant installation as Britain's national Willy'.

One of the more complicated and fraught issues facing scholars interested in the matter of race in Shakespeare's works emerges in relation to Shakespeare's dramatic representations of Jews. Two essays reprinted in this volume, James Shapiro's 'Shakespur and the Jewbill' and Laurence Lerner's 'Wilhelm S and Shylock', direct our attention to the contentious place Jews hold in the national discourse and the racial imagination of modern England. In 'Shakespur and the Jewbill', James Shapiro examines the role Shakespeare performs in the debates surrounding the Jewish Naturalization Act of 1753, also referred to as 'the Jew Bill'. Shapiro's historical overview of the genesis of the bill, the political controversies that emerged around the bill, and the use to which Shakespeare was put offers us a profound insight into one of the vexing questions facing Shakespearian studies – the place of anti-Semitism or racism in Shakespeare's canon.

In his insightful discussion, Shapiro reminds us that eighteenth-century English attitudes towards Jews should be viewed in terms of the modern notions of race and racism. Centred on the question, 'What is an Englishman?' debates over the Naturalization Act resound with familiar cultural stereotypes, analogies and pronouncements. Central to all of these tactics is a long-standing notion that Jews were funda-mentally, immutably distinct from the English – no matter that the Jew was born in England, as were his ancestors. Rooted in the broader discourse of racism and anti-Semitism sweeping European societies, English discourse about Jews linked itself to this modern ideology even as it drew upon its own literary past, in this instance, Shakespeare's *The Merchant of Venice*, to create a peculiarly English perspective *vis-à-vis* English Jews. The production of this play during the height of the debates over the Naturalization Act became a vivid reminder of a prevailing negative mythology about Jews: 'the threat of Jews circum-cising Englishmen, taking Christian servants, and racially contaminat-ing the English nation' (p. 128). This production became an integral part of the propaganda campaign to protect England and its English-ness, in essence a 'racialized nationalism' (p. 135).

Laurence Lerner's 'Wilhelm S and Shylock' offers a contrasting view in his analysis of the uses to which Shylock and Shakespeare have been put in the name of 'racialized nationalism'. Lerner's method in the essay is quite similar to Soyinka's: Lerner refers to Shakespeare as 'Wilhelm S', locates Shakespeare's talents/genius in a 'Nordic pro-fundity', and establishes Shakespeare's connection with Nazi Germany. Lerner begins his discussion by noting that what 'led Nazi Germany to congratulate S for his understanding of racial psychology was *The Merchant of Venice*' (p. 140). This reading of Shakespeare's play, despite its obvious ironic (almost tongue-in-cheek) style, raises a number of insightful questions about paradoxes engendered by the political dimensions of *The Merchant of Venice*. Lerner's critique is directed at the uses to which Shakespeare's play has been put, especially decidedly political interpretations and the interpretative community that generates those interpretations. As Lerner notes,

Wilhelm S offers us an anti-Semitic *Merchant of Venice*, and we, reacting like good liberals, are upset by it. My 'thought experiment' was a way of asking how important is the difference between writing an anti-Semitic play, and offering an anti-Semitic interpretation of a play written in 1597. (p. 144)

For Lerner there is a difference and it is history which provides that distinction.

The essays of Shapiro and Lerner, despite their divergences, also respond to the vexing question associated with Shakespeare's plays: is Shakespeare racist and/or anti-Semitic?[2] Carefully dissociating themselves from the reductive and, not surprisingly, visceral reaction – 'authorial intention' – Shapiro and Lerner remind their readers that every commonplace has its complex historiography. The commonplace invocation and deployment of *The Merchant of Venice* to discriminate, persecute and redefine definitions of humanity through an ideologically driven campaign against people of Jewish heritage must be seen as precisely that, and not an essential attribute of the playwright. In other words, it is the play and not the man that bears the burden of nineteenth- and twentieth-century anti-Semitism.

POST-MODERN SHAKESPEARE

Important studies such as Harris's and Hunter's, not surprisingly, lay dormant as Shakespearian scholars and critics embraced the tenets of New Criticism, structuralism, and Russian Formalism in the 1960s and 1970s. Questions of politics, history and race quickly gave way to questions of language and form. In the late 1980s, two theoretical methodologies, cultural studies and New Historicism, inspired a 'next generation' engagement with race and Shakespeare. The effect was to revive interest in the scholarship of individuals such as Hunter, Harris, Winthrop Jordan and Samuel Chew. It would not be inappropriate to argue that Celia R. Daileader's 'Casting Black Actors: beyond Othellophilia' and Ania Loomba's ' "Delicious Traffick": Racial and Religious Difference on Early Modern Stages' reflect this revival and the nature of the current critical and scholarly practice in what can be termed the study of race in Shakespeare criticism.

Ania Loomba's ' "Delicious Traffick" ' begins definitively: 'For at least the last two hundred years, "race" has functioned as one of the most powerful and yet most fragile markers of social difference' (p. 203). Exploring what she terms the 'mirror-dance on the stages of Shakespeare's time – a time which can be characterized as either the last period in history where ethnic identities could be understood as fluid, or as the first moment of the emergence of modern notions of "race" ' – Loomba cogently brings together postcolonial theories, feminism and the problems of historiography to frame her analysis of the iconography of race on the Elizabethan and Jacobean stages. Loomba's essay is less an argument than an overview of the place race had on the stage in Shakespeare's culture. Where Loomba skilfully reminds her readers of the fluidity of racial iconography is in her discussion of the problematics of the 'Moor'. In contrast to Everett's essay, Loomba draws our attention to the literary conjunction of Moor and blackness, despite the diversity of 'skin colour' across Islamic cultures and the political agenda this conjunction is intended to serve. As Loomba argues:

Othello does not move from a glamorous black to a hated Turk; rather, we need to notice how both blacks and Turks can be glamorized as well as hated in contemporary representations, and how the two were interconnected, both in *Othello* and in the culture at large, via the Spanish discourse on Moorishness, via medieval stereotypes of black Turks, or Egyptians, and also by more recent developments in global relations. (p. 206)

Loomba's comment on the importance of 'recent developments in global relations' echoes the remarks of G. K. Hunter and Bernard Harris. Like these two earlier critics, Loomba enlarges her reading of Shakespeare's drama through careful attention to the global politics shaping late sixteenth- and early seventeenth-century English culture. Where Loomba exceeds the reach of Hunter and Harris is in her inclusion of gender in the critical matrix for reading Shakespeare's drama. As Loomba cogently suggests, there are two sites around which early modern anxieties and obsessions with 'race' can be identified: conversion and sexuality. With regard to the former, Loomba writes that 'conversion was viewed as a perpetually unstable condition: converts to Christianity were suspected of covertly practising Judaism or Islam, or of interpreting Christianity in the light of their previous faiths' (p. 209). Furthermore, she contends, 'it is precisely when faith could be improvised that the question of authenticity became especially urgent' (p. 210). That is, when 'inner faith' could not be 'match[ed to] exterior show' conversions became increasingly suspect. Thus, Loomba observes, 'a Marrano or a Morisco cannot be a quintessential Renaissance man even though he may represent the essence of Renaissance self-fashioning' (p. 212).

It is, however, the problematics of race and its association with gender, in particular the depiction of the converted woman, where Loomba offers her most significant contribution to explorations of race and Shakespeare. Her analyses informed by the work of feminist Shakespearians such as Lynda Boose and Mary Jane Metzger, Loomba traces the ways in which the 'exchange of women', which 'has always signalled the vulnerability of cultural borders', 'took on new urgent meanings in an early modern England which was simultaneously looking outward and consolidating its national culture in linguistic, religious and ethnic terms' (p. 218). Women characters such as Tamora in *Titus Andronicus* and Cleopatra 'highlight a tension' between ethnicity and colour, between politics and gender, and between religions; yet, as Loomba concludes, the 'convertible body of women' becomes 'the "delicious traffick" between cultures, religions and races' on the Shakespearian stage (p. 219).

Where Loomba's reading addresses the dramatic parameters of Shakespeare's 'global' politics, Celia R. Daileader's essay, 'Casting Black Actors: beyond Othellophilia', localizes the politics of race and Shakespeare in the physical body of the black actor on the modern English stage. Daileader focuses on the two media through which the late twentieth-century spectator's and actor's racial gaze is/can be constructed through Shakespeare's drama, in particular *Othello*: stage and photography (the latter effecting a kind of permanency that the former lacks). This gaze so constrains almost any actor playing Othello that, according to Daileader, he seems 'to be playing the same character in [whatever Shakespeare play he acts] – and the more one looks at that character, the more he looks like Othello' (p. 178). Daileader labels 'this phenomenon' 'Othellophilia' and, in an insightful discussion, she illuminates the degree to which racial ideologies become inescapable for the 'black' actor once he performs the role of Othello.

Central to 'Othellophilia' are the problems engendered by the concept of 'colour-blind casting'. Directing her attention to the Royal Shakespeare Company (RSC), Daileader organizes the essay into four sections: the first section provides a historical account of RSC tradition in casting black males in Shakespearian roles; the second explores black/white imagery and the related theme of sexual purity as played out in *Othello* and echoed in *Troilus* and in *White Devil*; and sections three and four focus on the ways in which the RSC productions 'replicate' the 'racialized language' of Shakespeare's text. It is Daileader's aim to 'reconstruct the scene of the casting crime in *Troilus*,' and to illustrate the 'way Othellophilia, with its attendant opportunities for something approaching biracial porn, functions to exploit both white women *and* black men' (p. 179).

Daileader's reading of *Othello* and *Troilus and Cressida* reminds us of the powerful effect directorial decisions in lighting, costume, music and setting have in setting the limits of meaning in these two plays. Black actors (whether British or American), as Daileader astutely shows, are quickly interpellated as erotic objects of and for the spectatorial gaze in the way the RSC casts and costumes, and importantly the way critics respond to the casting and costuming. As Daileader notes, despite the fact that Hugh Quarshie and Ray Fearon 'achieved a measure of success in the RSC *without* playing Othello', both actors remain shadowed by 'Othellophilia' until they have portrayed the Venetian General (as Fearon did in 1999, after this essay was written). What is strikingly notable in Daileader's argument is that, contrary to the 'liberal intentions' behind colour-blind casting, 'a director with truly liberal intentions in casting a black actor [in any Shakespearian role] will have to work hard to surmount audience preconceptions' (p. 195). In other words, the deeply embedded racial assumptions and expectations about the place, status and behaviour of blacks effectively circumvent any well-intentioned efforts on the part of a 'liberal' director.

In matters of race and sex, Daileader suggests, the inclination towards 'Othellophilia' is a factor of both the long historical shadow Shakespeare's play has cast on the performance of 'race' in Shakespearian theatre and the ideologies that figure blackness as erotic and dangerous. As a consequence, whether Ray Fearon plays Francisco in Kenneth Branagh's filmed version of *Hamlet* or Paris in the RSC's *Troilus and Cressida* or Romeo in the RSC's 1997 *Romeo and Juliet*, critics and spectators will inevitably view his performance through the lens of Othello's blackness and all that it entails. It is this inevitability which prompts Daileader to coin 'the term Othellophilia' and to remark that while she 'was not initially conscious of the fact that it ended in a homophone for Shakespeare's famous female suicide', as the essay's argument clarified itself, 'the feminizing and self-destructive suffix seem[ed] appropriate' (p. 199), given the recurring erotic display of the black actor's body as part of the Royal Shakespeare Company's response to his skin colour.

As Ania Loomba's essay demonstrates, there has been a return (so to speak) to contextual evidence, that is, the archive, in the scholarly study of 'Race and Shakespeare'. In my own work on Shakespeare and the question of race, I have not only begun to re-read (and read anew) critical studies such as those of Bernard Harris and G. K. Hunter, but also texts published during the years Shakespeare wrote. What I have discovered is that there is still much work to be done on the question. The one area which interests me and which I believe remains under-scrutinized is the epistemological and philosophical conceptualization of race in the early modern period. As an example, I want to trace briefly how a philological inquiry can shed light on the multivalent nature of the idea of race in Shakespeare's England.

In 1591 Richard Percyvale published *Bibliotheca Hispanica. Containing a Grammar, with a Dictionarie in Spanish, English and Latine, gathered out of divers good Authors: very profitable for the studious of the Spanish toong.*[3] Despite its obvious indebtedness to the idea behind traditional bilingual lexicons, Percyvale's work marks a new trajectory in English vernacular and cultural history. For, unlike earlier compilers of lexicons and dictionaries (which were primarily Greek and Latin), Percyvale produced a dictionary not for the grammar school or university student but for the lay-person who might require fluency in Spanish. In other words, Percyvale's intended audience was the merchant, lawyer, sailor or soldier whose livelihood took him to Spain or its territories or who had dealings with Spaniards in England. There are a number of striking elements to Percyvale's dictionary: its familiarly modern layout, its ease of use and its attempt to be inclusive. What stand out, however, are two aspects which are seemingly unrelated yet when juxtaposed become a vivid reminder of the significance of race to Elizabethan society. The first aspect is Percyvale's detailed account of the origins of the Spanish language,[4] and the second is the curious absence of the Spanish word *raza* – 'race' – as a main entry in the dictionary.

On first glance Percyvale's dictionary appears remarkably apolitical in its handling of semantics. Words are familiarly cross-referenced, entries when needed have sufficient diversity of English analogues to permit the reader's understanding of a word's complexity, and the pronouncing key is easily comprehended. Yet this organizational apoliticism, I would argue, begs critical attention. A reader who turns to the Spanish section to look up the Spanish equivalency for the English word 'race' discovers that it is not listed as a main entry. Upon further scrutiny, our reader finds that 'raza' does surface, however, on a number of occasions in the dictionary, in both its Spanish and English sections, but only as a synonym for other main entries.

While we can only speculate as to why Percyvale decided to omit 'raza' as a main entry in the Spanish section of the dictionary, it would not be presumptuous to suppose that he assumed his readers would be familiar enough with the word's Italian spelling and signification that inclusion in his dictionary was not warranted. Whatever the reason, Percyvale's other entries which cite 'raza' – *casta, abolengo* and *abolorio* – provide an understanding of what 'raza' signifies, even if indirectly. In each entry, Percyvale notes as English linguistic equivalents the words 'a race, a lineage, a breed, genus'. The situation takes on a different shading if we recognize that the absence of an entry for 'raza' may be explained by looking to the word's problematic semantics in Spain. As a number of critics have shown, 'raza' in Renaissance Spain[5] was already signifying a complex (and often contradictory) classification system, which included ethnicity and phenotype. Perhaps, inhabiting a society still wedded to conceptualizing race in terms of lineage or genealogy, Percyvale was not yet convinced that this signification was important enough to his English readers.

John Minsheu, on the other hand, in his continuation of Percyvale's dictionary, was apparently under no such illusions. At first glance, Minsheu's *A Dictionarie in Spanish and English. First published into the English tongue by Ric. Percivale gent. Now enlarged and amplified with many thousand words* (1611) appears to make only minor or slight changes to Percyvale's *Biblioteca Hispanica*, yet a careful scrutiny reveals that Minsheu's entries are far more significant additions to Percyvale's lexicon than his title page suggests.[6] In his dictionary, Minsheu includes not only an entry for 'raza' but one other term which will have major ideological consequences in the long run, 'mestizo'. Minsheu's handling of the Spanish 'raza' and English 'race' does indeed 'enlarge' on what is missing in Percyvale. For example, in the Spanish-to-English section, the entry for 'raza' (or 'raca') is defined as 'a ray or beame shining through a hole. Also a race, stocke, kinde or breede'. Additionally, in the English-to-Spanish, Minsheu writes, 'line or race – vide Casta, Raca'; and under the entry titled 'race or stocke' he directs the reader to 'vide Raca, caste, Abolorio, Abolengo'. In doing so, Minsheu creates a dictionary which offers its users as much information as they will need to comprehend all the vagaries of the Spanish language and its racial lexicon, even going so far as to provide definitions for subsets within entries. Yet every entry seems to reiterate a prevailing semantics; whatever Spanish word one uses – *casta*, 'raza', *abolorio, abolengo* – it will inevitably signify in English 'a race, a linage, a breed, issue of one's bodie, a progenie, a stocke an offspring' or 'pedigree, stocke, or descent of kindred'.[7]

I want to highlight one more instance of augmentation on the part of Minsheu. As I noted earlier, in his *Bibliotheca Hispanica*, Percyvale does not provide entries for the Spanish terms familiar to postmodern readers – such as *mulatto* and *mestizo*. Minsheu, interestingly enough, includes *mestizo* but not *mulatto*. Moreover, in his definition of *mestizo* Minsheu does not cross-reference other Spanish terms or offer English equivalents. Instead, he writes, 'mestizo m. that which is come or sprung of a mixture of two kinds, as a blacke-Moore and a Christian, a mungrell dog or beast'. What Minsheu does in defining *mestizo* this way is to dissociate the word (and thus the concept) from the term (and concept) 'raza'; in effect, 'raza' (and its English equivalent, race) is used to connote class-based genealogy, while *mestizo* (and 'kind') registers an identity rooted in species or, intriguingly, religion.

What Minsheu's definition misses, or to be more accurate, misrepresents, is that, in the period under scrutiny, the word *mestizo* was rarely applied to anyone born of sexual relations between African (or Moor) and Christian; in fact, the term generally referred to offspring of Spanish and American Indian unions. Second, it was rare for *mestizo* to signal non-human sexual relations. What Minsheu seems to do is to draw upon a number of different terms in the Spanish and Portuguese racial lexicons (*mestizo, mestico, mulatto* and *morisco*), blend their meanings, and offer his English readers a hybrid explanation. As Minsheu constitutes it, *mestizo* functions as a less than desirable term of reference. To categorize a person as a *mestizo*, then, is not only to point to a problematic genealogy but to deny that individual a 'racial' history.

The emergence of dictionaries such as Percyvale's and Minsheu's, and their attempts to carefully delineate (and limit) the meaning of race, is not a coincidence. On the contrary, these dictionaries represent a major attempt to localize the semantic possibilities of the word 'race' in the face of increasing perturbations within existing social relations. In fact, I would further contend that these lexical efforts are linked initially not just to the colonial practices under way in the Americas but also to changing class and social dynamics in England itself. Between 1560 and 1660, England's political economy and social institutions underwent a radical realignment. The English nation–state was no longer firmly rooted in a feudal mode of production; capitalist economic relations and institutions were beginning to shape all aspects of its social relations. Merchants, lawyers and other professionals (especially as civil servants) were an important defining presence in Tudor/Stuart culture. Though an increasing number of merchants and financiers came from the nobility or the gentry (younger sons), the majority of this class were 'commoners'. The increased wealth of this emergent class produced fundamental changes in a social fabric once thought immutable. Money enabled these 'commoners' to live in a manner once thought solely the privilege of the nobility, to acquire the trappings of 'civility' (land, education, luxury goods), and, more importantly, to procure titles (either through service, purchase or marriage).[8]

The patriarchal feudalism which had given rise to the word 'race', and its social legitimacy, was inexorably being transformed by the dynamics of mercantile capitalism and the class that it was to engender, the bourgeoisie. It is no coincidence, then, that the word 'race' and its conceptual semantics require lexical elucidation at the same time that the English capitalist/mercantile class is just beginning to solidify its presence as a political, cultural, and social power as a consequence of its economic hegemony. And it is this ambiguous, or more accurately, rather flexible semantic possibility which may have prompted sixteenth- and seventeenth-century English lexicographers, such as Percyvale, Minsheu and John Florio, to undertake the onerous task of constructing a taxonomic system for the word 'race' that was prescriptive yet, when necessary, inclusive. 'Race', these dictionary compilers seem to suggest, is capable of accommodating whatever shifts may arise in the emerging political economy. Thus early modern writers can deploy the word in a variety of ways without once having to evince concern for the political contradictions which may surface.[9] In effect, because of these types of lexical and semiotic interventions, the word 'race' required just enough semantic augmentation to permit the possibility of delineation specific enough to mark a person's class but general enough to allow it to be used for other purposes.

Of the various semantic registers, typology provided the most efficacious means of defining social differences as the seventeenth century progressed. More and more, phrases such as 'the English race', 'the Irish race', 'race of women', appear with greater frequency. Furthermore, as a result of the colonial and imperialist endeavours of the English, phrases such as 'black race' or 'white race' begin to displace 'Moor', 'Ethiopes', or the 'English nation' as taxonomic classifications. These 'shifts' are rarely reflected upon in later dictionaries and lexicons for, I would argue, one telling reason: from the outset, the dictionary was explicitly designed, politically and ideologically, to be a discursive investigation into a word's semantic and etymological origins. Having set out the terms of race, compilers of dictionaries left to their literary, philosophical and historical counterparts the task of implementing a word's cultural and philosophical value, to embellish or restrain meaning.

I end this introductory essay with this brief account of the word 'race' and its lexical history in Elizabethan society because, in many ways, it adumbrates the complex theoretical problematic that goes into a critical reading of 'race' and Shakespeare. Like Percyvale's and Minsheu's dictionaries, this volume reveals that our understanding of race in Shakespeare's canon (and his England) is built upon the continuing contributions a generation of Shakespeare scholars can make to our epistemological understanding of the history of a social ideology. In one of the most engaging and thoughtful analyses of racist discourses, David Theo Goldberg asserts that 'race is a fluid, transforming, historically specific concept parasitic on theoretic and social discourses for the meaning it assumes at any given moment'.[10] In other words, in order for race to be understood it must pretend to universality. Race ensures the idea of commonality by negating or effacing the differing interests of a group of individuals. However, there is an inherent paradox in this push for commonality. In order to invest race with meaning, modern societies must frame visible (and, quite frankly, minor) differences among people in terms of antithesis. Consequently, race becomes at once transcendentally immutable and historically mutable. Furthermore, this, at times, contradictory 'truth' becomes preternaturally astute in sustaining itself through the illusion of essentialism.

Comprehension of this theoretical avatar produces sets of questions different from those one might normally ask with regard to early modern English literature: for example, we might well inquire why literary works such as Shakespeare's *Othello* and *Titus Andronicus* or John Webster's *The White Devil* are treated as texts which deal almost exclusively with race and racism, while Philip Sidney's *Arcadia* or Edmund Spenser's *Faerie Queene* are treated as primarily concerned with matters of nationalism and Englishness. On this and related issues, we might also ask whether modern cultural and social critics of early modern literature, by extending the racial taxonomies and ideologies which have shaped post-Enlightenment social subjectivity to pre-Enlightenment subjectivity, have fashioned earlier social formations in our own image.

Questions such as these, of course, become the catalyst for additional epistemological problems and queries: what if our assumption, our 'understanding', of Shakespeare's (and thus early modern England's) concept of race is incomplete? What if, in attempting to sort out the significance of early modern English literature to a post-Second World War, global political economy, we have misread, or not read at all, some of the transgressive signs of racial subjectivity in Shakespeare's canon? Is it possible that too narrowly a defined notion misrepresents and engenders a misreading of the complexity and ambiguity of the word 'race' as well as its social and cultural articulation in seventeenth-century England?

To pose these and other questions about the racial implications of any early modern text is also to inquire into how audiences (then and now) might have construed and recognized the concept of race and its linguistic inflections. As I have argued elsewhere, early modern English usage of the word 'race' reveals a multiplicity of loci, of axes of determinism, as well as metaphorical systems to aid and abet its deployment across a variety of boundaries in the making.[11] As an expression of fundamental distinctions, the meaning of 'race' varied depending upon whether a writer wanted to specify difference born of a class-based concept of genealogy, a psychological (and essentialized) nature, or group typology. Nonetheless, in all these variations, race is envisioned as something fundamental, something immutable, knowable and recognizable, yet we only 'see' it when its boundaries are violated, and thus race is also, paradoxically, mysterious, illusory and mutable. All of this, perhaps, was well known to Shakespeare.

NOTES

1 William Shakespeare, *Othello*, ed. Gerald Eades Bentley (New York: Penguin, 1958), p. 17.
2 One of the continuing points of debate in 'race studies' is whether Jews constitute a 'race' and thus anti-Semitism should be considered racism. See James Shapiro's brilliant *Shakespeare and the Jews* (New York, 1996).
3 Richard Percyvale, *Bibliotheca Hispanica. Containing a Grammar, with a Dictionarie in Spanish, English and Latine, gathered out of divers good Authors: very profitable for the studious of the Spanish toong. By Richard Percyvall Gent. The Dictionarie being inlarged with the latine, by the advise and conference of Master Thomas Doyley Doctor in Physicke.* Imprinted at London, by Iohn Iackson, for Richard Watkins. 1591. Folger Library copy.
4 Percyvale begins his rationale for the dictionary by stating that, 'it would be a tedious peece of worke, to search out what shoulde be the proper language of the Spanish nation; the countrie having bin mastered by so many dyuers kinds of people, as either of ambition to enlarge their dominions, or

of necessitie to seeke habitation for such surplus, as their owne lymits coulde not conteyne: haue been invited to make inuasions'. Not surprisingly, he then goes on to do exactly what he claims 'would be a tedious peece of worke' – pursue the origins of the Spanish language. The 'Spanyard', Percyvale writes, 'as in things he standeth highly upon his reputation; so he glorieth not a little of his antiquitie'. Percyvale's shift from linguistics to ethnicity is not surprising to anyone familiar with the political dynamics shaping late sixteenth-century England; yet that he engages in this discursive strategy in the preface to the reader stigmatizes Percyvale's text in ways no other dictionary of the period is marked. Percyvale's political gesture ideologically defines the terms of his project, as he moves from a linguistic to what would now be defined as a racial exegesis for the origins of the Spanish language.

5 See Verena Stolcke, 'Invade Women: Gender, Race, and Class in the Formation of Colonial Society', in *Women, 'Race' and Writing in the Early Modern Period*, ed. Margo Hendricks and Patricia Parker (London and New York, 1994), pp. 272–86, and Paul Julian Smith, *Representing the Other: 'Race', Text, and Gender in Spanish and Spanish American Narrative* (Oxford, 1992).

6 The full title is rather daunting: *A Dictionarie in Spanish and English: first pvblished into the English tongue by Ric. Percivale gent. Now enlarged and amplified with many thousand words . . . together with the accenting of every word thorowout the whole dictionarie, for the true pronunciation of the language, as also for the diuers signification of one and the selfesame word: and for the learners ease and furtherance, the declining of all hard and irregular verbs; and for the same cause the former order of the alphabet is altered, diuers hard and vncouth phrases and speeches out of sundry of the best authors explained, with diuers necessary notes and especiall directions for all such as shall be desirous to attaine the perfection of the Spanish tongve. All done by John Minsheu . . . Hereunto for the further profit and pleasure of the learner or delighted in this tongue, is annexed an ample English dictionarie, alphabetically set downe with the Spanish words thereunto adioyned, as also an alphabeticall table of the Arabicke and Moorish words now commonly receiued and vsed in the Spanish tongue.* I have used the Folger copy, STC 19619, copy 1.

7 Other Renaissance dictionaries also engage in similar techniques. See John Florio's *A World of Wordes, Or Most copious, and exact Dictionarie in Italian and English* (1598), and Thomas Wilson's *A Christian Dictionarie* (1616), for example. Florio's work, in particular, illustrates how concerned later compilers were to include all possible meanings of words such as 'race'. Florio's definition of the Italian word *razza* goes as follows: 'Razza, Raza, as Raggia, a kind, a race, a broode, a blood, a stocke, a name, a pedigree.' The anomaly in this series is the word Raggia, which Florio defines as 'a fish with whose skin fletchers smooth their arrowes called a ray or skate. Some have taken it for the thornbacke. Also resin [which he defines as] a tree in Arabia, whereof there is but one found, and vpon it the Phenix sits.'

8 See Richard Grassby, *The English Gentleman in Trade: The Life and Works of Sir Dudley North, 1641–1691* (Oxford, 1994). As Grassby writes, of North, this

'gentleman trader . . . accepted the prevailing norms of his society and he reconciled the demands of business with his personal desires, his family obligations, and the public interest. To [this man] money was never the measure of his life, but it served as an outward sign of success in a society which honoured wealth but not the skills by which it was created', p. 285. See also, Felicity Heal and Clive Holmes, *The Gentry in England and Wales, 1500–1700* (Stanford, 1994) and Marvin B. Becker, *Civility and Society in Western Europe: 1300–1600* (Bloomington and Indianapolis, 1988).

9 This did not foreclose, however, the possibility of exploiting the other meaning of 'race', kind. One has only to explore the corpus of Edmund Spenser to find instances where the plurality of meaning of 'race' abounds. Even William Shakespeare's employment of the term, though primarily figuring lineage, is occasionally marked by ambiguity. Nonetheless, when we encounter the word 'race' it is usually understood to signify a group of characteristics associated with a particular socio-economic group, namely the aristocracy.

10 David Theo Goldberg, *Racist Culture: Philosophy and the Politics of Meaning* (Oxford and Cambridge, Mass., 1993), p. 74.

11 Margo Hendricks, 'Obscured by Dreams: Race, Empire, and Shakespeare's *A Midsummer Night's Dream*', *Shakespeare Quarterly* 2:1 (Summer 1996), 37–60.

CHAPTER 2

A portrait of a Moor

Bernard Harris

In 1956 the Shakespeare Institute acquired a portrait of the Moorish Ambassador to Elizabeth in 1600 – a portrait which is of considerable interest to students of history, of art and of the theatre (fig. 1).[1] For the historian it gives character to an episode, nowhere fully recorded, in the diplomatic relations between England and Barbary. It forms, too, a handsome and out-of-the-common addition to the gallery of Tudor portraits. For those concerned with the theatre its interest is twofold. First, although it lacks the direct relevance to stage-history attaching to Peacham's sketch of Aaron, it may well assist a producer of *The Merchant of Venice* when he comes to the stage direction, 'Enter Morochus, a tawny Moore all in white.' The second point of theatrical interest is at once more speculative and much more significant. The picture presents 'ocular proof' of what the Elizabethans saw as a Moor of rank, one whose presence with his companions in London a year or so before the usually agreed date of *Othello* caused much contemporary comment. Idle speculation, of course, must be curbed; but at least we are entitled to wonder whether an audience alert for the topical would not look for a true Barbarian on their stage. This ambassador from Mauretania, we have to remember, was Othello's countryman. Iago refers to his master as a 'Barbary horse' and elsewhere uses the term 'barbarian'; after the dismissal from Cyprus, he tells Roderigo that Othello is going to Mauretania, a lie designed to imply the general's final disgrace – his loss of high office among Christians and his ignominious return to his own people.

Obviously Othello's character is the invention of Shakespeare's imagination; obviously, too, the account of his general life and crime, with details concerning his rank and race, come from Cinthio's *Il Moro*. Yet we still argue about Othello's features, on which the source is silent and the play confusing. We know that he is black and a Moor; that the Elizabethans were inexact in their use of the terms 'Moor' and 'negro';

that in glossing 'Moor' as 'negro' Onions seems to cut this knot, but really leaves us with two loose ends which an inconsistent stage practice has never tied up. Through all this ambiguity of terminology and stage tradition the portrait of the Moorish ambassador reminds us of the common acquaintance of the Elizabethans with real, as distinct from fictional, Moors; and here interest in the picture goes beyond speculation.

To recount the story of the embassy in some detail is to take us nearer to Shakespeare's England, perhaps even, in a sense, to Shakespeare's Moor.[2] Cinthio's is not the whole tale after all; the fundamental dramatic contrast of racial difference is Shakespeare's first departure from his source. Primarily this derived from the mind which had conceived Shylock, yet it was a contrast in contemporary reality, not in cosmopolitan Venice but in insular England; an incompatibility illustrated in 1600 by the reception and behaviour of the Moorish visitors.

Relations between England and Barbary, of which Morocco was part, had been characterized by commercial ambition and diplomatic expediency from the time of the first voyage made by *The Lion* in 1551. James Alday, who had apparently inspired the traffic, complained bitterly that while the great sweat kept him from the ship at Portsmouth, 'Windam had her away from thence, before I was able to stand upon my legges, by whom I lost at that instant fourescore pound.' The prize was indeed great, but the race was for the strong, and many notable merchant families were soon embarked on it. The trade, much of it in imported sugar and exported cloth, was contested by Spain and Portugal, whose spheres of influence it transgressed; it was further complicated by merchant rivalry, by changes in foreign policy, and endangered by pirates of all nations.

In the fifty years since *The Lion* had first sailed, many problems of mutual concern for England and Barbary remained unresolved. The Barbary Company of 1585, headed by the Earls of Leicester and Warwick, achieved little regulation of affairs and was never incorporated, its first charter expiring in 1597. Many of its members were naturally also trading for the dominant Levant Company, whose success perhaps implied the commercial defeat of the Barbary Company. Certainly the trend of political opinion in the last decade of the sixteenth century was against an overt alliance of arms for further assault on Spain. By 1600, when the Barbarian ambassador came to suggest joint aggression, Elizabeth was already wary of the dangers presented by a weakened Spain and an ascendant France. She had not invited the embassy, but

1 Portrait of the Moorish Ambassador to Queen Elizabeth, 1600–01.
English School. Oil on panel, $44\frac{1}{2} \times 34\frac{1}{2}$ inches

welcomed it no doubt as offering a means of insurance, although one for which the policy was unlikely to mature.

Diplomatic relations between England and Barbary had always been a compromise, in a sense compromising. The questionable alliance was put in terms of the advice offered Elizabeth in 1586, that 'Her Majesty in using the King of Fez, doth not arm a barbarian against a Christian, but a barbarian against a heretic.' But the heathen hand, though welcomed against Spain, was rarely taken in public. The military prowess of the Moors, typified in the battle of Alcazar, coloured the drama of the day. But diplomatic exchange waited upon emergencies. The Armada brought a Moroccan emissary to England, and Essex's raid on Cadiz in 1597 inspired eventually the embassy of 1600. For two years later, emboldened by England's success, and hopeful of her active support, Muley Hamet, King of Barbary, proposed the grand design of the total conquest of Spain.

Elizabeth was then corresponding with him upon more mundane affairs; one, of long standing, was the release of some captives from the Low Countries; another concerned a dispute over the estate of a merchant Southern, about whose goods his partner Richard Tomson and the official agent John Waring were wrangling.

The Tomson brothers, Richard, George and Arnold, with their kinsman Jasper, were merchant adventurers. Richard, a servant of Cecil and holder of monopolies in almonds, dates, capers and molasses, had been accused of bringing into the trade as many interlopers as there were members of the Barbary Company. Doubtless the Tomsons' service to Cecil gave them safety at home, and gun-running made them popular with the Moors.

It was to Jasper that the King of Barbary confided his ambition. Jasper had been in the campaign of Mahomet III against the Emperor in 1596, and Muley Hamet was naturally interested to learn details of this encounter between heathen and Christian arms. In a letter of June 1599 Jasper relates to Richard Tomson how the King, his chief adviser Azzuz, his principal secretary (the future ambassador) and an interpreter between them kept him up all night in conversation. He did not share the Moors' enthusiasm for an armed alliance, protesting that the Cadiz raid had been a reprisal for the Armada, not an attempted invasion. Talk of an army of 20,000 Englishmen and 20,000 men and horses from Barbary put Jasper out of his depth. When he suggested that such matters ought to be discussed at a higher level he was asked if he had friends close to the Queen – and hence he requests Richard, presumably through Cecil, to canvass the idea at Court, if only for amusement's sake.

Rumour of alliance soon arose. In October 1599 the Venetian ambassador in Germany reported that Elizabeth had use of a port in Barbary from which to harass Spanish shipping. This probably met Elizabeth's needs. She continued to write to Muley Hamet about Southern's estate, the return of prisoners, and the restitution of money robbed from two Englishmen in Morocco.

The King countered with proposals for an embassy, to be disguised as a trade mission to Aleppo, calling at England for the sake of mutual regard. Letters of recommendation, assurance of safe-conduct, and transport for the whole party – including nine returning prisoners – were requested. Merchants were desired to ship them to England, to Aleppo, and home again. The real business of the embassy was too secret for correspondence, and a formal letter of June 1600 explains that the ambassador in person would treat of proposals for an alliance. The Ambassador was the King's secretary, Abd el-Ouahed ben Messaoud ben Mohammed Anoun, supported by al Hage Messa and al Hage Bahanet, and accompanied by an interpreter Abd el-Dodar, by birth Andalusian.

George Tomson, writing to his brother Richard for Cecil's information, gives an informal description of these principal members of the embassy. He did not think the Ambassador a very good choice. Although 'a natural Moore borne' he was a Fessian, which 'the natural Moore houldeth baseness'. Azzuz was his superior in council. Sharpwitted and literate, el-Ouahed flattered for advantage and was conceited. He had solicited letters from Moroccan agents to their masters in England on his behalf, and George's letter is partly to counterbalance his own composition in this kind.

In fact, the old man Messa 'was thowt should have gone for principall', but after many such employments had recently disgraced himself by hiding from the King two *balas* rubies purchased abroad. Messa and Bahanet were to conduct the business in Aleppo, and were also authorized to deal with English merchants who had precious stones to sell.

Of the real business of the embassy George had no idea, 'Here yt is so secreat that none knoweth the grounde of their goinge', but in view of Jasper's foreknowledge such profession of ignorance was probably diplomatic.

The interpreter, described as being 'of more sense than all the rest and a verie honest man', had soldiered in Italy, according to Juan de Marchena, and would speak Italian to the Queen, though ordinarily using his native Spanish. The Ambassador knew a little Spanish, too, but scorned to speak it except with inferiors. His King lacked even this accomplishment.

A higher opinion is held by Thomas Bernhere in recommending el-Ouahed to the famous Edward Wright, though we must bear in mind that his letter was probably one of those solicited. El-Ouahed here is described as being capable of understanding Wright's navigational inventions; Bernhere declares that he had been instructed to select certain instruments for his own and the King's use. These might be brought back to Morocco for engraving, or completed in England, since the Ambassador 'being a perfect penman can set the Arabique letters figures and words down very faire'. He was also likely to be interested in 'the experiments mathematical of the load stone'. Bernhere's letter in general emphasizes the enduring Arab learning in scientific navigation, essential to their journeying 'over a Sandy sea'.

The letters of both Tomson and Bernhere show that the purpose of the embassy was more than diplomatic, and that its contact, as much as at Court, would be with such merchants as Alderman Edward Holmedon, Grocer, of the Levant and Barbary Companies.

At the end of June 1600 the sixteen members of the embassy, together with the prisoners, sailed from Morocco in *The Eagle*, under Robert Kitchen. The news that Spanish ships had cruised to intercept them in the Straits brought Muley Hamet home in consternation from the field. But the danger was avoided, and the embassy reached Dover harbour on 8 August.

There was some embarrassment at their coming. Sir Thomas Gerard, who in April 1600 had overcome problems set by the eighty members of the French Ambassador's train and a shortage of horses, now found greater social difficulties in receiving the small party of Barbarians. By 11 August the preparations were incomplete, when he wrote to Cecil, 'I have moved the merchants for the Ambassador's diet, but they all plead poverty, and except her Majesty discharge it, it will rest upon himself. My Lord Mayor has taken Alderman Radclyffe's house for him.' Anthony Radcliff had been Sheriff in 1585–6. The fact that in 1601 the Privy Council considered his house in the Strand, near the Royal Exchange, a suitable residence for Count de Beaumont, the French Ambassador, upon its vacation by the Duke of Lennox, the Scots Ambassador, must be weighed against the allegation of a contemporary letter-writer, probably Winwood, that the Moors were to be entertained 'without scandall, and for that purpose they are lodged in a house apart, where they feed alone'. The relationship between domestic privacy and segregation was probably close, but the usual diplomatic hospitality was offered to the Moors. Gerard and a group of merchants met them at Gravesend on 14 August, and brought them into London on the following evening tide. Rowland White commented to Sir Robert Sidney, 'no Tyme yet appointed for their Audience; they are very strangely attired and behauiored'.

Five days later they had their first audience of Elizabeth at Nonsuch, and White gives a detailed account:

The Embassador of *Barbary* had Audience vpon Wednesday last; here was a roiall Preparacion, in the Manner of his receuing; rich Hangings and Furnitures sent for from *Hampton* Court; the Gard very strong, in their rich Coatees; the Pentioners with their Axes; the Lords of the Order with their Collars; a full Court of Lords and Ladies. He passed thorough a Gard of Albards to the Cownsell Chamber, where he rested; he was brought to the Presence, soe to the Priuy Chamber, and soe to the Gallery; where her Majestie satt at the further End in very great State, and gaue them Audience.

The 'Winwood' letter quoted above adds the detail that 'At the end of his Audience, her Majesty for a further grace to the States Agent, caused him to be present, and soe she receaved [the nine captives] of the Barbarian with one hand, she gave them to him with an other.'

Although the interview was conducted in Spanish through Lewkenor, White remarks that before departing 'the Interpreter of the Embassy spoke *Italian*, and desired to deliuer some Thing in priuate, which her Majestie granted. On which Mr *Lewknor* and the Lords removed further of. Yt is giuen out, that they come for her Majestys Letters to the *Turke*, to whom a brother of this King of *Barbaries* is fled, to complaine against him.'

On 31 August the ambassadors requested another audience and seemed anxious to arrange for their eventual departure. Still surrounded by mystery, they were received at Oatlands on 10 September. Admitting that the business of the Moors 'hath bene very secretly handled, which is not yet come to Light', White offers a new version in which:

yt is sipposed, that he makes good Offers to hir Majestie, yf she will be pleased to Ayde hym with Shipping, fitt for his Portes, to conduct in safety some Treasure he hath by Mines, in Part of the *Indies* conquered by hym, which now he is forced to carry by Land, and to maintain an Army to safconduct yt, and sometyme yt is taken from hym by Force.

This information of White's is nearer the true business of the embassy as set out in a memorandum of el-Ouahed's, of which a translation is endorsed by Cecil '15 Sep. 1600. The Barbarie Embassadors proposition to the Queen, delivered to Mr Secretarie Harbart and me'. The main proposal was for an alliance between England and Barbary against Spain. Muley Hamet declared that he possessed a great army of proven quality, all manner of munitions, materials for shipbuilding, and iron. If an English fleet could be provided, he would take the war to Spain. England and Morocco, once united in arms, could seize from Spain both the East and West Indies and divide the spoils. The whole memorandum is exploratory and tentative. Elizabeth is invited either to send her own ambassador to Morocco to discuss a treaty further, or to conclude one in England with a different envoy from Barbary, while el-Ouahed continues his pretext of a journey to Aleppo. But the latter is at Elizabeth's disposal if she prefers him to escort an English envoy to Morocco. In any event, Muley Hamet cautions that el-Ouahed's route should be by Aleppo. A later note of the Ambassador's, when Elizabeth had decided to employ her own negotiator to the King, seeks a reassurance that the other members of the embassy will be shipped to Aleppo if the Queen requires el-Ouahed to return direct to Morocco.

This insistence upon preserving a useless pretext, and the Moors' need of transport, became a great embarrassment to the Privy Council. On 22 September they requested the help of the Levant Company, and were refused. Captain Edward Prynne, a pensioned seaman in Cecil's service, who was in charge of the arrangements for the Moors' hospitality, offered passage on a friend's ship. But the Council had instructed him to arrange for a warship under Captain King to be got ready. This scheme had the approval of the Lord Admiral, the Earl of Nottingham, who pointed out to Cecil that it was not fit for the Queen's honour that the embassy should return in other than a man-of-war, that the proposed salt ship was inadequately armed, and that the warship could do useful service on the return journey by spying out Spanish preparations. But the Moors shrank from such a bellicose leave-taking, and the Council had to instruct Lord Buckhurst, the Lord High Treasurer, to reimburse Captain King for his preparation of the warship, and cancelled the whole plan on 8 October.

New complications soon arose. The Russian Embassy from Boris Godunov arrived the next week, and may have extinguished some of the interest in the Barbarian visitors. White reported that the Moors would take their leave of the Queen on either 15 or 16 October, and on 15 October in fact John Chamberlain assured Dudley Carleton:

The Barbarians take theyre leave sometime this week, to goe homeward, for our merchants nor mariners will not carry them into Turkie, because they thinck it a matter odious and scandalous to the world to be friendlie or familiar with Infidells but yet yt is no small honour to us that nations so far removed and every way different shold meet here to admire the glory and magnificence of our Queene of Saba.

On 21 October Chamberlain wrote again that 'The Barbarians were yesterday at Court to take theyre leave and wil be gon shortly; but the eldest of them, which was a kind of priest or prophet, hath taken his leave of the world and is gon to prophecie *apud infernos* and to seeke out Mahound theyre mediator.'

Messa's death, uncharitably referred to here, must have delayed the Moors' going, though this was clearly awaited on 1 November, when Nicholas Mosley, the Lord Mayor of London, wrote to Cecil in the following terms:

I have thought good, before the departinge of the Barbarie Imbassador, to let your Honour understande that, upon your Honours letters for repaiment, I have caused to be delivered unto Captain Primme, at sundrie times, the some of 230^{li} toward the defraying of the Imbassador his charges, which will not discharge all that is owinge. And Mr Ratlefe, in whose howse he is lodged, expecteth some consideracon for the use of his howse, and spoile made by them.

By this date the Ambassador would seem to have outstayed his welcome in official quarters, and certainly with Alderman Radcliff; and Philip Honyman had already noted that 'The merchants took little pleasure in his being here.' Honyman alleged, indeed, that the commercial purpose of the embassy was more serious than the diplomatic, and that the Ambassador's 'dryft was, under colour of thir formall voyadge, to lerne here how merchandize went, and what gaine we made of their sugors, that he might raise the prices accordingly'. Stow repeated this charge of the merchants, with the embellishment that the Moors:

during their half yeares abode in London, . . . used all subtilities and diliggence to know the prises wayghts measures and kindes of differences in such commodities as eyther there country sent hither or England transported thither. They carried with them all sorts of English wayghts measures and samples of commodities.

It seems likely that the persistence of the Moors resulted in the warning issued by the Privy Council, during the period of the embassy, to Alderman Edward Holmedon and other merchants, about the manipulation of sugar prices.

However, unpopular on all sides, the Barbarians stayed on to the end of the year, and courtesy was somehow maintained. Stow records that on 'the 17th November being the Queen's day the Queene being then at Whitehall, a speciale place was builded only for them neere to the parke doore to behold that day's triumph'. Of the same occasion, using new-style dating, de Boissise, the French Ambassador, informed his king that on 'le 23 de ce mois la Royne est arrivée en ceste ville avec la cérémonie et pompe accoustumée voire avec plus grande à l'occasion des Ambassadeurs de Moscovie et de Marroc, ausquelz elle a voulu monstrer sa magnificence'. With consummate timing, dating his preface 'At London this three and fortieth most ioifull Coronation-day of her sacred Maiestie', the young John Pory brought out *A Geographical Historie of Africa*, a translation of the fifty-year-old work 'Written in Arabicke and Italian by John Leo a More, borne in Granada and brought vp in Barbarie'. In his dedication of these 'first fruits' to Cecil, Pory declares that 'at this time especially I thought they would prooue the more acceptable: in that the Marocan ambassadour (whose Kings dominions are heere most amplie and particularly described) hath so lately treated with your Honour concerning matters of that estate'. A lost book, entered on 4 September as 'the widow of England and her seven sons strangly tormented to Death by the Turkes in Barbary', may represent a less cultured attempt to make capital out of the Moors' presence.

By all accounts they were difficult guests. The 'speciale place' accorded them at the triumph in Whitehall was doubtless again a courtesy and a convenience. Stow, the chronicler nearest in time to the embassy, is also the fullest and most hostile, claiming that:

Notwithstanding all this kindness shown them together with their dyet and all other provisions for six moneths space wholly at the Queenes charges, yet such was their inveterate hate unto our Christian religion and estate as they could not endure to give any manner of alms, charitie, or relief, either in money or broken meat, unto any English poore, but reserved theire fragments and sold the same unto such poore as would give most for them.

Such behaviour was no doubt unfavourably regarded in London, and other personal customs excited curiosity, such as that 'They killed all their own meat within their house, as sheep lambs poultry and such like, and they turned their face eastward when they killed anything.'

Stow's final conjectures, first, that 'being returned it was supposed they poysned their interpreter, being born in Granado, because he commended the estate and bounty of England', and second, that 'the like violence was thought to be done unto their reverend aged pilgrime least he should manifest England's honour to their disgrace', are careful to acknowledge their basis in unsympathetic rumour. But common opinion probably endorsed his conclusion that 'It was generally judged by their demeanors that they were rather espials than honourable ambassadors for they omitted nothing that might damnifie the English Merchants.'

Stow's reference to their six months' stay is our best indication of the date of their departure, probably at the beginning of February 1601. A warrant of the Privy Council in May 1601 declares that 'the Ambassadour doth by her Majesty's leave and permission take with him one John Rolliffe, a mann of learning, and Richard Edwards, an apothecary, to serve the Emperour his master', and further orders 'every of you to whom it shall or may appertaine to suffer the foresaid John Rolliffe and Richard Edwards to go forth of the realme and attend on the said Ambassadour with such apparrell, bookes and other necessaryes as they do carry with them for their use. Whereof wee require you not to faile.'

The warrant is unlikely to have been issued retrospectively, so that Rolliffe and Edwards must have followed the Ambassador to Morocco, for on 27 February 1601 Muley Hamet wrote to tell Elizabeth of the embassy's safe arrival home, and of their favourable report upon her reception of them. The King accepted her excuse of inconvenience to merchants for her failure to ship the Moors to Aleppo. Elizabeth, in a letter of 20 October 1600, had instructed Henry Prannell, an agent resident in Morocco, to continue discussions about an alliance, and some idea of the nature of her diplomatic handling of the King of Barbary is to be gained from the memorandum in response, which he attached to his letter of 27 February. She first stipulated that England's help should be kept secret from Spain, an implausible but sensible necessity since she was simultaneously negotiating for peace with the King of Spain; she set the cost of equipping a fleet at £100,000, to be provided in advance, against her credit, out of prize money taken by the Moors from Spanish possessions; she needed the treasure immediately.

Muley Hamet was equal to the bluff; the money, he said, was at hand, only it was difficult to transport it safely. Elizabeth was asked to send a tall ship, under some person of responsibility, and in secret. Meanwhile, he requested the Queen to think further about the military aspect of the proposed treaty, and reminded her that the purpose should not be to sack Spain and her territories, but to take and hold them for ever. His final request was for her special ambassador, to carry into being the prospect of an omnipotent alliance of England and Barbary.

The unreal vision soon faded. When Elizabeth resumed the correspondence after the settlement of the Essex affair, it was only to write of such matters as the release of prisoners and the difficulties of some English merchants in Morocco. Even in these simple matters her ambiguous diplomacy continued. After the embassy had gone home an Act of the Privy Council had arranged the deporting of 'negars and blackamoores', whose great numbers in England irritated Spain, and fostered trouble against her. Elizabeth's release of Moorish captives later had the double advantage of conciliating both Spain and Barbary.

Within two years of the embassy both Elizabeth and Muley Hamet were dead, and Barbary was engulfed in civil wars. George Tomson came home penniless to recover debts from the merchants in London, and George Wilkins began his account of *The Three Miseries of Barbary*.

Officially, the embassy of 1600 was forgotten. Camden recorded it with formal resonance, in the hollow phrases '*Ab austro enim Hamettus Rex Mauretania Tingitanae, a Septentrione Boris Pheodorici Imperator Russiae, omni studio amicitiam ejus ambierunt.*' Thomas Gainsford put both embassies in his list of such distinguished foreign tributes in *The Glory of England* of 1618, though noting of Barbarians and Russians alike that they 'from a stubborn bestialitie seemed to vilipend the managing of many affaires by outward forme; yet were driven to applaude our generall happines'.

Informally, among the merchants, the Barbary Embassy was remembered for a precedent when argument arose concerning the payment for the Turkish Ambassador's entertainment in 1607. Then Richard Stapers, of the Levant Company, reminded Salisbury that 'in the late Queen's time there came an Ambassador from the King of Barbary, to whom she gave maintenance all the time he was here, and 100 *l.* at his departure, and yet he gave nothing here'.

It seems impossible that the Moors should have come empty-handed, yet it may be true. Rowland White's description of their audiences has no mention of such customary gifts as those presented by the Russian Ambassador, who, White tells us, gave Elizabeth 'in open Sort, a Timber of Sables, and one sengle Paire of excellent goodnes'. We remember that the presents sent by the Great Turk in 1583 had included '4 lyons roiall, 12 turkish swords, 4 cases of knives, 12 unicorns horns, 20 hangings of cloth, A Bed for a Galley all of cristal and gold, 1 chest of Chrystal,

2 Horses', and that Stow accused the Moors of neglecting the poor. Along with their 'stubborn bestialitie' went considerable naïvety, as is shown by White's account of their visit to Hampton Court, 'where they saw and admired the richnes of the Furniture; and they demanded how many Kings had built yt, and how long it was a Doing'. Certainly behind the bombastic diplomatic mission lay only shrewdness and commercial cunning; and behind that, if the rumours had any truth, was insensitivity and cruelness, even murder.

To Elizabethan Londoners the appearance and conduct of the Moors was a spectacle and an outrage, emphasizing the nature of the deep difference between themselves and their visitors, between their Queen and this 'erring Barbarian'. When Shakespeare chose, for this audience, to present a Moor as his hero, he was not perhaps confused in his racial knowledge, simply more aware than his contemporaries of the complex pattern made by white and black.

First published in *Shakespeare Survey 11*, 1958

NOTES

1 The portrait in oils of the Ambassador appeared as Lot 65, 'Portrait of Abdul Guahid, Moroccan Ambassador to the Court of Queen Elizabeth I', when it was sold at Christie's on 11 November 1955. The purchaser, Mr George Higgins, after having it completely cleaned and restored, exhibited it at the Ruskin Galleries in Stratford-upon-Avon during the autumn of 1956, when, through the co-operation of Mr Higgins and Mrs Constance Thomson, it was acquired by the Shakespeare Institute.

The portrait is on a panel $44\frac{1}{2}$ in. × $34\frac{1}{2}$ in. To the left of the head is inscribed '1600', 'Abdvl Gvahid', and 'Aetatis 42': to the right is the description 'Legatvs Regis Barbariae in Angliam'. The artist is unknown, but the giving of the Ambassador's age, not known from other documents, suggests an authoritative portrait, rather than a casual painting.

2 The sources from which the account of the embassy is taken have been listed here, rather than in the numerous and repetitive footnotes otherwise needed: *Les sources inédites de l'histoire du Maroc, Angleterre*, 3 vols., ed. de Castries (Paris, 1918–35); *PRO, State Papers, Domestic*, Elizabeth, vol. CCLXXV; *State Papers, Foreign*, Barbary States, vols. XII and XIII; *Cal. of SP*, Spanish, vol. VII; Venetian, vol. X; *Acts of the Privy Council*, ed. Dasent, vol. XXX; *HMC Cal. Cecil MSS.*, Parts IX, X, XI; *The Sidney Papers*, ed. Collins, 2 vols.; John Chamberlain's *Letters* (Camden Society), LXXIX; J. Nichols, *Progresses and Public Processions of Queen Elizabeth*, 3 vols.; A. B. Beaven, *The Aldermen of the City of London*, 2 vols.

STC 4496 Camden, *Annales*; *STC* 11517 Gainsford, *The Glory of England*; *STC* 15481 Johannes Leo, 'Africanus', *A geographical historie of Africa*; and *STC* 23337 Stow, *Annales*.

The writer wishes to acknowledge the kindness of the Earl of Leicester who gave permission to consult MS. 678 in the Library of Holkham Hall; of Dr W. O. Hassall, of the Bodleian Library, librarian at Holkham Hall; of Professor Leslie Hotson, who supplied references and comment, and of Mr David Lockie, who gave further assistance and provided a quotation from the Calendar of the Cecil MSS. at Hatfield House for the year 1607.

CHAPTER 3

Elizabethans and foreigners

G. K. Hunter

'The three corners of the world'

The impact of foreigners on a community or a culture is affected, obviously enough, both by the opportunities for contact and knowledge that exist, and by the framework of assumptions within which information about foreign lands and customs is presented and received. The period with which we are concerned here – let us say the sixteenth and early seventeenth centuries – is well known as one in which the amount of scientific information about the world increased dramatically. In the Renaissance period England, like the rest of Europe, acquired modern-style maps; trade-contacts with Turkey[1] and Russia[2] became a commonplace feature of economic life; visitations of Red Indians, Eskimos and Negroes,[3] an influx of refugees from Europe, plantations in the New World, and knowledge of other European ventures of a similar kind – all this might seem to give the average Englishman of the early seventeenth century almost as much expertise in physical geography as is possessed by his modern counterpart. But this is to reckon without the 'framework of assumptions'. It is probably true to say that by the early decades of the seventeenth century more scientific information was available than could be digested within the terms in which the world was traditionally conceived; and it is certainly true that the facts of physical geography which were accepted by sailors as useful in practice were very difficult to accommodate within the sophisticated and complex traditions that form the natural background to literature.

What was the framework of assumptions concerning foreigners? When we look at medieval writings seeking for information that bears on the question, 'what attitudes to foreigners were traditional in English literature?' we find little evidence; and this very absence must be our starting-point. Most medieval literature is located in a dimension that cares little for the compass. It is true that Chaucer's Knight had been:

37

> At Alisaundre . . . in Pruce.
> In Lettow hadde he reysed and in Ruce,
> No Cristen man so ofte of his degree.
> In Gernade at the sege eek hadde he be
> Of Algezir, and riden in Belmarye.
> At Lyeys was he, and at Satalye,
> Whan they were wonne; and in the Grete See.[4]

And of his Wyf of Bath he tells us:

> thryes hadde she been at Jerusalem;
> She hadde passed many a straunge streem;
> At Rome she hadde been, and at Boloigne,
> In Galice at seint Jame, and at Coloigne.[5]

But the interest of these journeys is not geographical; the points mentioned are only important as points of connection with the Divine.[6] The typical travellers of the Middle Ages – the pilgrim and the crusader – often brought back information which the modern geographer sees to be of scientific value, but this information was only a by-product (and they saw it as a by-product) of movement on quite another plane. There is no point in complaining that the sixth-century monk Cosmas, 'should have known better'[7] (a phrase we shall often meet in this study) than create a *Christian Topography*[8] which Sir Raymond Beazley has stigmatized as 'systematic nonsense',[9] as a marvel of 'scientific supernaturalism'.[10] It is true that Cosmas Indicopleustes ('he who has sailed to India') was a notable traveller: he had travelled to Malabar and Ceylon, and then back again to Egypt before he settled to write his account of the world. And it is equally true that he did not use this geographical experience to influence his Bible-centred model of the world. But why should he? If the Bible gives the most important information about the world, then it is proper to avoid the snares of mere sense impression, by clinging (so far as is possible) to biblical texts and intentions. It may be proper to remember here the famous scholastic exercise on the word Jerusalem: 'Literally, it is the city of that name; allegorically it represents Holy Church; tropologically, it signifies the faithful soul of whosoever aspires to the vision of eternal peace; anagogically, it denotes the life of the dwellers in Heaven who see God revealed in Zion.'[11]

What is, on a map, only a physical position (neither more nor less important than any other) acquires intensity of meaning by the superimposing of spiritual senses over the physical one; the undifferentiated physical fact has to aspire to spiritual meaning in order to become important. The medieval *mappa mundi* is an excellent demonstration of this view of geography. It details an image of the world as Christendom, centred on Jerusalem, not only because Ezekiel 5.5 reads, 'Thus saith the Lord God; This is Jerusalem: I have set it in the midst of the nations and countries that are round about her', but because the Holy Land represents the natural hub of Christian experience, which spreads out from this centre to the fringe of circumambient waters (for 'God said, Let there be a firmament in the midst of the waters' (Gen. 1.6)) where Pagans live, close to Leviathan (both whale and Devil), together with Negroes, apes, semi-homines and others whose distance from full humanity could be measured by their geographical distance from that area where humanity had been most fully realized in the life of Christ.

Other aspects of medieval geography and ethnography bear witness to the same basic assumptions.[12] That primitive view of the Ptolemaic 'threefold world'[13] which saw the continents as populated by the sons of Noah – Africa by the descendants of Ham, Asia by those of Shem, Europe by those of Japhet – *could* have been used as the starting-point for a science of ethnography. But the interest of the medieval mind was less in exploring the racial differences than in categorizing theological statuses. And to some extent we ought to be able to understand the force of this preference, even today. That explanation of the black skin of the Negro which sees it as a mark of God's disfavour, visited on the descendants of Ham, remains potently attractive, even in an allegedly scientific world. In the medieval world, it was the scientific fact that was the sport, present but useless. The *mappa mundi* in Hereford cathedral categorizes Europe and Africa by these names; but the words *Europa* and *Affrica* are interchanged – 'an "error"', remarks Denys Hay, 'which could scarcely have occurred if the words had meant anything'.[14]

The *mappa mundi* survived for longer than might have been expected.[15] Competent *portolani* or coastal charts exist from the end of the thirteenth century, and probably existed even earlier;[16] but though these might be useful to mariners, it did not follow that the learned would consent to take notice of them.[17] Indeed if we see the *mappæ mundi* as primarily 'emblems of man's spiritual world', there is no good reason why the two kinds of knowledge should conflict. As in the parallel case of Ptolemy and Copernicus, the two maps showed remarkable powers of co-existence, even though they were (seen on a single plane of 'truth') mutually exclusive.

The capacity of the individual mind to remain quite happy in the possession of incompatibles is a source of endless fascination when we read the Tudor voyagers and their propagandists. Dr John Dee, scientific colleague of Ortelius and Mercator, was at the same time a myth-bound and credulous charlatan.[18] Sir Walter Raleigh was a competent navigator and explorer; and yet he asserted his belief that there were headless people on the Caora river, 'with their eyes in their shoulders, and their mouthes in the middle of their breasts', giving as one reason for the belief that 'such a nation was written of by Mandeville'.[19] Sir John Mandeville's *Travels* was the most popular of all the travel books; Josephine Waters Bennett records twenty-five English editions before 1750.[20] Richard Hakluyt, a hero of modern geography, included Mandeville's *Travels* in the first edition of his *Principall Navigations* (1589), alongside more modern travellers and observers whose standards were quite different from his. John Stow, the painstaking and accurate antiquary, recorded in the margin of his copy of Norden's *Description of Hertfordshire* (1598) his opinion that Mandeville's 'travayles in forraine regions and rare reportes are at this time admired through the world'.[21] In the same way, when Stephen Batman in 1582 reissued Trevisa's medieval translation of Bartholomaeus Anglicus' *De Proprietatibus Rerum*, he included additional material from such painstaking modern observers as Sir Humphrey Gilbert, Stow, Gesner and Ortelius, seeming not to notice that the new patches tore away the substance of the old, fabulous material.[22] The result is a hotch-potch, neither entirely spiritual nor scientific, but in a Limbo somewhere between. Geoffroy Atkinson, in his survey of the French geographical literature of the Renaissance, has noted: 'La survivance des idées de l'ancienne géographie et des "Images du Monde" côte à côte avec les vérités nouvelles est responsable d'une partie de la confusion qui caractérise ce domain littéraire, surtout avant 1560. Mais jusqu'en 1609 les ouvrages "géographiques" présentent, à nos yeux d'aujourd'hui, un mélange du croyable et de l'incroyable.'[23] If anything, the confusion in France is more obvious than that in England, though not different in kind. No English figure focused as sharply the contradictions of the age as did André Thevet, 'grand voyageur' and Cosmographer Royal. Thevet's *Cosmographie universelle, illustrée de diverses figures des choses plus remarquables veuës par l'auteur* (1575) is a wilderness of marvels. The work was criticized by the geographers of the day, but the author won the acclaim of Ronsard, Jodelle and de Baif.[24]

The learned did not come clearly to the aid of the practical traveller, by establishing rational boundaries to assumptions about foreigners; neither did the practical man use his experience to correct his frame of reference about what might be expected. The travellers, as Wittkower has told us:

from the Dominican and Franciscan monks of the thirteenth century to Columbus and Fernão de Magellan, went out to distant countries with a preconceived idea of what they would find. Many of the travellers were learned; they had a knowledge of classical authors, they knew their Christian encyclopaedias, their treatises on natural science, their romances, they had seen on their maps the wondrous nations in those parts of the world to which they were travelling – in short, their imagination was fed from childhood with stories of marvels and miracles which they found because they believed in them.[25]

Writers on early geography tend to be disdainful of this 'frame of reference', to be implacably progressivistic in their viewpoint. Penrose never tires of castigating Columbus for the 'curious medievalism' of his thought – elsewhere his 'perverse medievalism' or his 'warped medievalism'[26] – but the interest of our period would seem to lie precisely in this overlap between the medieval world and the modern one, an overlap which allowed development and smooth progression rather than jarring disruption.

The new information which the English voyages of the sixteenth century brought to the national culture had to be fitted, as best it could, into a received image of what was important. This means that the facts were not received in quite the same way as they would have been in the nineteenth century. Historians of the last century were much taken with the idea of the Elizabethan imagination liberated by the voyagers. But there is little evidence of this outside the unhistorical supposition, 'that's how I would have reacted'. The voyages certainly did expand the physical horizon, but it is not clear that they expanded the cultural horizon at the same time. Englishmen became aware of India, Brazil, and the Spice Islands as possibly exploitable sources of wealth; to some they suggested possible avenues of imperial expansion (this we may take to be the master impulse in Hakluyt);[27] there was a small but influential circle interested in the technical (map-making, economic, astronomical) arrangements that had to be involved. But none of these were close to the traditional areas of culture; and to many of those who were close, it seemed that the new activities offered only new opportunities for baseness. George Buchanan spoke for many of the wisest minds when he declared that it was Avarice that had discovered America.[28] The image of man in his theological, political and social aspects could not be much affected by the discovery of empty or primitive lands; the aim of travel in this period is usually stated to be the observation of courts, universities and other sophisticated societies; and America could not offer anything of this kind. Atkinson has shown how small a proportion of French geographical literature in the period 1480–1609 was actually concerned with the New World.[29] In France in this period there were twice as many books published about the Turks[30] as there were about both the Americas, and four times as many about Asia in general. What is more, the proportion of books devoted to America actually drops as the period advances. The same balance seems to exist in Italian and Spanish literature also,[31] and there is no reason to suppose that the English figures are very different; the 'framework of assumptions' made the facts of physical geography seem uninteresting to the average cultured man of the period, a source neither of instruction nor of illumination.

Geographical exactitude was no part of the literary tradition, and even those writers who 'should have known better' show astonishing carelessness about place-names and modes of transport, using them for their associations, not for their reality. It may be that we can now 'exonerate' Shakespeare for shipwrecking Perdita on the sea-coast of Bohemia,[32] but it remains hard to find Helena a reasonable route from Rousillon to Compostella which goes via Florence,[33] or explain Proteus' sea-journey from Verona to Milan.[34] But Shakespeare is not exceptional, this is only common form in the period. Barnaby Rich's Don Simonides sails from Venice to Genoa (possible, I admit) and only a few hours from Venice is shipwrecked 'in a wilde deserte . . . onely inhabited with brute and savage beastes'; there he wanders for seven days before he meets another human being.[35] And yet Rich had served abroad in Holland and France and had been at sea as a privateer.[36] Henry Roberts was an author who spent most of his energies recording voyages and singing the praises of seamen. He was a sea-captain himself, and had been to Algiers, to Brazil and the Canaries.[37] But when he comes to write a romance, such as *A Defiance to Fortune* (1590), he makes his hero take ship from Siena,[38] while his *Haigh for Devonshire* (1600) describes a journey from Bordeaux to Rouen via the forest of Ardenne.[39] Thomas Lodge wrote his *A Margarite of America* (1596) while at sea with Cavendish: 'Touching the place where I wrote this, it was in those straits christned by *Magelan*; in which place to the southward many wonderous Isles, many strange fishes, many monstrous Patagones withdrew my senses . . . so that as there was great wonder in the place wherein I writ this, so likewise might it be marvelled . . .' It is obvious enough from the tone of this description that it is the legendary strangeness of the place rather than its factual existence that, for Lodge, makes it worth literary mention. The *America* of his romance has nothing to do with geography. The Empire of Cusco is no more Peruvian than that of Mosco is Russian; both (as C. S. Lewis has remarked) 'are conceived as high pagan civilizations in some undefined period of the past'.[40]

Marlowe is well known to have had a map.[41] He seems to have written *Tamburlaine* with Ortelius' *Theatrum Orbis Terrarum* open in front of him.[42] It was a trait of scholarship to use the most scientific atlas for his thesaurus of names; but he used it as a poet, not as a geographer, arbitrarily selecting quite unimportant towns to stand for the regions he intended.[43] There is little or no sense of reality in the places where Tamburlaine operates. Babylon, Natolia, Zanzibar, the Terrene and the Euxene seas – these, the last enchantments of the atlas, fitly convey the magic of 'the sweet fruition of an earthly crown'; but it adds nothing to imagine the physical reality of such places.

Sometimes, however, the new facts did cohere with assumptions already existing, and already prepared for in terms of emotional impact. The search for a Terrestrial Paradise was one of the motifs which the early voyagers caught easily from their fabulous predecessors.[44] And even the facts of American life could not wholly disabuse the imagination of the dream of an ideal natural civilization:

the people most gentle, loving and faithfull, voide of all guile and treason, and such as live after the maner of the golden age.[45]

. . . soo that (as wee have sayde before) they seeme to lyve in the goulden worlde, without toyle . . . without lawes, without bookes, and without Judges.[46]

The history of the New World seemed to give body and reality to this old dream, especially where (as in England and France) it provided a nationalistically attractive contrast between the ideal innocence of the exploited Indians and the corruption of the 'civilizing' Spaniards, who 'in stead of spreading Christian religion by good life, committed such terrible inhumanities, as gave those that lived under nature manifest occasion to abhor the devily character of so tyrannical a deity'.[47] To be fair to the Spaniards, one must note that the *History of the Indies* by Las Casas is one of the most eloquent documents in the whole of this literature; but Las Casas can hardly be taken as representative of the Spanish colonizers; and it is to the countries excluded from conquest that we must look for further development of this theme. Sir Thomas More's *Utopia*, Montaigne's *Essays* (especially that on the Cannibals) and Shakespeare's *The Tempest* all show a view of the 'savage' which is powerful, because they see him in relation to European sophistication, as an implicit criticism of European ways of life. In this respect the figure of the exotic foreigner is very like that of the pastoral shepherd; Gilbert Chinard has made this point in respect of Ronsard's *Isles Fortunées* (of 1553):

> ses sauvages ne ressemblent pas plus aux vrais sauvages que les bergers de tout le XVIe siècle ne ressemblent aux pastours de l'Ile-de-France ou ceux de Sannazar aux pâtres italiens. Si la vie et l'observation avaient fourni quelques traits, un point de départ assez difficile à situer, l'imagination poétique n'avait pas tardé à tout embellir et à tout magnifier.[48]

The foreigner could only 'mean' something important, and so be effective as a literary figure, when the qualities observed in him were seen to involve a simple and significant relationship to real life at home. Without this relationship, mere observation, however exact, could hardly make an impact on men caught up in their own problems and their own destiny.

The image of the world as a Christian entity centred on Jerusalem, and awareness of foreignness only in the sense of devil-prompted infidelity – this was, it is true, a vision which bore little relation to the general hatred of 'strangers' – even Christian strangers[49] – and the mass persecution of them, which went on all through the Middle Ages. But it is equally true that these eruptions of man's base nature were not canonized by theory, and so did not emerge in literary expressions. Europe retained a strong common culture well into the seventeenth century. Chaucer was widely read in at least three European literatures, but he shows little awareness of cultural distinctions, and he is probably right enough in failing to do so. Erasmus and More do not seem to have thought of one another as 'foreigners', and even such later humanists as the Scaligers, or Lipsius, or Casaubon knew 'the foreigner' only in the sense of 'the boor', the man whose Latinity fell below an international standard of excellence, such as today applies only to hotel cuisine.

But this common culture seems to exist in the seventeenth century largely as a hangover from the period of a common faith; the fragmentation of faiths in the period of the Reformation had its eventual result in the fragmentation of national cultures. The career which carried Isaac Casaubon (1559–1614) from international scholarship to Anglican apologetics[50] may serve as a model of the whole drift of interests. The national claim to represent a separate (and better) religious tradition – the development of 'God's Englishman' to set against Popish wickedness

– made the old organization of the West as Christendom, centred on Jerusalem, seem unsuitable, even in theory. When Jerusalem is set 'In England's green and pleasant land' it becomes obviously desirable to create another, England-centred, intellectual pattern of European races. But we should beware of supposing that a pattern of races emerged readily from the Europe that Christendom had become, a pattern capable of supplying moral discriminations rich and complex enough for literary use. There were, of course, intellectual patterns by which the main European nations could be related to one another. There was the ancient climatic contrast[51] which set Northern phlegm against Southern blood, and which was much invoked to contrast the grossness of the Teutons with the passionate conduct of the Latins. But this does not take one very far; more detailed relationships of place and temperament, such as John Davies of Hereford's 'never yet was fool a Florentine'[52] have the air of being climatic glosses on an existing cultural image. Surveys of the time are fond of making lists of French, English, Spanish, etc., national characteristics, such as we find in Portia's review of her suitors,[53] or at the end of Fynes Moryson's *Itinerary*,[54] as a mode of rhetoric in Thomas Wilson's *Art of Rhetoric*,[55] or as a poem in Turler's *The Traveller*.[56] But such lists hardly go beyond journalistic generalizations about superficial mannerisms (e.g. clothing, or eating habits):

> The Dutchman for a drunkard
> The Dane for golden locks,
> The Irishman for usquebaugh
> The Frenchman for the [pox].[57]

Here is material for caricature, but hardly for character.

Modern authors sometimes create profoundly revealing conflicts out of the clash of racial *mores*; for a modern author may see civilizations as representative of possible lines of development in human consciousness: Godbole, Aziz and Fielding in Forster's *A Passage to India* or Lambert Strether and Mme de Vionnet in Henry James' *The Ambassadors* provide obvious examples of this. But the complexity of valuation and the withholding of immediate judgement that these works require is a rare gift at any time; the Elizabethan urge to moralize was normally served most easily by presenting the foreigner in terms derived from simple nationalism. The European foreigner appears in post-Reformation English literature, in fact, as part of a process of vulgarization (in both senses of the word). He comes into literary focus caught between the xenophobic poles of Fear and Derision, which had always operated where Englishmen and Foreigners came into contact, but which was new as a literary image. And this applies not only to plays like *Jack Straw* (> 1593) and *Sir Thomas More* (*c.* 1596) which take anti-foreign feelings as their subject-matter, but is inescapable in any work showing the foreigner living in England; in such a context the 'stranger' could be shown to be a villain or a clown, but little else.

William Haughton's run-of-the-mill comedy *Englishmen for my money: or, a woman will have her will*, which he seems to have written for Henslowe about 1598, may be taken as a fair example of stock attitudes (of the more genial kind) to foreigners who tried to live in England. It tells the story of Pisaro, a 'Portingale' usurer-merchant resident in London,[58] whose three daughters are (illogically enough) totally English in outlook. They are wooed on one side by three English gallants, and on the other by three foreigners, a Frenchman, a Dutchman and an Italian. The daughters prefer the English suitors, the father promotes the foreigners; and the plot thus consists of the usual New Comedy type of intrigue and counter-intrigue. In the end the Englishmen (of course) win the girls and the foreigners accept this proof of superiority. What is interesting about this play in the context of a general consideration of foreigners is the superficiality of the colouring that their nationalities provide. We can recognize the plot of the usurer's fair daughter as a recurring stereotype. Usually the father's choice is rich and old, and ridiculous for these reasons; Haughton has added foreignness to the list of disqualifications, but it does not appear really different in kind from the other qualities of a standard pantaloon. Foreignness is no part of the moral structure, but is only an intriguing local colour.

Sometimes, though less frequently (as is understandable in any literature that aims to be entertaining rather than disruptive), the foreigner living in England is shown as more malignant than comic. In such cases he is seen (as always) to be dangerously 'cleverer than us', as slick, devious and lacking in integrity. In Robert Wilson's *Three Ladies of London* we meet Artifex, an honest English tradesman, who cannot sell his honestly made wares, 'for there be such a sort of strangers in this country / That work fine to please the eye, though it be deceitfully'.[59] When Artifex has been brought near enough to starvation he succumbs to these foreign wiles and is instructed by the Franco-Scottish Fraud how to make trashy goods look attractive. In the sequel-play, Wilson's *Three Lords and Ladies of London* Fraud reappears, this time (dressed as 'an old French artificer') deceiving the honest English clown Simplicity.[60] The moral structure of these plays derives from a very different convention from that of *Englishmen for my money*, but the 'foreignness' of

Fraud is as incidental as that of the suitors in Haughton's play. He is not wicked because he is foreign but foreign because he is wicked.

At the same time, however, as these prejudices were invading literature from the marketplace, increased national separateness was making foreign culture *more* attractive. The sense that foreigners are 'cleverer than us' can also be taken to mean that we must learn from them; rustic integrity can also be seen as provincial backwardness. 'Home-keeping youth have ever homely wits', says Shakespeare,[61] and the vision of courtly culture that he gives us in his high comedies is always set abroad. The New Learning substituted classical for biblical holy places as points of pilgrimage (geography was only taught in the period as ancillary to classical history and literature).[62] But the cultural image of Rome could not obliterate its politico-religious significance sufficiently to turn it into a second Jerusalem. Throughout the period there is a strong ambivalence in the attitude to travel. The obvious educational advantages are seen; yet (as S. C. Chew has remarked) 'It is difficult to discover in the literature of the period any whole-hearted and unqualified commendation of travel.'[63] The power of European and especially Popish corruption to mar the youth of England was much mulled over by moralists; and travel itself (even in the abstract) is seen as of doubtful spiritual utility;[64] it was dangerously close to *curiositas* – that spending of effort on matters no way essential to salvation. The bottom panel of the engraved title page of Samuel Purchas's *Pilgrimes* (1625)[65] seems to provide a useful emblem of this ambivalence. Purchas was, of course, a clergyman as well as a propagandist for the voyagers, and the two roles were not entirely coherent. On one side the title page tells us that 'soldiers and Marchants [are] the worlds two eyes to see it selfe'; in the middle it shows us Purchas reading verses from Psalm xxxix, 'for I am a stranger with thee, and a sojourner, as all my fathers were', and 'verily every man at his best state is altogether vanity', and from Hebrews xi, 'they were strangers and pilgrims on the earth'. We are still close to the medieval attitude, even here among the documents of the new geography.

I have suggested that the clear emergence of the foreigner in post-Reformation English literature was part of a process of *vulgarization*. Vernacular and popular prejudices invaded literature, to deprive those who were known from close contact with English life of any status save that of failed Englishmen. And the more intimately these strangers are known, the less their *strangeness* seemed intriguing, the more it seemed despicable. The Irish, the Welsh and the Scots were normally seen as

absurd deviations from an English norm; and the better-known Europeans acquired the same status.

The inhabitants of the Low Countries ('Dutch' and 'Flemings')[66]
were the best-known strangers in Elizabethan England. In the census of
1567 there were 2,030 Dutch in London out of a total of 2,730 aliens in
all;[67] in Norwich at the same time there were about 4,000 Flemings[68]
and there were considerable numbers distributed throughout East
Anglia and the southern counties. In 1573 there were said to be 60,000
Flemings in England.[69] But neither the Low Countries nor their inhabitants appear to have much significance in the literature of the time. Of
course there are plenty of 'butter-box' fat Dutchmen in the drama,
characters with names like Hans van Belch,[70] usually drunk, and unable to speak English even when sober; but these waterfront humours
do not add up to anything like a serious image of what it is like to be
Dutch. With the exception of Marston's 'Dutch Curtezan'[71] I know of
no seriously used character in the period alleged to be Dutch; and I
cannot think of a single play or romance which is set in contemporary
Holland or Belgium.

It seems as if the Dutch were too close to the eyes of the English
beholders for anything more than detailed idiosyncrasies to be observ-
able. France, whose Huguenot refugees soon began to rival the Dutch
and Flemings in numbers, was not in very different case. Insofar as the
French fitted into the southern climatic stereotype of hot-blooded, fiery-
tempered, subtle, dandified, smooth-tongued and Roman Catholic, their
role duplicated that of the Italians (see below); but France as a country
was too well known to be complex and divided in itself to provide a
fitting background for the full development of these characteristics.
The Elizabethans seem to have been aware of France as a great and
complex polity, working out in its history approximately the same
problems as beset England. Marlowe's *The Massacre at Paris* (1593) and
Chapman's political plays are set in France, but are not 'foreign' in the
sense that they are self-consciously un-English. France is in these cases
a convenient locale for the pursuit of political and religious conflicts
that could not be safely dealt with in an English setting. The locale and
the history are real and so avoid the escapist emphasis of Ruritanian
settings, but French national characteristics play little part in the effect.
The casts of such plays have little or nothing in common with characters
like Dr Caius in *The Merry Wives of Windsor* or the Dauphin in *Henry V*,
who appear in contrast to the English and whose national characteristics
are as superficial as those of the Dutchmen we have already discussed.

It seems to be the great virtue of Italy as a setting for literature of this period that everyday experience (and prejudice) supplied so little check and limitation to imaginative rendering. The number of Italians living in London was very small. In the census of 1567 there were only 140 Italians recorded;[72] and by 1580 the number had dropped to 116.[73] There was no traditional relationship between the countries, not even the relationship of war (as with France and Spain), and no strong economic links (as with the Low Countries and the Hanseatic ports). Italians are rarely mentioned in the petitions in which London merchants regularly complain of the unfair competition of aliens and strangers; and when Hand D (commonly supposed to be Shakespeare's) in the play of *Sir Thomas More* makes Sir Thomas speak of possible reprisals against English merchants abroad, he does not even mention Italy as a possible scene of such activity:

> go you to ffraunc or flaunders to any Iarman
> *pro*uince [to] spane or portigall nay any where.[74]

The absence of these varieties of knowledge gave all the greater strength to the cultural image of Italy as the land of wit (in all the variety of meanings that the word contained), of pleasure and of refinement, the home of Petrarch and Bembo and Castiglione and Ariosto, of Machiavelli and Guicciardini. It was an image which could be turned various ways (like the word *wit* itself), towards romance or towards diabolism, for use in comedy as well as in tragedy. The absence of a clearly defined central government in Italy further increased the malleability of the image, for it was only in a cultural sense that Italy was a 'country' at all. There, the high life of courts could be portrayed without intruding questions of responsibility (as they could hardly be in France or Spain, let alone England), whether in a mood of elegant idleness (the Milan of Shakespeare's *Two Gentlemen*) or in one of criminal selfishness (the Venice of Marston's *Antonio and Mellida*). And in the conflicts between these states there was no question of aligning one side or another with the English way of life. Italy as an image was sufficiently remote from England not to enforce immediate and invidious comparisons of national detail; but its way of life was (especially in tragedy) strange enough to force comparison with English life at a general moral and social level. The ambivalence of which I have already spoken in relation to travel, the simultaneously held desire to know, and fear of knowing, operated at maximum pressure in relation to Italy. For here there was a plethora of imaginative material and very little of that practical experience which might have limited its use.

I have elsewhere[75] developed the view that the 'Italy' of Elizabethan and Jacobean tragedy is related to England in the same way as the abstract world of the morality play (say Skelton's *Magnificence*) is related to real life (say the court of Henry VIII). I have suggested that just as the Renaissance search for 'reality' led Bishop Bale to substitute Stephen Langton and Pandulphus for Sedition and Private Wealth,[76] just so the developing sense of geographical 'fact' led from the 'Gargaphie' of *Cynthia's Revels* to the 'Italy' of *The Revenger's Tragedy* – though both should be seen as providing basically only the physical name for an abstract idea (in this like the medieval 'Jerusalem'). That argument was concerned principally with the corrupt Italian courts which are so common a feature of Jacobean tragedy; I do not wish to repeat here the interpretations essayed there; but there is a parallel line of argument centred on the mercantile world of Venice which should make the relationship between England and the image of Italy sufficiently clear.

Robert Wilson's late morality, *The Three Ladies of London* (*c.* 1581), focuses neatly the observed relationship between Venice and London. This play shows the gradual domination of London by the Lady called Lucre (who may be taken to stand for the acquisitive instinct) and the exiling of her virtuous sisters, Love and Conscience. Among the new servants who flock to serve Lucre is one called Usury, and in conversation with him she reveals her genealogy:

> *Lucre.* But, Usury, didst thou never know my grandmother, the old Lady
>   Lucre of Venice?
> *Usury.* Yes, madam; I was servant unto her and lived there in bliss.
> *Lucre.* But why camest thou into England, seeing Venice is a city
>   Where Usury by Lucre may live in great glory?
> *Usury.* I have often heard your good grandmother tell,
>   That she had in England a daughter, which her far did excel.[77]

The point is then made that what Venice has been in the past London is now becoming; and nowadays, Lucre concludes,

> I doubt not but that you shall live here as pleasantly,
>   Ay and pleasanter too, if it may be.

It is clear enough that Venice is here a type-name for 'the commercial society' and represents an ethos which could create a 'Venice' in London, by the same route as might establish 'Jerusalem' in England's 'green and pleasant land'.

It is the dynamism of this threat to life as it is that gives force and propriety to the most rigorous development of this morality image – to the Venice of Jonson's *Volpone*. Jonson has painstakingly documented the topography of a real Venice; but, as often with Jonson, the texture of physical reality is only a surface. The social habit on which the plot turns (legacy hunting) belongs to the Roman Empire, not at all to the Venetian Republic. But it matches the Venetian background, for it turns the acquisitive instinct into the sole dominating force of social existence. Obsessed by their mania for money, these characters achieve their Venice by losing their humanity. At the level of achievement they are Magnificos, Avvocatori, etc.; but beneath the Venetian robes lie the predatory fur and feather and membrane of fox and flesh-fly, raven, gor-crow and vulture. The merchant as predator today holds Venice in fee; but tomorrow (the moral seems to run) it may be called London. As if to drive home this point Jonson throws into his animal city an English innocent abroad and his resolute tourist wife. This pair, Sir Politic and Lady Would-be, measure not only the distance of Venice from London, but also the ease with which it could be traversed. Their virtue is protected by nothing but their ignorance, not even by their will to be virtuous, for what they 'would be' is Politic, that is, Italianate, that is, amoral.

Shakespeare's *The Merchant of Venice* is clearly less rigorous in the use of the Italian setting to focus the meaning of the play. The Venetian world is here self-sufficient and does not ask to be brought into relation to London. But the setting is not without propriety for all that. What we have here (and in this the play is comparable to *Volpone*) is a world of Finance, where lovers, Christian gentlemen, friends, enemies, servants, daughters, dukes, fathers, Jewish usurers, all express themselves in terms of financial relationship; and where the differences between love and hate, bounty and selfishness, Mercy and Justice, Christianity and Jewry are all treated in terms of money and how to handle it. Shakespeare focuses his Venice, however, not by pointing it back to England, but by pointing it out to the remoter world of 'blaspheming Jews',[78] whose non-Christianity, like that of pagans, infidels, Moors and Turks, gave depth of meaning to 'foreignness' that mere difference of European race could hardly do.

I have suggested that the Elizabethan awareness of foreigners was closely conditioned by a traditional religious outlook on the world; and that much 'new knowledge' lay fallow or was treated in a merely superficial manner because of this. The European nations were inexorably emerging from the matrix of Christendom; but they did not yet stand distinct enough from one another to allow simple dramatic opposition. Even Italy supplied a distinct moral image only in the small areas of power-politics or commercial practice. These were hardly to be seen as the fruits of a deeper level of national wickedness; an Italian on the stage had to do more than announce his racial identity before his moral status was known. For such large-scale contrast the Elizabethan author had to go beyond Europe, and draw on oppositions that were older than ethnographic differences, on the conflict between God and the devil, between Christian and anti-Christian.

Shakespeare's *Merchant of Venice* treats its Italians as Christians (though merchants) and therefore 'like us'. For the opposition is with a figure who stands outside Christianity altogether, and whose commercial practice is seen as a part of his religious attitude – legalistic, obdurate, revengeful. In sixteenth-century England the threat of the infidel outsider still had the general effect of stilling internal European oppositions and stressing the unity of Christendom. When the Turks attacked Malta in 1565 the English dioceses appointed prayers to be read 'every Wednesday and Friday' 'to excite all godly people to pray unto God for the delivery of those Christians that are now invaded by the Turk':

Forasmuch as the Isle of Malta . . . is presently [*at the moment*] invaded with a great Army and navy of Turks, infidels and sworn enemies of Christian religion . . . it is our parts, which for distance of place cannot succour them with temporal relief, to assist them with spiritual aid . . . desiring Almighty God . . . to repress the rage and violence of Infidels who by all cruelty and tyranny labour utterly to root out not only true Religion, but also the very name and memory of Christ our only Saviour, and all Christianity.[79]

When Don John of Austria (Philip of Spain's half-brother) defeated the Turks at the battle of Lepanto, England was in the middle of a life-and-death struggle with Spain and the Pope (this was the year of the Ridolfi Plot); Elizabeth might treat the news with the wry awareness that the balance had been tilted against France,[80] but the popular reaction was one of rejoicing:

The ninth of November a sermon was preached in Paules Church at London, by maister William Foulks of Cambridge, to give thanks to almightie God for the victorie, which of his mercifull clemencie it had pleased him to grant to the christians in the Levant seas, against the common enimies of our faith, the Turks.[81]

Present at this service were the Lord Mayor with the aldermen and the craftsmen in their liveries:

And in the evening there were bonefiers made through the citie, with banketting and great rejoising, as good cause there was, for a victorie of so great import-ance unto the whole state of the christian common-wealth.[82]

Foulkes's sermon took as its text, Psalm xvi. 4: 'Their sorrows shall be multiplied that hasten after another god.' The force of the old conception of the world is too obvious on such an occasion to require comment. And throughout the period, the glory of Lepanto did not fade. James I wrote a famous poem on the subject. In 1593 Gabriel Harvey can ask the very rhetorical question, 'Who honoureth not the glorious memory and the very name of Lepanto: the monument of Don John of Austria, the security of the Venetian state, the Halleluia of Christendome, and the welaway of Turky?'[83] And Thomas Randolph can sum up for us the general nostalgia for Lepanto when he says (well into the next century), 'The last valour show'd in Christendom / Was in Lepanto'.[84]

Shakespeare in *The Merchant of Venice* uses the figure of the Jew rather than the Turk to represent the pressure of infidel forces on the Chris-tian dispensation. This was necessary if the play was to turn to inter-pretations of a mode of conduct, not on the tragical arbitrament of war. But the point of infidelity is the same. Congreve's Lady Pliant was picking up an old tradition when she pursued her husband with the string of names, 'heathen . . . Turk, Saracen . . . Jew'.[85] In medieval representations the Jew swears by Mahomet, and he does so as late as in Wilson's *Three Ladies of London*;[86] in Marlowe's *Jew of Malta* Barabas and Ithimore make a point of the common Jewish-Turkish interests: 'we are villaines both / Both circumcized, we hate the Christians both'.[87] The two catch phrases, 'to turn Turk' and 'I am a Jew if . . .' were making precisely the same point – of betraying one's baptism, or selling one's soul to the devil.

Modern scholars often labour to document the exact racial back-ground of Shylock (or Othello); and certainly we can say that Shake-speare *could* have learned many true facts about these remote races. But the evidence of the plays suggests that the old framework of assump-tions about Jews, Turks and Moors – and this means theological assumptions – provided the controlling image in his mind.

It is clear that few Elizabethans had met a Jew (or a Turk, or a Moor); Jews provided no economic threat to the country. And so a modern historian can legitimately wonder at the residual prejudice through which 'Shakespeare could stir the blood of his audience by the spectacle of a Jewish usurer, three hundred years after there had been

Jews in the land'.[88] This is only a difficulty, however, if we ignore the point made by Dr Michelson: 'the New Testament and nothing but the New Testament is to be blamed for the peculiar psychology of the Jew in literature . . . down to and inclusive of Shylock this psychology was never based on observation, but simply taken over from the New Testament'.[89] To the Bible-readers and sermon-attenders of the Elizabethan age there was no difficulty in recalling the nature of the Jewish threat, a threat which was never-ceasing, for as Christ himself had remarked of the Jews, 'Ye are of your father, the devil',[90] and between the devil and the godly no peace could be imagined. In the medieval English *Play of the Sacrament* the Jew Jonathas is depicted as a rich man; but his wealth is not directly involved in his sin, which is simply the ritual re-enactment (with a consecrated wafer) of the central and never-to-be-forgotten sin of Jewry – the betrayal and murder of Christ.

When in 1594 Dr Lopez was arraigned for attempting to murder the Queen, Sir Edward Coke did not fail to raise his Jewishness in the argument against him: 'This Lopez, a perjured traitor and Jewish doctor, worse than Judas himself, undertook the poisoning.'[91] But it is the biblical sin that is still the key to the attitude. Again, when Lopez was at the gallows he 'declared that he loved the Queen as well as he loved Jesus Christ, which coming from one of the Jewish profession [= confession] moved no small laughter in the standers-by'.[92] What the audience could not forget was the relationship between the Jew and Christ; his activities in the world of the present could only be understood in the light of this. Shakespeare in *The Merchant of Venice* hardly mentions religion; but the contrast between the man who gives his life for his friend and the self-justifying legalist is squarely based on Scripture, however glossed with economic and psychological probability. And Jewish usury itself was seen by Shakespeare's contemporaries as more than an economic fact. It was an anti-Christian practice only proper to Jews, not because they were forced to live by it, but because Judas their eponym had sold Christ for thirty pieces of silver. And a usurer is a Jew whether he is racially (confessionally) Judaic or not. Bacon uses the verb 'to Judaize' of usury in general.[93] 'Lombard-Jew' is a typical conflation of appropriate nationalities, since (as Langland tells us), 'Lumbards of Lukes . . . lyven by lone as Iewes',[94] and in the Elizabethan period we find the same compound in Nashe,[95] and in Beaumont and Fletcher's *The Laws of Candy* – 'an usurer or Lumbard-Jew'.[96]

The acceptance of the idea 'Jew' as a fairly blank norm of villainy[97] gave authors an opportunity to play an effective theatrical trick on the audience's expectations, dramatizing the idea 'worse than a Jew'. In Wilson's *Three Ladies of London* we meet Mercatore, a Christian merchant from Italy who undermines English sturdiness by importing knick-knacks, 'Musk, amber, sweet powders, fine odours, pleasant perfumes, and many such toys: Wherein I perceive consisteth that country gentlewomen's joys'.[98] Mercatore cheats Gerontus, a Jew, of the money for these imports, and when Gerontus meets up with him in Turkey, and asks for his money, the Christian threatens to 'turn Turk' (quite literally) and so (in spite of Turkish abhorrence) escape the debt. Gerontus, rather than see such a shocking breach of Christian faith, cancels the debt. This is wildly unrealistic, of course; but it is a good indication of the extent to which the Jew in this period is an idea or a norm rather than a person.

Another sophisticated use of the Jew figure can be seen in Marlowe's *The Jew of Malta*, where Jew and Christian once again (as in *Three Ladies*) face one another under pressure from the Turks. This time, however, everyone is much more realistic, meaning much more unpleasant. The Jew has all the wickedness that was traditionally associated with his nation; but the Christian is almost without his expected virtue. The author again uses the expected opposition only as a ground plan or *canto fermo*, over which he works sophisticated inversions and vari- ations.[99] Marlowe's play treats racial prejudice of a quite distinct kind from anything we know in the modern world; for the prejudice is not so much based on observation of what Jews actually do, as on assump- tions about what kind of things people with this theological status are expected to do. This kind of unobserved *a priori* assumption obviously lends itself to dramatic inversion.

A pamphlet of the seventeenth century bears the curious title, *The blessed Jew of Marocco, or a blackamoor turned white.*[100] The two paradoxes in the title are obviously seen as parallel; and what I have said already about the attitude to Jews can be (in large) applied to 'Moors' also. Indeed I wish to go farther and point to *Othello* as the most magnificent specimen of the dramatic 'inversion of expected racial values' which I have discussed above in relation to 'Jew' plays. In order to make this point one must first note that in Elizabethan drama before *Othello* there are no Moor figures who are not either foolish or wicked. Eleazer in *Lust's Dominion* (*c.* 1600), Aaron in *Titus Andronicus*, Muly Hamet in *The Battle of Alcazar* (*c.* 1589) supply the norm of dramatic expectation – of a man whose colour reveals his villainy as (quite literally) of the deepest dye. We can have no doubt, of course, that Shakespeare's Othello, like the 'Moors' I have already mentioned, is not conceived of as a 'sheikh of Araby' type of coloured man, but as 'the thick-lips', 'the devil', with 'collied' complexion – in short, as a coal-black Negro.[101] The word 'Moor' was very vague ethnographically, and very often seems to have meant little more than 'black-skinned outsider', but it was not vague in its antithetical relationship to the European norm of the civilized white Christian. Elizabethan authors describe Moors as existing in many parts of the globe: we hear of the 'Mores of Malabar' from Spenser,[102] of Moors in Malacca from James Lancaster,[103] of Moors in Guinea from Eden,[104] of Moors in Ethiopia from Lodge,[105] of Moors in Fukien from Willes,[106] of Moors in America from Marlowe[107] and sundry others. There seem, in fact, to be Moors everywhere, but only everywhere in that outer circuit of non-Christian lands where, in the *mappæ mundi*, they appear with the other aberrations – 'salvage' men, satyrs, apes, skiapods, and the creatures that Othello knew of old:

> The Anthropophagi, and men whose heads
> Do grow beneath their shoulders.

Throughout the Elizabethan period, indeed, there seems to be a considerable confusion whether the Moor is a human being or a monster. In the 'plat' of *Tamar Cam* (1592) we are told of an entry of 'Tartars, Geates, Amozins, Nagars, ollive cullord moores, Canniballs, Hermophrodites, Pigmies', etc.[108] a characteristic medley; in *Volpone* we have a list of undesirables that Volpone has coupled with to produce his Fool, Dwarf and Hermaphrodite; the supposititious parents are 'beggers, / Gipseys and Jewes, and black-*moores*'.[109] In the street-pageants and processions of the time, Moors played a considerable part – but again a part that was often interchangeable with that of the Devils, Greenmen, etc. As Withington has remarked: 'The relation between wild-men, green-men, foresters, Robin Hood, the Moors, and the devil is very difficult to clear up. A great many cross-influences must exist; and it seems obvious that all these figures are connected.'[110]

Finally, we have the evidence of the English folk-play. In this, the enemy of St George is variously called 'The Turkish Knight, Black Morocco Dog, Morocco King, Black Prince of Darkness, Black and American Dog'.[111] Such confusions are obviously parallel to those which surround the Jew figure; and the reason, I would suggest, is the same in both cases. The Moor, like the Jew (but with less obvious justification), is seen in primarily religious terms. The epithets that Jonson and Shakespeare apply ('superstitious Moor' and 'irreligious Moor')[112] seem to me the basic ones. And the Moor had a very obvious advantage for the presentation of *a priori* wickedness; however large was the 'bottle nose' that Henslowe used to present the Jew of Malta on the stage,[113] it could not have been as impressive as the total sable of the Moor; which was seen as an emblem of Hell, of damnation, as the natural livery of the devil. Thomas Heywood may be taken to represent the general view when he speaks of 'a Moor, Of all that bears mans shape, likest a divell'.[114] Indeed, we may remove the *like* qualification; the devil himself appeared to many in the body of a Moor. Reginald Scott in his *Discovery of Witchcraft* (1584) tells us that 'A damned soule may and dooth take the shape of a blacke moore',[115] and that Bodin 'alloweth the divell the shape of a blacke Moore, and as he saith he used to appear to Mawd Cruse, Kate Darey, and Jone Harviller'.[116] St Birgitta (of the fourteenth century) tells us in her *Revelations* that she saw the devil in the form of 'an Ethiope, ferefull in syght and beryng'.[117] St Margaret had the same experience.[118] In Shakespeare's own day the Enemy was still using this form. Sara Williams, one of the possessed women described in Harsnet's *Popish Impostures* (well known as a source of diabolical names in *King Lear*) was said to have seen 'a blacke man standing at the doore, and beckning at her to come away';[119] this was a demon, of course. Later, another black figure tempted her to break her neck down the stairs, and (at another time) to cut her throat.[120] Samuel Butler, with characteristic acidity, summed up the whole belief in a couple of lines:

> Some with the devil himself in league grow
> By's representative, a Negro.[121]

If this is a fair summary of received expectations about black men, we can see how Shakespeare is using this background in his *Othello*. Iago presents the civilized, white, Christian viewpoint in just these terms. But, as in the parallel case of Gerontus in *The Three Ladies of London*, the supposed outcast turns out to be the true Christian, while the nominal Christian with the white skin appears as the devil's representative. And again, as in Wilson's play, the Turks provide a pressure that sharpens the moral issues. Othello appears not only as noble, gracious, courtly, Christian, loving, but he is even the leader of Christendom in the last sense in which Christendom had any meaning – in the Crusade against the Turks, 'hellish horseleaches of Christian blood'.[122] The play thus may stand as one of the latest (as it is the supreme example) of representations of foreigners, using the old assumption that foreigners are meaningful because of their status in God's Providence. The play does not assent to this proposition; but Shakespeare accepts what the older geography could give him – a freedom to concentrate on essential moral problems – where the new geography could only give him facts. There is enough 'Moorish' and 'Venetian' colouring to prevent us losing our sense of the here-and-now in place and character; but this is only a starting-point for an exploration of what such characteristics imply. The 'overlap' in Renaissance geography of which I have already spoken, the co-existence of radically different and scientifically incompatible views of the world, allows Shakespeare to explore, swiftly and coherently, the image of the foreigner, the stranger, the outsider in a dimension which is at once terrestrial and spiritual.

First published in *Shakespeare Survey 17*, 1964, with accompanying illustrations.

NOTES

1 The Levant Company was established in 1579.
2 The Russia Company had its first privileges confirmed in 1569.
3 See Sidney Lee, 'Caliban's Visits to England', *Cornhill Magazine* n.s. 34 (1913), 333–45.
4 Prologue, A. 51–9.
5 *Ibid.* A. 463–6.
6 Cf. C. R. Beazley, *The Dawn of Modern Geography* (London, 1897–1901): 'Devotional travel was as little in sympathy with exploration for the sake of knowledge as the theological doctrines of a scriptural geography . . . were in sympathy with the formation of a scientific theory of the world's shape' (I, 13).
7 B. Penrose, *Travel and Discovery in the Renaissance, 1420–1620* (Cambridge, Mass., 1952), p. 7.
8 Translated in Hakluyt Society, vol. XCVII (1897).
9 Beazley, *Dawn of Modern Geography*, I, 32.
10 *Ibid.* p. 252.
11 Gilbert de Nogent (Migne, *Patrologia Latina*, CLVI, 25) quoted in Caplan, 'The Four Senses', *Speculum* 4 (1929), 283.
12 See, for example, the 'Beatus' maps, whose radical purpose was 'the delineation of the twelve apostles, their dioceses and their distribution over the habitable world as "sowers of the word"' (Beazley, *Dawn of Modern Geography*, II, 563).
13 R. R. Cawley, *Unpathed Waters* (Princeton, N.J., 1940), pp. 75 ff., traces the prevalence of this idea in English literature up to 1641.
14 Denys Hay, *Europe, the Emergence of an Idea* (Edinburgh, 1957), pp. 54–5.
15 John Cayworth's Christmas masque of 1636, *Enchiridion Christiados* (BM Add. MS. 10311), is the latest use that I have found. The masque is illustrated by a T–O type map, showing Christ's descent through the

world from Heaven (at the top of the map), his descent into Hell, and his re-ascension into Heaven. As Cawley remarks, 'Cayworth would have gone far to seek a design which would suit his purposes quite so perfectly' (*Unpathed Waters*, p. 76). It is clear that Cayworth intends his map-form to be spiritually effective, and this implies (what is more interesting there) that he expected it to be intelligible as a world-shape to his patron and to his generation. Another interesting volume, pointing to the late diffusion of these medieval notions is *STC* 17297 – *Mappa Mundi: otherwyse called the Compasse and Cyrcuet of the worlde, and also the Compasse of every Ilande, comprehendyd in the same* [R. Wyer, 1535]. This is advertised in the colophon as *Very necessary for all Marchauntes and Maryners. And for all such, as wyll labour and traveyle in the countres of the worlde.* But in spite of much invocation of the name of Ptolemy, the image of the world provided is the medieval one, centred on Jerusalem (sig. A3^{v}), with the Terrestrial Paradise in the East, and Hell 'in the myddes of Affryke under the earth'. Africa is the land 'of dyvers shape of people, and many great wonders' (sig. A4^{v}), and America has no mention at all.

16 See M. C. Andrews, 'The Study and Classification of Medieval Mappae Mundi', *Archaeologia* 75 (1924–5), 64.

17 'None of [the early printed world maps] is influenced by the advances in geographical knowledge . . . There is thus no group of printed maps based on Spanish, Portuguese or Italian portolans, notwithstanding their proximity in time' (Erich Woldan, 'A Circular, Copper-Engraved Medieval World Map', *Imago Mundi* 11 (1954), 13).

18 On Dee's gifts to geography see E. G. R. Taylor, *Tudor Geography, 1485–1583* (London, 1930).

19 'The Discovery of Guiana', in Hakluyt, *The Principal Navigations . . . of the English Nation* (Glasgow, 1903–5), x, 406.

20 Josephine Waters Bennett, *The Rediscovery of Sir John Mandeville* (New York, 1954).

21 Quoted in M. Letts, *Sir John Mandeville* (London, 1949), p. 13.

22 See esp. Bk 18, chap. 48, 'De Faunis et Satiris'.

23 Geoffroy Atkinson, *Les nouveaux horizons de la Renaissance française* (Paris, 1935), p. 14.

24 See, for example, Gilbert Chinard, *L'Exotisme américain dans la littérature française au XVIe siècle* (Paris, 1911), p. 10.

25 R. Wittkower, 'Marvels of the East', *Journal of the Warburg and Courtauld Institutes* 5 (1942), 195.

26 Penrose, *Travel and Discovery*, pp. 78, 86, 90.

27 See G. B. Parks, *Richard Hakluyt* (New York, 1928).

28 *De Sphaera*, I, 182, quoted by C. S. Lewis, *English Literature in the Sixteenth Century* (Oxford, 1954), p. 16. Cf. Atkinson, *Les nouveaux horizons* 'L'idée maîtresse des voyageurs de la Renaissance fut sans doute l'ambition de faire fortune' (p. 135).

29 Atkinson, *Les nouveaux horizons*, pp. 9 ff.

30 The Renaissance period was fascinated by the Turkish Empire, as combining the features of a diabolical portent with those of a remarkably efficient politico-military organization. Knolles's great *Generall Historie of the Turkes* (1603) nicely catches this ambivalence in his opening phrase about 'the glorious Empire of the Turkes, the present terrour of the World'.

31 See (on Spain) Angel Franco, *El tema de América en los autores españoles del siglo de oro* (Madrid, 1954), and M. A. Moringo, *América en el teatro de Lope de Vega* (Buenos Aires, 1946); on Italy see Rosario Romeo, *Le scoperte americane nella coscienza italiana del Cinquecento* (Milan and Naples, 1954).

32 See S. L. Bethell, *The Winter's Tale* (1947), p. 33.

33 *All's Well that Ends Well*, 3.4.4 and 3.5.34.

34 *Two Gentlemen of Verona*, 2.3.30.

35 *The straunge and wonderfull adventures of Don Simonides* (1581), sig. M3ᵛ.

36 See Cranfill and Bruce, *Barnaby Rich* (Austin, Tex., 1953).

37 See L. B. Wright, 'Henry Robarts', *Studies in Philology* 29 (1932), 176–99.

38 Sig. E4.

39 Sig. C2.

40 Lewis, *English Literature in the Sixteenth Century*, p. 424.

41 M. E. Seaton, 'Marlowe's Map', *Essays and Studies* 10 (1924), 13–35.

42 *Ibid.* p. 28.

43 *Ibid.* pp. 27–8.

44 See G. Boas, *Essays on Primitivism and Related Ideas in the Middle Ages* (Baltimore, 1948); Luis Weckmann, 'The Middle Ages in the Conquest of America', *Speculum* 26 (1951), 130–41.

45 Hakluyt, *Principal Navigations*, VIII, 305.

46 Peter Martyr [Anglerius], *The decades of the newe world or West India*, trans. R. Eden (1555), sig. E1ᵛ.

47 Fulke Greville, *Life of Sir Philip Sidney* (1652), ed. Nowell Smith (Oxford, 1907), pp. 116–17.

48 Gilbert Chinard, *L'Exotisme américain*, pp. 123–4.

49 The word *foreigners* is not at all common in the sixteenth century; *strangers* is the normal expression. Indeed the first three examples of the former word in *OED* (that is, up to 1637) are all qualified by the latter word, as if to provide a clue to the meaning.

50 Mark Pattison, *Isaac Casaubon* (Oxford, 1892).

51 J. O. Thomson, *History of Ancient Geography* (Cambridge, 1948), pp. 106 ff. Charron, *Of Wisdom* (trans. Samson Lennard; ent. Stationers' Register 1606), has an interesting discussion of this (Bk 1, chap. 42).

52 John Davies of Hereford, *Microcosmos* (ed. Grosart, 1878), p. 32.

53 *The Merchant of Venice*, 1.2.32 ff.

54 Fynes Moryson, *An itinerary, containing his ten yeeres travell* (1617), III (Glasgow, 1907), 448 ff.

55 Thomas Wilson, *The Art of Rhetoric* (1585), ed. G. H. Mair (Oxford, 1909), pp. 178–9.

56 *De Peregrinatione* (Strassburg, 1574); *The Traveiler of Jerome Turler* (1575).

57 John Marston, *The Malcontent* (1604), 5.2.1–4.

58 It is worthwhile noticing that this 'Portingale' seems to be a Jew, in fact, though the word 'Jew' is never used. He is called 'Signior Bottle-nose' (Hazlitt's Dodsley, x, 522) and elsewhere he is said to have 'a snout / Able to shadow Paul's, it is so great' (p. 481).

59 Hazlitt's Dodsley, VI, 279.

60 *Ibid.* pp. 438–9, 499.

61 *Two Gentlemen of Verona*, 1.1.2.

62 Foster Watson, *The Beginnings of the Teaching of Modern Subjects in England* (London, 1909), p. 91. F. de Dainville, S. J., *La géographie des humanistes* (Paris, 1940).

63 S. C. Chew, *The Crescent and the Rose* (New York, 1937), p. 29.

64 Foster Watson has a useful survey of attitudes to travel in the period (*Beginnings*, pp. 128–35).

65 Cf. the MORS written round the Hereford *Mappa Mundi*.

66 *Dutch* simply meant (in this period) 'German-speaking' (distinguished when necessary into 'High-Dutch' and 'Low-Dutch'). Most of the refugees were, however, from the nearest area of Teutonic-speaking population, i.e. were 'Dutch' in the modern sense. But Elizabethan vagueness in these matters defies simple explanation. Thus in Dekker and Webster's *Northward Ho* (1605) the 'Hollander' has his home in Augsburg.

67 Huguenot Society Publications, vol. x, part i (1900), p. 365.

68 *Social England*, ed. Traill and Mann (London, 1903), III, 500.

69 E. Eckhardt, *Die dialekt- und ausländertypen des älteren Englischen dramas*, Teil II (Materialien zur Kunde des älteren Englischen dramas, vol. XXXII) (Louvain, 1911), p. 48.

70 In Dekker and Webster's *Northward Ho*.

71 I cannot even guess why Marston represented Franceschina as Dutch. It is entirely proper to her part that she should be foreign, a stranger to the bourgeois comforts of the Subboys and Freevills, but I do not know why Holland should be the foreign country chosen.

72 Huguenot Soc. x (i), 365.

73 W. Besant, *London in the Time of the Tudors* (London, 1904), p. 80.

74 MSR lines 250 ff. Cf. the petition against Aliens printed in Besant, *London in the Time of the Tudors*, Appendix III, which lists those by whom the realm is pestered as 'Frenchmen, galymen [? = allemandes], pycardis, flemings, keteryckis [? = Caterans (Highlanders)], Spaynyars, Scottis, Lombards'.

75 G. K. Hunter, 'English Folly and Italian Vice', in *Jacobean Theatre*, ed. John Russell Brown and Bernard Harris (London, 1960), pp. 85–110.

76 In his *King Johan*.

77 Hazlitt's Dodsley, VI, 268–9.

78 *Macbeth*, 6.1.26.

79 *Liturgical Services of the Reign of Queen Elizabeth*, ed. W. K. Clay (Parker Society (1847)), pp. 519–23.

80 *CSP* (*Spanish 1568–1579*), p. 359.

81 Holinshed's Chronicle (1808 edn), IV, 262.

82 *Ibid.*

83 *A new letter of notable contents* (1593) (*Works*, ed. Grosart, I, 262).

84 *The muses looking glass* (Oxford, 1638), act 3, scene 4 (*Works*, ed. Hazlitt, II, 232).

85 *The double dealer*, act 4, scene 4. Cf. Brandt/Barclay in the *Ship of Fools*, where in the section 'Of straunge Folys and infydels as sarasyns, paynems, turkes and suche lyke' we may read the following:

> The cursed Iewes despysynge christis lore
> For theyr obstynate, and unrightwyse cruelte
> Of all these folys must nede be set before
> The nacion of Turkes next of them shall be
> The sarrazyns next . . .
> The Scithians and also they of Sarmatyke
> And they of Boeme, by fendes fraudolent
> Ar led and blynded with an errour lyke . . .
> The owgly Mauryans ar also of this sect etc.
>
> (1874 edn, II, 188–9)

86 Hazlitt's Dodsley, VI, 345.

87 Ed. Tucker Brooke, II, 979–80.

88 Besant, *London in the Time of the Tudors*, p. 239.

89 H. Michelson, *The Jew in Early English Literature* (Amsterdam, 1926), pp. 4–5.

90 John 8.44. Cf. Thomas Ingelend, *The Disobedient Child* (*c.* 1560) in which the Devil says:

> All the Jews and all the Turks,
> Yea, and a great part of Christendom,
> When they have done my will and my works,
> In the end they fly thither, all and some.
>
> (Hazlitt's Dodsley, II, 310)

91 See G. B. Harrison, *Second Elizabethan Journal* (London, 1931), p. 289.

92 *Ibid.*, p. 304.

93 'Of Usury'.

94 C text. Passus 5.1.194.

95 'Lenten Stuffe' (1599), in *Works*, ed. McKerrow, III, 211.

96 4.2.32–3; *Works*, ed. Waller and Glover, III, 283.

97 It is worth noting a correction in Jonson's *Every man in his humour*, where the quarto text (1601) reads *I am a Jew* (3.1.40) where the Folio (1616) reads *I am a knave* (3.3.48).

98 Hazlitt's Dodsley, VI, 330.

99 'The theology of Marlowe's *Jew*', *Journal of the Warburg and Courtauld Institutes* (1964).

100 (1648); Wing, s. 545.

101 It is sometimes supposed that the Elizabethans made a regular distinction between a blackamoor and a tawny moor. Morocco in *The Merchant*

of Venice is called a tawny moor, and the New Arden editor glosses this 'in contrast to a black one'. Portia, however, says that he has 'the complexion of a devil' and in any normal usage this would mean 'black' (see text below). The word *tawny* often seems to mean little more than dark. Thus in *King Leir*:

> As easy is it for the Blackamoore
> To wash the tawny colour from his skin.
>
> (MSR 1271 f.t)

Eleazer, in *Lust's Dominion*, is clearly black; yet he is called *tawny* (ed. Brereton (Louvain, 1931), line 231); he comes from Barbary (229), but is said to be an *Indian* (1819, 2316).

102 *Faerie Queene*, 6.7.43.

103 Hakluyt, *Principal Navigations*, VI, 399.

104 Peter Martyr [Anglerius], trans. R. Eden, *The History of travayle* (1577), fol. 348^v.

105 *Works* (Hunterian Society), II, 52.

106 Hakluyt, *Principal Navigations*, VI, 321 (where it is quite clear that 'Moorish' means 'Mahommedan').

107 *Doctor Faustus* (in *Works*, ed. Tucker Brooke), p. 150 (cf. the 'black Indians' in Brewer's *The lovesick king* (Bang's Materialien (1907), 952–6), in Googe's translation of Kirchmeyer's *The popish kingdom* (1570) (1880 edn), p. 39, and the African Indians in *Sir Thomas Stukely* (TFT 2169)).

108 *Henslowe Papers*, ed. W. W. Greg (1907), p. 148. Cf. the 'Negro-Tartars in *Gesta Grayorum*' (MSR 46) – 'Negarian Tartars' on p. 52.

109 *Volpone*, 1.5.44–5.

110 R. Withington, *English Pageantry* (Cambridge, Mass. and London, 1918), I, 74. Cf. the collocation of ideas in Wilson's *Three Ladies*, where Mercatore proposes to travel in search of profit:

> me dare go to de Turks, Moors, Pagans, and more too:
> What do me care, and me go to da great devil for you?
>
> (Hazlitt's Dodsley, VI, 306)

111 E. K. Chambers, *The English Folk Play* (Oxford, 1933), p. 28.

112 Ben Jonson, *Sejanus*, 5.1.712; Shakespeare, *Titus Andronicus*, 5.2.121.

113 *Jew of Malta* (ed. Tucker Brooke), 1229.

114 *The Fair Maid of the West* (Part II) (Pearson Rpt p. 350).

115 *The Discovery of Witchcraft* (1584), p. 535.

116 *Ibid.*, p. 89.

117 EETS o.s. 178 (1929), 43. I owe this reference to Mr B. F. Nellist.

118 Scott, *Discovery of Witchcraft*, p. 456.

119 Samuel Harsnet, *A declaration of egregious popish impostures* (1603), p. 177.

120 *Ibid.*, p. 178.

121 *Hudibras*, 2.1.399–400.

122 Hakluyt, *Principal Navigations*, V, 122.

CHAPTER 4

'Spanish' Othello: the making of Shakespeare's Moor

Barbara Everett

Many studies of *Othello* confront as a vital problem what they see as some inherent randomness in the play. The current agreement, too, that the work is a 'domestic tragedy' may more tacitly voice the same reaction, depending as it seems to do on Bradley's sense of the play as less great than the others of the Big Four, because the dramatist had not fully succeeded in universalizing his materials – a judgement that brings us back to that 'randomness' again. This widespread reaction among readers and critics is not my subject here; I want to use it only to suggest that if that randomness really does survive in *Othello* as an achieved work of art, then it surely originates from the play's main source, Cinthio's prose narrative. It is hard for a reader of Shakespeare not to define literary merit as quantity of meaning – even in a case like *Othello* where the 'meaning' in a higher sense is still distinctly moot; the play, despite all the doubt, means a good deal to us. Of merit or meaning in that sense Cinthio's story has little. Given what we cannot help finding the mere externality of its avowed moral, its only meaning lies in the purposiveness of the Ensign's love-jealousy; when Shakespeare removes or blurs this he leaves what remains of the narrative as a succession of events that are 'cruel', almost in the modern sense of 'absurd'.

Thus deprived of conventional motivation the story faced the dramatist with peculiar problems. There is even evidence (or so I hope to argue elsewhere) that Shakespeare rewrote his tragedy somewhere between the stages represented by the quarto and the Folio versions, simply in an attempt to release his hero from the degradingly passive and ridiculous role imposed on him by the ruins of the original intrigue situation. This degree of essential difficulty in the story ought perhaps to make any student of the play ask what it was in the source narrative that nonetheless so powerfully attracted Shakespeare as to make him decide to take it on. There may be many different answers to this question, and all of them will of course be both subjective and hypothetical:

but it seems to me all the same a question that needs asking. The answer that I want to put forward tentatively here has at least the support of different kinds of evidence. I want to propose that the dramatist's imagination was compelled – and compelled at once, beyond the point of no return – by the random premise of Cinthio's opening phrase, 'Fu già in Venezia un Moro', 'There was in Venice a Moor.' Here, surely, with the Moor who is, in the Italian, left as character-less as he is nameless but for his race-title, must Shakespeare too have begun. It is worth remarking that in the dramatist's own lifetime the play seems to have been universally known not as *Othello* but as *The Moor of Venice*. And similarly, the elegy on Burbage speaks of him as the creator of 'young Hamlett' and 'kind Leer', but *not*, interestingly enough, of jealous Othello: the role is that of 'the Greved Moore', a phrase which retains both the passive stance and the race-typification of the source-story's character.[1] There may be some support too from within Shakespeare's own career for the assumption that what drew him to Cinthio's story was essentially its beginning with a 'Moor in Venice'. We do not know when the dramatist read Cinthio's narrative first, but we tend to assume he read it at least most fruitfully immediately before he began to write his own tragedy. This is a point in time from which he might look back at *The Merchant of Venice* as already an achieved success nearly a decade earlier in a busy past: when the 'Venice' it contained and the 'Moor' it presented would certainly contribute something of their own rich meaning to Cinthio's threadbare narrative, and yet were far enough behind not to hinder the emergence of an altogether new poetic possibility, in which 'Moor' and 'Venice' reacted together in their new context to make an original poetic world. For Othello is as different from Morocco (or, for that matter, from Aaron, further back still) as he is from the Moor of Cinthio's narrative.

The difference between the two writers is of course not confined to their central characters. To agree that Shakespeare used Cinthio's random story is to recognize also how much the prose story's emptiness does not hold or foreshadow the strange polarities of *Othello*, its brutal farce as well as its high tragedy, its fierce romanticism and its cool mundaneness. The play is often alluded to as simple, but is not; those critics who call it simple may differ strikingly among themselves in their very description of this 'simplicity'. Indeed, it is a leading characteristic of the work to seem simple and yet to produce very different responses from the equally sensitive and intelligent persons it has numbered among its readers.[2] An explanation of this may lie in the peculiar relation of the work to its source. What we call the 'source' of a great work of literature may never be its true source: which is instead to be found within those great accretions of experience and idea which constitute a writer's consciousness. The strength and richness of these stores of idea and experience may depend on those very qualities which tend to make them hard of access, their depth from the surface and their dislocation from each other. The value to Shakespeare of a story like Cinthio, such as we call his 'source', may have lain essentially in its relative unlikelihood – its thinness, simplicity, its functionalism: its capacity in short to activate by some clue or other all the otherwise unhandlable resources below consciousness; and by its lack of other merit not to obtrude on this activity once it was well begun. I am suggesting that Cinthio's 'Moor in Venice' acted as precisely such a clue, and that there was nothing in the impoverished narrative that follows that was talented enough to get in Shakespeare's way: the play was begun, and the dramatist stayed with it whatever inordinate difficulties occurred.

Beneath the 'simple' surface of *Othello* there are problems which are also its life, its vitality: any of which it is therefore unwise to ignore. The quality that we call, in moral terms, randomness; the play's shifting from tragic mood to comic and back again; the aspect of the being and relation of Othello and Iago that has caused criticism of the play to be filled with the whole incidental debate of 'nobility' and 'ignobility' – all these underlie the play's 'simplicity'. I do not intend even to try to solve any of them. What I want to do is to suggest that they are all directly related to what I argue is the play's essential beginning: Shakespeare's acceptance of the subject of the 'Moor in Venice'. And this was so, I shall suggest, because 'Moorishness' was a condition that had a meaning, for Shakespeare and his audiences, once casually familiar though long lost to us. It was the subject of the Venetian or – more largely – *displaced* Moor which, given certain contemporary circumstances, at once fused together rich and diverse potentialities within the dramatist's mind, and called his new tragedy into being.

The true source of a poet's creativity is a subject perhaps both over-large and over-hypothetical. It can be translated into approachably smaller matters of fact by asking of Shakespeare's finished text of *Othello* a few questions so simple that it is surprising they have not been asked before. If we read the play the first word that we meet after the opening stage direction is the speech-prefix *Roderigo*. Why should the dramatist have bestowed on his Venetian gull a *Spanish* name? The answer must be that Roderigo, who does not exist in Cinthio, depends wholly on his role as 'feed' (in all senses) to the character called in Cinthio the Ensign: here made not the friend of the Moor but his subordinate, almost his servant. The gull provides the necessary social extraversion for this underhand character now newly called Iago. Roderigo has a Spanish name, in short, because Iago has. But here a much more striking question arises. How then does Iago come to have a Spanish name? – and *such* a Spanish name, at that?

For it must be noted that Shakespeare has given his villain the same name, in Spanish, as his new King possessed: and the writer who will take pains to interrupt his tensely economical *Macbeth* with a courtly compliment to his new royal patron is not going to donate that actual or future King's name to a villain without noticing what he is doing. Furthermore, Shakespeare is careful to reiterate these Spanish names several times over in his play's first scene, which re-echoes with 'Roderigo', 'Iago' and 'the Moor', as if the writer were intent on implanting them well within the consciousness of his audience. And Shakespeare was unlikely to have been protected from the risk involving *lèse-majesté* by his own ignorance or that of audiences, for at that time 'Iago' was of all names the most recognizable both as Spanish and as James. St James was of course the patron saint of Spain, and was extensively commemorated by such shrines as that of Santiago de Compostela, in the north-west of Spain, after Rome the second-largest such centre in existence: made pilgrimage to by an incessant stream of the devout, of whom the dramatist's own Helena is one, setting out as she does for 'St Jaques le Grand'. It is by considering the importance of St James or Santiago in Spain that we may light on some facts of relevance to *Othello*.

Santiago was adopted as patron saint on the basis of a handful of widely publicized though somewhat apocryphal historical events, of which the most renowned was his appearance to encourage and assist the Spaniards in the eleventh-century battle of Clavijo. The interesting thing is that this was perhaps the most significant encounter in the long struggle against the Moors; and that – so the historian of St James in Spain tells us – 'after this battle the apostle was commonly known in Spain as Santiago Matamoros, St James the Moor-killer'.[3] It seems possible, therefore, that if 'Roderigo' came into Shakespeare's play because of Iago, then 'Iago' came into the play because of Othello – the Moor-killer along with the Moor. And, if the dramatist was content to risk the dangerous associations of the name Iago, then the reason that suggests itself is the name's affiliation to the Moor. But this is so *only* if we understand that 'Moor' could have in Shakespeare's world a peculiarly Spanish connotation. On that basis we can say that the reechoing, in the play's first scene, of 'Roderigo . . . Iago'. . . the Moor' gave to the work and its hero a Spanish resonance that nothing else could effect so briefly and successfully. Every time the name 'Iago' drops with helpless unconsciousness from the Moor's lips, Shakespeare's audience remembered what we have long forgotten: that Santiago's great role in Spain was as enemy to the invading Moor, who was figurehead there of the Muslim kingdom.

There is a limit to the amount of significance that may wisely be read into the names of romantic drama; but Romeo's 'What's in a name?' hardly stops Juliet from dying. Shakespeare's dramatic nomenclature, in short, is interesting because it reflects certain harsh facts in the world outside the plays; and these facts help to extend that imaginative resonance possessed by mere names. During the sixteenth century Spain was the leading power of Europe, holding an eminence barely challenged by the English themselves at the Armada, and as such played a huge part in the Elizabethan consciousness; so that a 'Spanish' name would in any case sound very different in Elizabethan ears from what it would in our own; and to this general consideration we must add a very particular one. During the very years that we presume *Othello* to have been written, from 1602 to 1604, London had a ringside seat (even if an oblique one) at a crisis in the affairs of the Spanish Moors. It was in these very years that the French spy, Saint-Etienne, was in London attempting to persuade the English government to give assistance to the rebelling Moors of Valencia: though at length Robert Cecil was forced to decide that in view of his new King's pro-Spanish policy he could do no more for the rebels than give money and advise application to their other, because similarly Protestant, potential ally, Holland.[4] Saint-Etienne's attempt itself came at the end of, and is partly explained by, a sequence of years during which Protestant England, the defeater of the Armada, seems to have become something of a political asylum for refugee Moors from Spain: so much so as to produce two royal edicts (in 1599 and 1601) effecting – for a time – the transportation of these refugees from the country, on the grounds that:

the Queen's Majesty is discontented at the great number of negars and blackamoors which are crept into the realm since the troubles between her Highness and the King of Spain, and are fostered here to the annoyance of her own people, which want the relief consumed by these people . . .[5]

It was the common English habit from the Middle Ages on into the seventeenth century to categorize Moors as 'negars and blackamoors' (in the words of the edict); but in fact these refugees would not have been anything that we would recognize as 'black', though a less ethnically experienced Elizabethan crowd might conceivably see olive skins and predominantly Arab features in this light. For the ancestors of these Spanish Moors, the Moors who invaded and conquered the peninsula in the eighth century, were principally of the Berber strain: and the culture they establish there, Islamic.[6] I make the point about what one must conceive the appearance of these Spanish Moors to be because it seems to me of great importance to Shakespeare's play. And this, not because that appearance is of any significance in itself – just as it does not really matter whether Othello is 'black' or 'tawny', an issue I shall return to in due course – but because the appearance of these Spanish Moors reflects their peculiar 'belonging' in their own country. If we visualize Othello as black, we see him as essentially standing out from the white faces around him. But the Spanish Moors who seem to have flooded Shakespeare's London did not so stand out from their countrymen. There can have been very little difference between a dark-skinned Spaniard and an olive-skinned Moor: and again, this fact is of interest as reflecting something essential about the position of the Moor in his own country. In fact the contemporary situation of the Spanish Moor is so significant as to demand a moment's brief consideration.

In 1556 Pope Paul IV referred in a fit of disaffection to 'that breed of Moors and Jews, those dregs of the earth' – and the people he was referring to were the inhabitants of nominally Catholic Spain. For many centuries after the Moorish conquest in the eighth, the area we can now call Spain was a coagulation of shifting states cohabited by Christian and Islamic peoples together, with the Jews as a third and intensely influential minority. During the Middle Ages these three peoples had co-existed on terms that changed constantly, but that included an unchanging element of deep mutual interdependence, on both economic and more largely cultural grounds. There is likely to have been some degree of interbreeding during the period between the eighth and the sixteenth centuries (the Spanish royal family in Shakespeare's time was believed, perhaps rightly, to have Jewish blood); and there was also the kind of cultural fusion that makes precise understanding of what 'Spanish Moor' actually means a decidedly difficult matter, given that Jews and Visigothic Christians were absorbed into Islam at the Moorish conquest, and their descendants reconverted when Catholic conquest succeeded Islamic, and Islamic tolerance gave way to Catholic 'Re-conquest'. For Spanish history from the eleventh century to the fifteenth is essentially the story of the *Reconquista*, the struggle of the Catholic kingdoms of the North to wrest the peninsula from the hands of the Infidel. And Reconquest was followed in the later fifteenth century by the imposition of Orthodoxy, as Spanish monarchs from Ferdinand and Isabella to the Philips of Shakespeare's lifetime fought to unify their great new single kingdom. Indeed, it was the very depth of the intermingling of Christian, Moor and Jew within Spanish culture that seemed to them to dictate the new criterion of orthodoxy: the fires of the Inquisition were lit to 'purify'.

By the beginning of the sixteenth century Spain had assumed the image it was to carry in Shakespeare's own lifetime. In 1492 Columbus discovered America; Granada, the last of the Moorish kingdoms in Spain, was finally overthrown; and all Jews who would not accept Christian baptism were expelled from the country. The three events formed one concerted nationalistic and imperialistic drive, a drive that produced Spain's 'greatness' and yet contained within itself an essential self-destructiveness. The expulsion of the Jews left the Moors the chief objects of Catholic animus. Not rich and intellectual as the Jews had been, the Moors – though their ancestors had given earlier Spanish culture so much of its brilliance – were now sunk to a mainly peasant population; but it was a numerically huge one. In Valencia, for instance, where the Moors provided most of the aristocrats' workforce, they counted for something like a third of the population. Nonetheless, after the expulsion of the Jews the Moors inherited the fury of Orthodoxy. At first nominal baptism seemed to solve the problem, and Moors became 'Moriscos', or Christianized Moors. But by the later 1560s it was recognized that the Moors would not withdraw from their struggle to retain some vestige of their cultural identity. The last decades of the century in Spain saw bitter racial and religious strife, that gradually worsened until in 1609 – a few years after Shakespeare's play was first performed – all Moors, baptized and unbaptized, were expelled from Spain.

One of Shakespeare's best-known sentences comes, as does his Moor, from Venice: 'When you prick us, do we not bleed?' That the dramatist may have imagined Shylock as a Marrano (or at least nominally con-verted Spanish Jew) one would not want necessarily to argue. But there are certain aspects of Othello's fellow-Venetian and fellow-outsider that approximate Shylock both to the Marranos and to the rebellious Spanish Moors of the dramatist's lifetime. Shylock is making, in this famous speech, a plea that he cannot himself live well by: he is arguing passionately for essential humanity in terms that allow – as Portia will show and his own extreme logic concedes – for essential inhumanity too. He is speaking, one might say, for the fierce indiscriminateness of the heart. Comparably, the tragedy of the real-life Spanish Moor was that he was, whatever his colour, in all important senses indistinguishable from his fellow-Spaniards; and this, not merely because in common practice he 'passed', he conformed to his society, but because that society was in itself infinitely unsimpler than the policy of the desperate Catholic states had to contend. Five hundred years and more of history in the peninsula had produced a 'Spain', in the age of nationalism, that was one intense national identity-crisis, of which the Moor was essentially no more than the point of breakdown – one who like other victims would kill to defend himself, and one whose expulsion further diminished his already sharply declining country. For Spain had never really recovered from the expulsion of the Jews.

Shakespeare's tragedy opens with Iago and Roderigo, two quasi-Spaniards by name, speaking with hatred, envy and derision of 'the Moor'. Doing so, they call up momentarily but with intensity an element in the contemporary political situation that must have been – judging by the royal edicts – as casually familiar to the playwright and his audiences as it is long unknown to us now. And, as Iago and Roderigo talk, it is not simply a 'black man' they are setting among 'the whites'. '*Moor*' means to Iago and Roderigo a civilized barbarian of fierce if repressed lusts – but to the dramatist himself it surely means something very different, a meaning entailed by his choice of names. The Moor is a member of a more interesting and more permanent people: the race of the displaced and dispossessed, of Time's always-vulnerable wanderers; he is one of the strangers who do not belong where once they ruled and now have no claim to the ancient 'royal siege' except the lasting dignity or indignity of their misery.

I have been trying to suggest how the story of 'the Moor' might appear if read within a world with a different mental geography from our own. In the world in which we read, America – only a century discovered in Shakespeare's time – is a great world power, and Africa perhaps beginning to become so: to think of a Moor is to set him essentially in an African context, and to impose on him something of the history of the American coloured peoples. It is to the point that since the Romantic period Othello does seem to have been viewed within precisely this

context and given precisely this history. The most valuable studies of
Othello as Moor, those by Eldred Jones and G. K. Hunter, equate
'Moor' with 'African'.[7] And this equation tends to bring along with it
an important subsidiary: it moves to the forefront what has become
known as 'the colour question', since we think of the Moor as 'African'
in his 'American' context – a black man, specifically, among white. I
do not want to linger here in discussing the intricacies of 'the colour
question' in *Othello*, beyond pointing out that Shakespeare seems to
have been, in writing the play, happy to do what he does many times
elsewhere, burn his candle at both ends – getting a maximal suggestiveness by implying things probably in fact self-contradictory. In *Hamlet*,
the Ghost seems to come from *both* Hell *and* Purgatory; in *The Tempest*,
the island seems clearly to be located *both* in the Mediterranean *and*
in the mid-Atlantic. In *Othello*, the Moor is a mixture of black and tawny,
of negroid and Arab; he is almost any 'colour' one pleases, so long as
it permits his easier isolation and destruction by his enemies and by
himself. And here we come to what is surely the vital point: Othello's
colour, which is to say his external being, is to some degree (in this
work of the imagination) not a literal factor, but a matter of social
assertion and reaction. He is, to repeat the phrase, 'almost any colour
one pleases': and this is precisely why Desdemona, who loves him, sees
his image in his mind (though in the world they live in, such inwardness
of seeing may be dangerous too); and why most of the few descriptions
we get of him come early in the play and are not to be trusted because
they come from enemies, from the 'Spaniards' Iago and Roderigo.
Roderigo's 'thicklips' (1.1.66) is an insult aimed by a rival in love incited
by Iago for sixty lines to think ill of the Moor; Iago's own 'old black
ram' makes Othello's oldness and blackness only as believable as his
tendency to bleat. Brabantio's first reaction is that a man who calls
Othello 'a Barbary horse' is a 'profane wretch', and he himself comes
to call the Moor a 'thing' with a 'sooty bosom' only when he learns that
Desdemona has preferred him to her father. Indeed, it is, in my view, a
particular part of the tragedy that Othello himself comes to share this
hard externalism which he thinks sophisticated, and to speak of himself
with a pathetic attempt at boldness as 'black'. But this is a discussion
that needs space elsewhere to elaborate.

If Shakespeare himself had been asked what colour his Moor was, I
think he would have answered that few actors in his experience would
permit a shade dark enough to hide the play of expression. Othello is,
in short, the colour the fiction dictates. And it is in order to make this

point that I have hoped to suggest that the Moor may be quite as much 'Spanish' as 'African'. It is only worth introducing some allusion to political affairs contemporary with Shakespeare in the hope of throwing light on what may have lain behind the apparent literalness of the dramatist's own allusions. The Moor is, of course, neither an African nor a Spaniard, but an actor on stage portraying the experiences of any-coloured Everyman: but our interpretation of those experiences will depend on how we read the words, and what presuppositions we bring as we begin.

I have been suggesting that Shakespeare's Moor should be seen as also 'Spanish', which is to say emerging from a situation that is as much political as ethnological – in which social relationship matters as much as colour. There is a further interest in conjecturing a Spanish background. Shakespeare adopts dramatically the situation that interested him politically – or perhaps this would be safer expressed in reverse: a writer may be attracted with peculiar sympathy towards political situations that his poetic gifts enable him to grasp and absorb. The heart of the tragedy of the real-life Spanish Moor was the ancient strength of the bonds which linked him to his fellow-Spaniards: bonds which ironically drove him (like Shylock) into a reactively defensive racism and nationalism. There is something deeply corresponding to this political situation in the way in which Shakespeare responsively *fuses* the Moorish with the Spanish, harnessing almost anything apprehended by him imaginatively as 'Spanish' to help characterize his Moor. This absorption of the 'Spanish' into his play gave it colour and substance; but more – it gave the work that puzzling multi-facetedness which underlies and enriches this apparently simple tragedy. For the Elizabethan image of Spanish things itself carried with it (or so I would suggest) an inherent self-division, shadowing that crisis of identity that was the pattern of Spanish history in the sixteenth century, at a moment which was one both of great wealth and achievement and of absolute and rapid decline. And it is, I believe, this sharply divided imagining of what it means to be 'Spanish' that helps to produce the very peculiar division of dramatic tone between tragedy and comedy in *Othello*.

To attempt to describe a whole phase of culture in a paragraph is of course ridiculous: nonetheless some of the most fruitful Elizabethan images appear to have been caricatures. It may merely be noted, for what suggestiveness the fact has, that in 1605, the year after that in which *Othello* was probably first performed, Cervantes published the first part of Spain's greatest single literary work. *Don Quixote* takes its

power from the profound ambiguity with which it treats a certain kind
of high romantic idealism, the way in which a given individual – gentle,
scholarly, obsessive – treats his ordinary daily existence as a perfect
Point of Honour. It does not explain the depth and richness of *Don
Quixote* to say that, in doing this, it summarizes its country's inward
history through the preceding century. The novel's jumping-off point
is the extraordinary effect which romance in fact had on Spanish
culture through the sixteenth century, serving to feed the spiritual pride
of Spain with high images of the life of heroic sacrifice, the stronger
for being divorced from traditional religion. When Philip II came to
England to marry Queen Mary, the main pleasure of the courtiers he
brought with him was to identify the sites of Arthur's imaginary adventures; and similarly when some years later the Spanish ambassador
wished to describe what he saw as the villainy of Elizabeth and her
government, he made his point by comparing them to characters from
Amadis de Gaule: the work which above all dominated the aristocratic
imagination of Spain in the sixteenth century. But the very extremity
and removedness of romance, and its obsession with the more external
questions of honour, made it in some way generate its opposite in
Spain at the end of this period: that toughly ironic treatment of honour
in an often quite startlingly realistic urban context which characterizes
the style and substance of Spain's new emerging and highly important
form, the picaresque.[8]

Something of that romantic–picaresque polarity and contrast which
must have comprised the English image of Spanish culture seems to me
to have found its way into *Othello*. It is nowhere there precisely or formally localized. Nor is there any question of the Moor and Iago forming
the kind of immortal twinning and pairing that we meet in Don Quixote
and Sancho Panza: although it may be important that Shakespeare
changed the Ensign from the friend of the hero to something parallel to
the servant of the Moor. By doing so he introduces into his tragedy
something of that vitally significant theme of the master and the man
which the Spanish (in *picaro* stories like *Lazarillo de Tormes* and in Tirso
de Molina's Don Juan play, *El Burlador de Sevilla*, as well as in *Don Quixote*)
introduced into European literature. The horror of Shakespeare's
'temptation scene' (*Othello* 3.3) is its corruption and inversion of the
master–servant relationship. A play too often treated as simple 'love-
tragedy' is in fact impregnated with the subject of power and social
hierarchies: and the master–servant relation of Othello and Iago compacts
these meanings into Cinthio's lucid and brutal story of sex-intrigue.

These possibilities opened up to Shakespeare, I believe, as soon as he envisaged his Moor as in some sense a Spaniard. Certain important corners of his new tragedy were at once flooded with a strange compound of the high-idealistic and the derisively picaresque. His Moor gained that wide and deep, that exquisitely painful awareness of the loss of honour that Cinthio's Moor (by contrast) is so devoid of; Othello's imagination is enormously, preposterously vulnerable to the sense of social shame. Shakespeare's play similarly begins to find room in itself for an experience which Cinthio again knew nothing of, that derisive, ugly back-street insolence which is a reactive response to an authority seen as at once over-absolute and unrespected. It is the picaresque common sense of the role (as Sancho Panza proves, in fact, a wiser governor than Quixote) that makes any reader or audience have to struggle so hard not to feel *some* sort of sympathy for that new wise underdog, the detestable Iago. And it is in part through this new 'voice from underground' that *Othello* gains its potentiality for frightful comedy, becoming at once the most romantic of Shakespeare's tragedies and the one most filled by an ugly obdurate vulgar Nashian humour, which leaves us deeply unprotesting as Emilia, Iago's mate, calls the Moor a 'gull' and a 'dolt': for indeed Othello *is* gulled, and *does* behave doltishly throughout the fifth act.

But there is another explanation than the spirit of Spanish picaresque for this peculiarly comic aspect of the tragedy. It has been pointed out that in creating the dramatic structure of this play Shakespeare utilized some of the forms of previous *comedy*, borrowing the scenic structures of *Much Ado About Nothing* and *The Merry Wives of Windsor*.[9] It may be similarly worth noting that two of the primary dramatic locations of *Othello*, the street and the harbourside, are those for centuries recognizable as belonging to Roman comedy, and to the Greek New Comedy before it. In a word, an audience that found themselves at this play's opening listening to Iago and Roderigo talking derisively in an Italian street about a Moorish captain would have felt no doubt at all as to what dramatic situation they were assisting at. For Roman comedy bequeathed to Italian learned comedy (which in time passed them on to the more popular *commedia dell'arte* routines) some of the most important elements we recognize in *Othello*. Learned Italian comedy of the Renaissance was distinguished from its Latin predecessors by its fostering of a new social type and situation, that of the cuckold or *cornuto*; and it often fused this role of the deceived husband with its new translation of a (dramatically) much older type, one found not only in Roman comedy but in the Greek before it – that of the braggart soldier. What makes Othello's 'Spanishness' of striking relevance here is that in the world of Italian learned comedy (and in popular comedy after it) this braggart who is often the deceived husband is also most characteristically a new national type: the *Spanish* soldier of fortune. For, as Boughner records in his valuable study of this character type in Renaissance comedy, 'Latin drama . . . was precisely the vehicle needed by the Italians for their mockery of the pitiless Spanish mercenaries that swept over the Peninsula in the sixteenth century and shook its civilisation . . .'[10] The braggart soldier in this guise became a directed Italian protest against the invading Spaniard, the 'barbaris hostis Italiae', 'tam ineruditus quam inflatus superbia gothica'; and he was reimagined for these comedies in a quite new guise as a pedantic and fantastic grandee of Castile, who added to a gravity of demeanour and decorum of speech and gesture a peculiar elegance that was believed to derive – as did so many civilized Spanish things – from those 'womanish men', the Moors.

The sense in which Othello is *not* a Spanish braggart captain will be obvious to any sensitive reader of the play. In this there is an obvious contrast between him and one of his other sources or prototypes, Morocco in *The Merchant of Venice*, whose boasting oath 'by this scimitar' and threat to 'outstare' and 'outbrave' set him well within the comic braggart type, and help to balance Portia's tartly racialist revulsion from him. And yet it would not have been surprising if some of the play's first audience, finding themselves listening to a soldier and his gentlemanly gull (a gull who might be straight out of a city comedy) both of them with Spanish names, and talking, in these back streets of Venice, of an apparently supremely arrogant Moor, had felt some disappointment to find the Moor so *little* a braggart; and had muttered, like Rymer later, that the play was 'a bloody farce, without salt or savour'. For only a certain grimness, a lack of the lightweight in Iago's intense tone, differentiates the circumstances at the play's beginning from those of scores of Italian learned comedies of the Renaissance. We might be in at the start of just such a comic–romantic story of jealous love as Bentivoglio's *Il Geloso* or Gabiani's *I Gelosi*, two among the many plays which such experts on the subject as Boughner or Marvin T. Herrick (in his *Italian Comedy of the Renaissance*, Urbana and London, 1966) class as absolutely typical and trivial representatives of the Spanish-braggart plays of the period. And, far enough away as these two comedies are from the enormous depth and power and meaning of Shakespeare's tragedy, it is a fact that *Othello* contains devices that seem a distant disturbing ironical echo of braggart conventions which two such trivial comedies exemplify. Behind, for instance, Othello's own wonderfully romantic and just possibly ironic rehearsal of the story that won Desdemona, the enigmatically splendid account of his heroic travels and battles, there lies the braggart's invariable evocation of the grandeur of his travels and campaigns: as Zeladelpho in *I Gelosi* boasts in his prose declamation of prizes won by scattering enemies protected by hundreds of cannon, of illustrious friends and patrons, and of campaigns and travels in faraway Africa, Egypt and Mesopotamia; or as the braggart captain in *Il Geloso* has his verse peroration concerning his achievements in Tunisia, in Barbary, in Vienna and Hungary, interrupted by the jeeringly undercutting echoes to his boasts by his valet, Trinchetto.[11]

Such echoes may be fortuitous. Marvin Herrick's wide-ranging study makes links between many of Shakespeare's comedies, and some of his tragedies, and both the Italian learned comedy and its popular successor, the *commedia dell'arte* – but finds *Othello* one of the few plays by Shakespeare not worth considering in this context: he simply fails to mention it. And yet it seems to me a detail striking enough to need some consideration that one of these two trivial comedies, Bentivoglio's *Il Geloso*, provided Ben Jonson with the characters who were the ancestors of his Bobadill and Kitely – and that one critic has suggested that it was from this very play, Jonson's *Every Man in His Humour*, that Shakespeare may have found the basis, in Thorello, for the name he gave his Moor, Othello.[12] The link at any rate adds to the materials for believing that these Italian learned comedies, in which the figure of the Spanish braggart was a principal attraction, were an important feature of that half-tragic and half-comic world that sprang to life within Shakespeare's energizing and unifying imagination. Already his Don Armado had shown how far an innately rich and delicate sensibility could refine the merely dramaturgical device of the coarse braggart into something at once far more truly 'Spanish' and far more individually Shakespearian. For Don Armado has something of that helpless imaginative refinement, that rigid vulnerability to idealism, which ten years later was to make the Don of Cervantes the great – the of course much greater – classic he remains. (And it may have been in response to the divided vision of Spain that Shakespeare impassively gives to Don Armado a servant-girl for a Doña, as Cervantes was to do with *his* knight.)

Othello also and much more darkly seems to reflect this double sense of what it might be to be Spanish: an experience of tension between a fastidious romanticism and an earthy and sometimes brutal directness.

Certainly there seem to me to be problem areas in the play which cease to be problems when seen simply as one aspect or another of this divided experience. So one might consider, for instance (and I mention here only a random handful of cases, differing in interest and scale) the strangely wordy gauche refinement, straight out of Don Armado, with which Othello himself anxiously denies on the day of his elopement that he could ever be subject to desire or 'heat, the young affects / In my defunct and proper satisfaction' (1.3.261–74, a speech that needs discussion though it has never to my knowledge had it: Othello's embarrassment actually creates verbal crux); Cassio's inexplicably intense and silly romanticism (2.1.61–82), emerging from a character for whom Shakespeare has invented a whore for him to keep company with; the calm social acceptance with which Desdemona follows the practice of earlier *comic* heroines in chatting with a clown, joining as she does in Iago's unfunny badinage at the harbourside; and most of all, the unerringness with which for dramatic reasons we find ourselves at once agreeing to complicity with our detached comic guide Iago, who on all human grounds is boring, shallow, vicious, and in no way whatever to be trusted.

All these are aspects of the play which seem wholly right in their context, and yet which continue to puzzle if we impose upon the tragedy some over-simplifying category. All are facets of the one central premise, and are necessitated by that originating idea which fused together in Shakespeare's imagination great diversities linked only by the code-word 'Spain'. Seen from any other angle, Cinthio's story offered Shakespeare scarcely anything but that meaningless line of intrigue-narrative which the tragedy holds on to with an impassivity in itself contributive; everything else, including the meaning, Shakespeare found for himself. But it was the intrinsic 'Spanishness' of that Moor-in-Venice opening ('Fu già in Venezia un Moro') that had begun his second great tragedy for him.

I hope that I do not seem in the foregoing to have argued that *Othello* is (as Rymer suggested) a comedy; or that its characters are in reality of Spanish birth, or that its hero is a braggart, or that he is black (or white). The intention of this essay has been merely to ask some questions about the formative period of one of Shakespeare's most brilliant plays: that phase of reflective reading-around while the dramatist was beginning to invent a new work. In doing so, I have had both a negative and a positive purpose. Negatively, I hope to challenge our

perhaps too simple 'African' sense of Othello. For a century and more
we have tended to see Shakespeare's play in the light of certain deep
even if tacit or indeed unconscious post-Romantic presuppositions which
in fact derive from a more or less modern myth of the Moor – the
Moor as essentially 'African' or 'black', in both a literal and a metaphorical sense. We have thus come to see Shakespeare's play, or so it
seems to me, as almost indistinguishable from a work that shares these
(as we may loosely call them) Victorian presuppositions: we see it as
much like Verdi's opera *Otello*, as a work that is simple, beautiful, full of
passion and of pain, lyrical and barbaric and above all, all about love.

Shakespeare's play does have some connections with this image: but
the image is far from a wholly true one, and as such may silently distort
and confuse. It is in an attempt to supplement that too partial image of
the play as about an 'African' Moor that I have tried to suggest that
Othello is in fact 'Spanish' as well. And this is a matter which reaches
back beyond the purely political context of Shakespeare's own time
into a great literary background that is vital to the play. If one deprec-
ates Victorian romance in the consideration of the play, this is not
because it is bad in itself but because it may serve to conceal that great
world of Renaissance romance which is not precisely the same thing,
but which surely contains some of the true sources of *Othello*. It is a
curious fact that the sole proof – if it is proof – that Shakespeare read at
least some Ariosto in the original is located in Othello's phrase about
the Sybil's 'prophetic fury'. It would not be surprising if the *Orlando
Furioso*, that great source of the Moorish for Italian learned (and hence
popular) comedy, taught much to a writer far greater than those comedies could provide. The background to *Orlando Furioso* is the perpetual,
dream-like war of Christian and pagan, and the pagans are Moors,
the wars being waged by the kings 'of Affrike and of Spaine' – this last
a phrase that re-echoes memorably through the poem; Rogero, for
instance, the inamorato of one of the two heroines, and a heroic pagan
whose colour is immaterial but clearly not black, is referred to as a
'knight of Affrike and of Spaine'.[13] His final conversion and marriage
to Bradamante concludes reasonably enough this great chronicle of
romantic courtesy that begins with the famous tender slightly ironical
image of the two 'auncient knightes of true and noble heart', one
Christian and one pagan, sharing one horse 'like frends'. Without
stopping to consider whether or not the poem might be called another
of the play's sources, one can say at any rate that this is surely the world
that Shakespeare's Moor – who is 'of Affrike *and* of Spaine' – in some

sense comes from, and in another sense would dearly like still to belong to. But Othello is *not* a knight, but a mercenary; and the realm he serves is not Ariosto's dreamily Charlemainean landscape of the past, but 'present-day' Venice, the great trade city – where, as the opening lines of the play make grimly clear, to be a 'frend' is to have 'my purse, / As if the strings were thine'. It is thus that we may say again that when Shakespeare read in Cinthio of a *'Moor in Venice'*, his tragedy was begun.

First published in *Shakespeare Survey 35*, 1982

NOTES

1 The relevant excerpt is given on p. 396 of the New Variorum edition of *Othello*.
2 The point is well made by Frank Kermode in his Introduction to the Riverside edition of the play: 'one can isolate a plot of monumental and satisfying simplicity without forgetting that the text can be made to support very different interpretations. The richness of the tragedy derives from uncancelled suggestions, from latent sub-plots operating in terms of imagery as well as character, even from hints of large philosophical and theological contexts which are not fully developed.' See also John Wain's Introduction to *Shakespeare: 'Othello', A Casebook* (London and Basingstoke, 1971).
3 T. D. Kendrick, *Saint James in Spain* (London, 1960), p. 24.
4 For the account of Saint-Etienne's attempt see Henry Charles Lea, *The Moriscos of Spain* (London, 1901), p. 287, to which I am indebted also in the general discussion which follows concerning the position of the Moors in Spain. See also J. H. Elliott's *Imperial Spain, 1469–1716* (London, 1963).
5 *The Calendar of Manuscripts . . . The Marquis of Salisbury* (1906), part ix, p. 569.
6 In the Introduction to his *Islamic and Christian Spain in the Early Middle Ages* (Princeton, N.J., 1979), pp. 14–15, Thomas F. Glick has a useful discussion of the problem of terminology which may be applied to a very different area of study. Explaining why he prefers the phrase 'Islamic Spain' even though 'it implies . . . a contradiction in terms', to those of 'Muslem', 'Arabic' or 'Moorish' Spain, he writes: 'the population was composed mainly of Hispano-Roman converts to Islam and Berbers and there were few Arabs in the population. Moorish Spain, besides being archaic and romantic (conjuring up images from Washington Irving's *Tales of the Alhambra*), is also misleading on a number of grounds. Strictly speaking, Moors were the Mauri, Berbers who lived in the Roman province of Mauretania; therefore its use stresses . . . the Berber contributions to Andalusi culture. In English, Moor has racial connotations (e.g. Othello, a negroid "Moor";

the "black-moor" of the standard English version of Aesop's fables) of black-ness, whereas many Berbers are fair-haired and blue-eyed. In Spanish . . . the term *moro* is derogatory.' Glick also writes (p. 3): 'Long after the enemy was vanquished, the Jews expelled, and the Inquisition disbanded, the image of the "Moor" remained as the quintessential stranger, an object to be feared.'

7 Eldred Jones, *Othello's Countrymen: The African in English Renaissance Drama* (London, 1965), also *The Elizabethan Image of Africa* (Virginia, 1971); G. K. Hunter, 'Othello and Colour Prejudice', the Annual Shakespeare Lecture from the Proceedings of the British Academy (1967).

8 See, for instance, A. A. Parker, *Literature and the Delinquent: The Picaresque Novel in Spain and Europe, 1599–1753* (Edinburgh, 1967).

9 Emrys Jones, *Scenic Form in Shakespeare* (Oxford, 1971), pp. 121–7.

10 Daniel C. Boughner, *The Braggart in Renaissance Comedy* (Minneapolis, 1954), p. 20; and *passim*.

11 Vincenzo Gabiani, *I Gelosi* in *Commedie Diversi* (Ferrara, 1560), p. 28^r: 'Tu dici il vero, che i priegiati, & horrevoli arnesi sogliono far riguardevoli i Capitani. Ma che mi curo di quello io havendo gia acquistato il credito, & fatto la riputatione? per havere condotto a fine tante imprese, & maraviglie, come fa il mondo. Senza che gli arnesi non sono quelli, che mettono i pari nostri avanti, appresso alle corone, & a gli scettri. Ma questa quà si bene, che importa il tutto. Va domanda in Acarnania, in Egitto, in Soria. Domanda di me in Aphrica, in Guascogna, in Boemia, & sopra tutto i Mesopotamia, et sentirai la relatione, che te ne sarà fatta.' Hercole Bentivoglio, *Il Geloso* (Ferrara, 1547), p. 18^v:

> O quante
> Altre gran prove hò fatte ch'or non dico,
> Che non è tempo: a Tunisi che feci
> Di Barberia? che feci ancho a Vienna,
> In Ungheria? non presi non uccisi
> Un numero infinito di quei Turchi
> Con questa spada . . .

12 Emrys Jones, *Scenic Form*, p. 149.

13 *Orlando Furioso*, trans. Harington, ed. Robert McNulty (Oxford, 1972), Bk 1, st. 6; Bk 30, st. 70. I am indebted to Emrys Jones for these quotations from his study (in preparation) of the relation of Shakespeare to Ariosto; as for other assistance kindly contributed towards this essay.

CHAPTER 5

Shakespeare and the living dramatist

Wole Soyinka

> Your statement is an impudently ignorant one to make. . . . Do
> you really mean no one should or could write about or speak
> about a war because one has not stood on the battlefield . . . ? Was
> Shakespeare at Actium or Philippi . . . ?[1]

That tart response from Sean O'Casey to Yeats will be familiar to
many. O'Casey is not of course a 'living' dramatist, but I am certain
that no one here expects a coroner's interpretation of that expression.
O'Casey could have picked no worthier defender of his arguments;
the universal puzzle of Shakespeare's evocative power often leads to
speculations – in various degrees of whimsy – about his real identity.
That is only another way of questing after the unrecorded things he
actually did in real life – especially in the area of travel. If Shakespeare
was never at Actium or Philippi contemporaneously with the events
which he dramatized on these sites, he must have stood on their ruins or
visited their living replicas in his wanderings – preferably press-ganged
into one of those notorious merchant ships while he was hanging around
the theatres, waiting to audition for a small role. Is it any wonder that
the Middle Eastern poets and dramatists claim that he must, at the very
least, have been a sometime visitor to North Africa and the Arabian
peninsula? How else, for instance, could he have encountered the
legend of Majnun Layla which he transformed – albeit without acknowledgement – into *Romeo and Juliet*? And so Ali Ahmad Ba-Kathir (who
died in 1969), an Indonesian-born poet who became a naturalized
Egyptian, restored to his adopted race what belonged to Arab literature
in the first place – he translated *Romeo and Juliet* into Arabic free verse.

One interesting poser for Ahmad Ba-Kathir arose from the fact that,
in the legend of Majnun's love for Layla, there was no history of family
feuds; not only that, Arabic custom prevents a Romeo-style declamation of love even into the empty expanse of the desert – this is bringing
dishonour to the girl and ruining the name and reputation of her

family. The fate of an Orlando caught in the act of hanging love-sick verses on tamarind trees is better left unimagined – still, such are the impieties to be expected when a gifted Arab like Shakespeare loses his roots among the English infidels!

The difficulties encountered by Arab dramatists as a result of the opposing nature of much of the conventions and mores of Arabic culture, not to mention the actual intervention of language for these poets and dramatists, heighten the phenomenon of the fascination of Shakespeare for Arab-speaking authors, both those who turned naturally to classical (i.e. literary) Arabic and others, like Gibran at the turn of the century, and the contemporary dramatist Tawfik-al-Hakim who have revolutionized the concept of Arabic literature with their adoption and enrichment of colloquial Arabic.

But I should make it quite clear that I am not about to discuss Arabic writers or their adaptations, about whom I have only very superficial knowledge. The phenomenal hold of Shakespeare on modern European and American dramatists and directors is however not merely well known but accepted as natural. The ideological interrogatories which a Marxist playwright like Brecht injects into his versions of Shakespeare, such as *Coriolanus*, are normal developments in European literary and dramatic sensibilities – Shakespeare is over-ample fodder for the creative browser. Indeed, the search for a moral anchor among the literary-inclined leads sooner or later to the vast arena of unresolved moral questions in his works and sometimes life. Thus, for Edward Bond, it was not enough that Shakespeare's *Lear* should be reworked through some ideological framework, however vague and ultimately cosseting. Clearly Bond's interest in *Lear* was only a temporary holding device for his real subject, William Shakespeare himself, whom Bond sees – despite some rather 'nice' disclaimers – as a petit-bourgeois Lear: 'Shakespeare's plays show this need for sanity and its political expression, justice. But how did he live? His behaviour as a property-owner made him closer to Goneril than Lear.' The explanation for this bizarre claim is that 'He supported and benefited from the Goneril-society – with its prisons, workhouses, whipping, starvation, mutilation, pulpit-hysteria and all the rest of it.' Like me? And you? Introductions and Prefaces are not of course the most helpful clues to an author's intentions or even thoughts, not even in the case of Bernard Shaw. The basic declarations of intent by Bond are valid enough: 'I wrote *Bingo* because I think the contradictions in Shakespeare's life are similar to the contradictions in us', complemented, for our purpose, by: 'Part of

the play is about the relationship between any writer and his society.'
That that relationship, in the case of Shakespeare, is closer to Goneril's
than Lear's carries for me, I must confess, the air of one of those
paradoxes which all writers – especially those with a poetic bent – like
to indulge in from time to time. Artfulness is indeed a stock-in-trade of
the self-conscious moralist; from Edward Bond we are instructed, in
similar vein, that 'Shakespeare created Lear, who is the most radical of
all society critics.' Well, Shakespeare's countryman should *know*, I suppose; so on that note I shall return to Shakespeare's distant cousins and
demand, like Hamlet: 'What's Hecuba to him, or he to Hecuba?'

Among other statistical and factual details of this fascination is this:
between about 1899 and 1950, some sixteen plays of Shakespeare had
been translated and/or adapted by Arab poets and dramatists. They
include plays as diverse as *Hamlet*, the ever-popular *Julius Caesar*, *The
Merchant of Venice*, *Pericles*, *A Midsummer Night's Dream*, *King Richard III* and
– need I add? – *Antony and Cleopatra*. There will have been others by
now because even the government of the United Arab Republic, fed up
with the number of embarrassingly inaccurate and inelegant translations, set up a committee to produce a scrupulous and complete translation of Shakespeare's works. So much for statistics, for much of which as
well as for other details I am indebted to an essay by Professor Bushrui,
formerly of the University of Ibadan, and to Dr Kole Omotoso, of my
own University and department.

But the Arab world was not content to adopt or 'reclaim' Shakespeare's works. M. M. Badawi, in an article in *Cairo Studies* (1964) titled
'Shakespeare and the Arab World', states that the matter goes much
further. Apparently it was not simply that Shakespeare stumbled on to
an Arab shore during his unpublicized peregrinations; he was in fact an
Arab. His real name, cleansed of its anglicized corruption, was Shayk
al-Subair, which everyone knows of course is as dune-bred an Arabic
name as any English poet can hope for.

Well, on our side, that is, in our own black Africa, we know that
Julius Nyerere did translate *Julius Caesar* into Kishwahili and I believe
there has been one recent adaptation of another of Shakespeare's plays
– I think it was *The Taming of the Shrew* – into a little-known language,
also in East Africa. But I have yet to hear of any claims that Shakespeare was a suspected progeny of a Zulu or Fulani herdsman or an
Ashanti farmer. A young Ghanaian cineast did adapt *Macbeth* for the
cinema, setting it in Northern, pastoral Ghana, but I believe the matter
was taken no further.

Well, there are the historical causes. The experience of colonized North Africa has been one of a cultural struggle between French and English cultures – beginning with their educational systems – wherein the literature is always centrally placed. Then there is the history of Arabic literature itself on which the Islamic culture placed a number of constraints from which the European culture became not merely a liberating but, in certain aspects, even a revolutionary force. At the heart of that literary culture – the European that is – stood Shakespeare, with his limitless universal themes, themes which were congenial to the Arabic epic – or narrative – tradition, promoting the romance of lyrical language for its own sake, as a tool of elegant discourse, formalized social relations and pious conduct. Arabic is the conscious vehicle of Islamic piety. The English language, even of King James's Bible, is not tied to any kind of piety; the Shakespearian use of it, however, makes it the very homeland of moral beings – we can see why the Arab poet felt an instant affinity with this language. It should be emphasized that modern, colloquial Arabic is so distinct from the classical that it makes a practitioner of both virtually bilingual – it was this classical form that was considered for a long time the only poetic vehicle fit to bear the colossal weight of Shakespeare, only this language could map the moral contours of the minds of tragic and romantic heroes and heroines, and their judges.

Earlier, in listing the plays which have been transformed by the pen of Arab dramatists, I gave a special kind of note to *Antony and Cleopatra*. Much of course is correctly made of the universality of Shakespeare's plays; here, I find myself more concerned with a somewhat less usual particularity, one with which, I am convinced, the Arabic, and most especially the North African, poet simply could not fail to identify. How could he? O'Casey makes a case for the art of the dramatist by reminding us that the greatest poetic illusionist of all, Shakespeare, did not require physical participation in the battles of Actium or Philippi; to the North African dramatist, especially if he is also a poet, *Antony and Cleopatra* must appear to belie O'Casey. Shakespeare, it seems, must have sailed up the Nile and kicked up sands in the shadow of the pyramids to have etched the conflict of Egypt and Rome on such a realistic canvas, evoking tones, textures, smells, and even tastes which were so alien to the wintry climes of Europe. This is a theme with which I find myself in more than a little sympathy.

Some years ago, I watched a production of *Antony and Cleopatra* at the Aldwych, by the Royal Shakespeare Company – and winced throughout the entire night. We all have our prejudices of course, but some of these prejudices are the result of experience. Perhaps the RSC knew that it had a problem in persuading even an English audience to accept any interpretation of Cleopatra by an English actress – so the actress sent up the whole thing – a sort of 'Look at me, we both know that this Cleopatra is not a character for real.' The production was very much of that order – a sort of variation of the play-within-a-play, only, this time, it was a director's critique-within-a-play – this Cleopatra was 'neither fish nor flesh; a man knew not where to have her'. If there was one female character that Shakespeare knew damned well where to have, it was Cleopatra. Come to think of it, I recall that my mind continually drifted off to a not too dissimilar occasion – this was the erotic, gastronomic orgy so sumptuously designed by the director of the film of Henry Fielding's *Tom Jones*. But at least that actress was trying her hardest, only I could not help superimposing on her performance the face and body of the actress Anna Magnani, one of the few European actresses of my knowledge who are truly endowed with a natural presence of erotic vulgarity. Shakespeare foresaw the problem, mind you:

> Saucy lictors
> Will catch at us like strumpets, and scald rhymers
> Ballad us out o' tune; the quick comedians
> Extemporally will stage us, and present
> Our Alexandrian revels; Antony
> Shall be brought drunken forth, and I shall see
> Some squeaking Cleopatra boy my greatness
> I' th' posture of a whore.
>
> (5.2.213–20)

The other side of the balance sheet, however, is an ironic one. The near-unanimous opinion of the Arabic critics themselves on the translations and adaptations of their 'compatriot' Shayk al-Subair's masterpieces is that they were, in the main, the work of 'scald rhymers' who 'ballad him out of tune'. But I am not qualified to pronounce upon that, knowing no Arabic beyond 'Salaam aleikum', a benediction which we must pronounce on Shakespeare's motions in his grave if what those critics say is true. The special fascination of Arabic literature with Shakespeare however, mends all, at least for those of us who are safe from a direct encounter with the early consequences.

Quite apart from language and colonial history, other theories have been offered, theories closer to the content of literature. For instance, it is claimed – as one of the reasons for endowing Shakespeare with Arab paternity – that only an Arab could have understood or depicted a Jew so 'convincingly' as in *The Merchant of Venice*. Similarly, the focus is sometimes placed on *Othello* – the Moor's dignity even in folly has been held up as convincing proof that no European could have fleshed out this specific psychology of a jealousy complicated by racial insecurity but a man from beneath the skin – an Arab at the very least. This of course would have to account for the unpredictability of a full-blooded Arab who suddenly turns against his kind in the portrait of Aaron in *Titus Andronicus*, reducing the representative of that race to unprecedented depths of savagery and inhuman perversion. No, I find that my judgement inclines to giving most of the credit to *Antony and Cleopatra* for the full conquest of the Arab poet-dramatist, and the reasons lie of course with that universally seductive property of the best dramatic literature – a poetic ease on the ear which, in this case, has been drawn to the service of a specific terrain. Throughout his career, this terrain held great fascination for William Shakespeare. I do not speak here of an inert geographical terrain, but of the opposing and contradictory in human nature. It is not entirely by accident that the physical terrain in *Antony and Cleopatra* was the meeting point of the Orient and the Occident – for Shakespeare, these had come to represent more than the mercantile or adventurers' stomping-ground; they are absorbed into geographical equivalents of the turbulences which the poet observed in human nature, that playground, and warring-ground of 'humours', of performance and intent, will and emotion: Angelo is the unfinished paradigm in *Measure for Measure*. The transfer by Shakespeare, obsessed apothecary, of the unstable mixture called humanity into the Elizabethan (i.e. European) exotic crucible of the Middle East was inescapable – the signs are littered in images throughout his entire corpus, and the Arab world acknowledged itself as the greatest beneficiary even when its dramatists held up the same models through opposing viewpoints.

Ahmad Shaqui, the poet laureate of Egypt who was hailed 'the Prince of Poets' and 'Poet of Princes' by his own peers, is often credited with introducing poetry into Arabic drama. Was it just a coincidence that the play in question was *Masra' Kliyupatra* (The Fall or Death of Cleopatra), and that it was inspired unequivocally by Shakespeare's own *Antony and Cleopatra*? It is true that he used material both from Egyptian and Arab-Islamic history but he did set out, according to our sources, to rewrite Shakespeare's own play. Fired by the Egyptian struggle for independence from the British, he recreates Cleopatra as a woman torn between her love of her country and her love for a man. In the end she commits suicide. For Shaqui, Shakespeare's Cleopatra was unacceptably unpatriotic, even a traitress, since she appeared ready to sacrifice her country on the altar of love. The emendations are predictable; they are of the same political and historically conscious order as, for example, the reversal of relationships which takes place when the theme of Caliban and Ariel is handled by anyone from the colonial or slavery experience, most notably in the West Indies. The case of the Arab world is however very different, owing its primary response not simply to politics or history, but to an order of visceral participation in the humane drama of its politics and history.

When one examines the majority of Shakespeare's plays very closely, there really is not much overt respect paid to 'local colour'. If anything, the colour is not infrequently borrowed from elsewhere to establish a climate of relationships, emotions or conflicts: 'Her bed is India; there she lies, a pearl' (*Troilus and Cressida*, 1.1.99). Where we encounter a localized immediacy we are wafted instantly away on a metaphoric bark to nowhere:

> Between our Ilium and where she resides
> Let it be call'd the wild and wand'ring flood;
> Ourself the merchant, and this sailing Pandar
> Our doubtful hope, our convoy, and our bark.
>
> (1.1.100–3)

Nestor finds Achilles' brains as barren as the banks of Libya while Ulysses considers it kinder fate that he parch in Afric's sun than be withered by the arrogance in Achilles' eye. Beyond two or three boastful and mutual admiration lines from Ulysses to Hector in act 4, scene 5, however, it is remarkable that in a war no less celebrated, no less legendary than Antony's scrap with Caesar, very little of the terrain of struggle is actually conveyed in Shakespeare's lines. I do not suggest that we miss it; on the contrary. The absent hills, moats, turrets and physical *belonging* all pass unnoticed thanks to the clamour of *machismo*, the conflicts of pride, the debates of honour and schemes of war. The atmosphere is replete, nothing appears missing. In *Coriolanus* we experience the city-state as a corporate entity against which one man is ranged, while the Rome of *Julius Caesar* could be anywhere, and the arguments of both, unchanged.

Compare these examples with the other remarkable exception, *Macbeth*:

Duncan.
  This castle hath a pleasant seat, the air
  Nimbly and sweetly recommends itself
  Unto our gentle senses.
Banquo.   This guest of summer,
  The temple-haunting martlet, does approve
  By his lov'd mansionry that the heaven's breath
  Smells wooingly here; no jutty, frieze,
  Buttress, nor coign of vantage, but this bird
  Hath made her pendent bed and procreant cradle.
  Where they most breed and haunt, I have observ'd,
  The air is delicate.

(1.6.1–10)

Shakespeare, drawing local colour into the service of fatal irony. The colours of *Antony and Cleopatra* belong however to a different segment of the spectrum and are applied on a more liberal canvas – after all, the whole world is up for grabs. But note that even where we encounter no more than what may be called a roll-call of names, there has been prior fleshing-out, so that the discomfiture of Octavius Caesar at the rallying of former mutual enemies behind Antony is real and problematic. It is historical personages that are summoned centre stage of the tapestry of events, not mere exotic names and shadowy figures from legend:

  He hath given his empire
  Up to a whore, who now are levying
  The kings o' th' earth for war. He hath assembled
  Bocchus, the king of Libya; Archelaus
  Of Cappadocia; Philadelphos, king
  Of Paphlagonia; the Thracian king Adallas;
  King Manchus of Arabia; King of Pont;
  Herod of Jewry; Mithradates, king
  Of Comagene; Polemon and Amyntas,
  The kings of Mede and Lycaonia, with a
  More larger list of sceptres.

(3.6.66–76)

The prior setting for what would otherwise be a mere catalogue of titles is contributive to the emergence of real figures from a mere bas-relief. For this is Caesar caught in a domestic dilemma involving his sister, using the arguments of war to get it into her head that she is neither an emperor's wife nor an ambassador but, quite ordinarily – a rejected woman. Caesar's passion is both that of a contemned protector of a weak woman, and a contender for empire on a larger-than-historic scale. And these empires become accessible, reduced to a human scale because of what Antony has done with the accumulated panoply of power: 'He hath given his empire / Up to a whore . . .' The whore? Cleopatra. Her other names – queen, whore, gipsy, Egyptian dish, the serpent of old Nile, ribaldered nag of Egypt, etc., one whose every act, whose every caprice, every clownish or imperious gesture confirms that she deserves every one of these accolades and more. And thus the kingdoms and empires which she draws into her fatal net through Antony partake of this same personal quality and expand our realistic conception and dimension of the drama being waged for possession of the world. Not without cause does Octavius Caesar envision, when the scale of war turns firmly in his favour: 'The time of universal peace is near.'

Shakespeare's enlargements of the ridiculous through sublime prisms are deft and varied; the process happens at bewildering speed, resolving seeming improbabilities through the credible chimeric qualities of the tragic heroine of the piece. Who can quarrel with the steely patriotism of Cleopatra even in defeat? Confronted with the stark choice between death and humiliation:

> Rather a ditch in Egypt
> Be gentle grave unto me! Rather on Nilus' mud
> Lay me stark nak'd, and let the water-flies
> Blow me into abhorring! Rather make
> My country's high pyramides my gibbet,
> And hang me up in chains!
>
> (5.2.57–62)

Ahmad Shaqui, poet and patriot, had most of his work already cut out for him; there really is not much left to do in mending whatever else appears to contradict this poise of nationalist dignity. Even the repulsive imagery has been turned to good account; the worst is evoked, and embraced – if that should be the only choice. How much more those other passages of contrasting physical evocation, those sumptuous, festal passages upon which Shakespeare has poured such haunting sensuousness. Have they not driven later poets and dramatists – notably T. S. Eliot – to an ambiguous relationship with their own literary heritage?

> The silken tackle
> Swell with the touches of those flower-soft hands
> That yarely frame the office. From the barge
> A strange invisible perfume hits the sense

> Of the adjacent wharfs. The city cast
> Her people out upon her; and Antony,
> Enthron'd i' th' market place, did sit alone,
> Whistling to th' air; which, but for vacancy,
> Had gone to gaze on Cleopatra too,
> And made a gap in nature.
>
> (2.2.213–22)

Does the palate tend to cloy a little? Possibly. But by now Egypt, whom all, including Octavius Caesar, have made us identify with Cleopatra totally, is quickly manoeuvred towards our reassurance that we are still in command of our faculties of judgement, then acquitted absolutely. Admittedly the foreman of the jury is none other than a prejudiced Enobarbus, but we know him also for a blunt-spoken soldier. Most importantly, that habitual juxtaposition of harsh lingual rigour with lines of ineradicable sublimity leaves no room for doubt that an objective assessment has been fairly concluded. In short, the advocate acknowledges faults, but witness how he phrases the extenuating circumstances:

> Age cannot wither her, nor custom stale
> Her infinite variety. Other women cloy
> The appetites they feed, but she makes hungry
> Where most she satisfies; for vilest things
> Become themselves in her, that the holy priests
> Bless her when she is riggish.
>
> (2.2.239–44)

That Cleopatra should match, in her final hours, the dignified poise of humility with a final thought (and abandonment) of defiance against the jealous gods is, in my view, both dramatically expected and aesthetically satisfying:

> No more but e'en a woman, and commanded
> By such poor passion as the maid that milks
> And does the meanest chares. It were for me
> To throw my sceptre at the injurious gods;
> To tell them that this world did equal theirs
> Till they had stol'n our jewel.
>
> (4.15.73–8)

But the awesomeness of the lines that follow can only be fully absorbed by an Egyptian, or one steeped in the esoteric cults of Egypt and allied religions, including Islam. Cleopatra is speaking figuratively here of the house of death, and then again, she is not. She is evoking the deeper mysteries of the cult of Isis and the nether kingdoms of an other-existence, and it spreads an eerie quality over the final tableau – unlike any comparable end in all of Shakespeare.

The following recites like any article of faith in the Resurrection:

> I have believed in Allah, and his angels, and His books, and His messengers, and the Last Day and the decree of its good and evil from Allah-ta'alla, and in the Rising after death. (*Islamic Book of the Dead*)

But the Arabic script that transcribes this *ayat* from the Hadith is composed like a high-prowed gondola with a crew of ritualized (hierographic-ally speaking) rowers.[2] What Islam in fact opposes in the 'Kafir' cults of Osiris and Isis have merely been transposed from their elaborate structures with all their sacrificial rites to a mystic opacity of liturgical language – in the Islamic exegesis of death, the kinship remains blatant. Their neighbours the pagan Greeks, who borrowed from them much of their cults and religions in any case, would have no difficulty in identifying the Osiris-prowed Hadithic boat of death with Charon's canoe, scything through the River Styx. Islamic injunctions, prayers and invocations on the theme of death more than compensate the exhortations to practical meagreness by their endless liturgy and lyrical wealth of going, and the aftermath of dissolution.

Cleopatra, whom we have watched throned as Isis, imbues the approach of death with a measured ritualism that is suffused with the palpable shadowiness of the crypt. Not just her contemporary worshippers at the shrines of Isis and Osiris, but their descendants, born into the counter-claims of Islamic religion, would therefore share more than a mere metaphor of language with Cleopatra's demand: 'Then is it sin / To rush into the secret house of death . . . ?' We can hear its echo in the following lines also from the *Islamic Book of the Dead*:

> It is said that every day the graves call out five times:
> I am the house of isolation. . . .
> I am the house of darkness. . . .
> I am the house of earth. . . .
> I am the house of the questioning of Munkar and Nakir . . .

I know of no parallel echo in the Christian offices of the dead. Arabic 'classical' poetry is however full of it, and of Shakespeare's sonnets, the ones which seem to attract the finest 'classical' poets among the Arabs seem to share this preoccupation with the imagery of death as a place of physical habitation. Sometimes they are outright translations but more often they are original compositions inspired by a specific sonnet of Shakespeare. And we find a consistency in the emphasis given to one part of Shakespeare's variations on the theme of love as against the main theme itself. Comparatively underplayed is the defiant sentiment:

> Not marble nor the gilded monuments
> Of princes shall outlive this pow'rful rhyme;
> But you shall shine more bright in these contents
> Than unswept stone, besmear'd with sluttish time.
>
> (Sonnet 55)

The humanistic verses of Omar Khayyám are considered worse than irreverent – they are termed heretical and subversive; nor does the graveyard humour of an Andrew Marvell hold much appeal for the True Islamic poet:

> The grave's a fine and private place
> But none, I think, do there embrace.
>
> ('To His Coy Mistress')

No, it is essentially the grave as a place, an abode in time, that taxes the poetic genius of Shakespeare's adapters, not as a spur to the demands of love, presented as an end which is worse for overtaking its victim loveless, against which is held the imperishable products of the Muse or the talisman of immortality in love's offspring. Elias Abu Shabbakah's 'The Song of Death' is aptly titled, though it derives from Shakespeare's Sonnet 71, 'No longer Mourn for me when I am Dead'. The contrast, despite the opening abnegation, is revealing:

My will, which I want you to remember, is to forget me when I am dead. And, if memories move you one day and your affection chooses to remind you of me, take the guitar of my inspiration into the dark night and go to my tomb in silence, and tap the guitar once; for it will let you hear a moaning sigh such as mine.

The unearthly moisture of suicide, the aspic's trail of slime on fig-leaves transports us to this totally alien earth, and I mean alien, not from the view of Shakespeare's culture alone. This is yet another world opening inwards from the mundane one into which we have already been inducted by some of the most unnerving imageries in poetic drama: a yoking of approaching bodily corruption with the essence-draining paradox of birth and infancy closes the fatal cycle of the union of opposites that began with the aspic's slime:

> Peace, peace!
> Dost thou not see my baby at my breast
> That sucks the nurse asleep?
>
> (5.2.306–8)

In this dark ceremonial, the crown which Cleopatra dons becomes not just a prop for composing herself for death as befits a queen, nor her robe the final cover for a soon-to-be-hollowed vessel, but ritual transformation steps towards the mystic moment of transition:

> Give me my robe, put on my crown; I have
> Immortal longings in me. . . .
> I am fire and air; my other elements
> I give to baser life. So, have you done?
> Come then, and take the last warmth of my lips.
> Farewell, kind Charmian. Iras, long farewell.
> Have I the aspic in my lips? Dost fall?
> If thou and nature can so gently part,
> The stroke of death is as a lover's pinch,
> Which hurts and is desired.
>
> (5.2.278–9, 287–94)

Iras has now preceded, and in that calm recital of Cleopatra:

> The stroke of death is as a lover's pinch,
> Which hurts and is desired

is heard the reprise and conclusion of that death aria which we have earlier descried. It commenced in the penultimate act, 'The crown o' th' earth doth melt. . . .' (4.15.63), and winds into the awesome darkness at the Osiric passage:

> Then is it sin
> To rush into the secret house of death
> Ere death dare come to us?
>
> (4.15.80–2)

In sustaining its threnody through one more act, despite the triumphant boots of Caesar and entourage, punctured by the country yokel humour of the aspic-hawking Clown, it becomes clear that our playwright has already inscribed *Finis* on the actual historic conflicts of power and passion. The crown of the earth has melted, and there is nothing left remarkable beneath the visiting moon. But in this setting, is that all? Beyond it? And beneath earth itself? The spectral power of Shakespeare's poetry remains to lead us into the 'other side' of the veil whose precedent reality, which is now seen as merely contingent, gives awesome splendour to the finale of an otherwise butterfly queen. The rest of *Antony and Cleopatra* is our excursion into that world, one which lies more innocently on the Egyptian reality of that time than on the most stoical, self-submissive will in the inherent or explicit theologies of Shakespeare's other drama:

> I am dying, Egypt, dying; only
> I here importune death awhile, until
> Of many thousand kisses the poor last
> I lay upon thy lips.
>
> (4.15.18–21)

Contrast this with the death of the genuine Moor whose folly was of a more excusable circumstance than Antony's:

> I kissed thee ere I killed thee. No way but this –
> Killing myself, to die upon a kiss.
>
> (*Othello*, 5.2.362–3)

One dirge-master is understandably Shayk al-Subair, the other William Shakespeare. Here most noticeably, the cadences of death in Shakespeare's tragic figures are as crucial to his poetry as his celebration of life, even when the celebrants are flawed and their own worst enemy of life. It is difficult to underestimate this property as one which the Egyptian dramatists identified in their own world, for in *Antony and Cleopatra* Shakespeare's sensuous powers climaxed to evoke not merely the humanity of actors of a particular history, but the glimpsed afterworld whose liturgy of resolution imbued them with their unearthly calm at the hour of death.

There are other minor but no less critical touches to the realistic evocation of a credible Egypt even within its very mythology. One need only examine the comparative sociologies of Shakespeare's stock characters – the Soothsayer for instance. In *Julius Caesar*, he simply comes off the street like a disembodied voice, and sinks back into urban anonymity once his dramatic role is fulfilled. Cassandra in *Troilus and Cressida* is a hysterical weirdo who, if anything, mars her cause with a melodramatic manner of revelations. Is she a member of the household? We do not really experience her – all these are not pejorative remarks, merely contrastive for a point of view. The Soothsayer in *Antony and Cleopatra* is an individual, a solid, recognizable persona. He follows Antony to Rome as his personal soothsayer and emerges more in the role of a shrewd psychologist than a mere mumbo-jumboist digging in eagles' entrails and seeing portents in the clouds. His analysis

of Antony's psyche is as detachedly clinical as Antony's own lecture on
the scientific achievements of his adopted home, which he delivers as a
cool, observant voyager to a curious stay-at-home:

> Thus do they, sir: they take the flow o' th' Nile
> By certain scales i' th' pyramid; they know
> By th' height, the lowness, or the mean, if dearth
> Or foison follow. The higher Nilus swells
> The more it promises; as it ebbs, the seedsman
> Upon the slime and ooze scatters his grain,
> And shortly comes to harvest.
>
> (2.7.17–23)

This mixture of clinical information on human beings and the cultivated soil alike makes the earth of Egypt dominate Rome and take over
the half-way house Misenum, making one suspect that Shayk al-Subair
cannot wait to get back to his own soil where his genius for this story
resides. He compromises by transferring a touch of Egypt to the no
man's land of Pompey's ship in Misenum. Between Enobarbus and
Antony – with a little help from Lepidus – the essence of Egypt continues to haunt the concourse of Rome, the Mediterranean and its
buccaneers. Does Shakespeare lavish any such comparative care in preserving the smells, sounds and allied definitions of a yearned for home?
We are not speaking now of rhetoric, even of the pathetic kind old John
of Gaunt expends in *Richard II*:

> This royal throne of kings, this scept'red isle,
> This earth of majesty, this seat of Mars,
> This other Eden, demi-paradise,
> This fortress built by Nature for herself
> Against infection and the hand of war,
> This happy breed of men, this little world,
> This precious stone set in the silver sea . . .
>
> (2.1.40–6)

nor of the philosophical, disinterested speculations on land and Nature
in *As You Like It*. No! To a people to whom land, fertile land, is both
worship and life, an Egypt of Shakespeare's *Antony and Cleopatra* cannot
be served by such rhetoric or abstract morality. And like morality, even
so those qualities that grace (or disgrace) humanity cannot be rendered
in the abstract but must be invested in characters and the affective
community – we need only contrast the following with Portia's peroration on the quality of mercy:

> For his bounty,
> There was no winter in it; an autumn 'twas
> That grew the more by reaping. His delights
> Were dolphin-like: they show'd his back above
> The element they liv'd in. In his livery
> Walk'd crowns and crownets; realms and islands were
> As plates dropp'd from his pocket.
>
> (5.2.86–92)

This, then, is the soul we recognize in Antony, so generous in giving that he loses all judgement. His rejection of pettiness over the defection of Enobarbus, his agonizing concern for the safety of his followers after defeat – these small redeeming features approve his humanity and contribute to a suspicion that our judgement of him may be lacking in that generosity which was his one redeeming grace. And what proud Egyptian, especially a poet, will fully resist the anti-chauvinist fervour of a one-third shareholder of the world, one who – no matter the motivation – declaims, both in word and deed:

> Let Rome in Tiber melt, and the wide arch
> Of the rang'd empire fall! Here is my space.
> Kingdoms are clay; our dungy earth alike
> Feeds beast as man.
>
> (1.1.33–6)

'Here is my space.' John of Gaunt's rhetorical flourish does not do half as much for the Englishman as Antony the Roman does, in that brief speech, for the land-proud Egyptian. The conqueror is himself conquered by the land in the person of her capricious Queen, the same land whose foulest ditch she would rather inhabit, upon whose highest gibbet she would rather hang, than be taken to grace the triumphal march of a conqueror (albeit a new one) in Rome. 'Here is my space' – it is at once a hint that the land has doomed him, and a taste of the largeness of a man whose bountifulness – as we come to know this – imbues our space with a heroic grandeur, even when events are trivialized by the humane weaknesses of our kind.

Only Shakespeare could contract the pomp and panoply of love and royalty into a gastronomic experience, yet unfailingly elevate both into a veritable apotheosis without a sense of the ridiculous or the inflated. Enobarbus, in Rome, unerringly predicts that Antony 'will to his Egyptian dish again'. The Egyptian dish herself boasts 'I was / A morsel for a monarch' without a hint of self-mockery, indeed with pride and womanly preening. When things go sour:

> I found you as a morsel cold upon
> Dead Caesar's trencher.
>
> (3.13.116–17)

Food, wine, violence, sexuality and putrefaction – both qualitatively
and in sheer quantity – this is a different landscape of human activities
from the more familiar settings of Shakespeare's. A moist land and
visceral responses. The transitions from the physical to the metaphys-
ical are unforced, and this is in no small measure due to the magnitude
of extremes with which the human vehicles are imbued. Is it not
through the same lips of the lustful gipsy, tripping credibly because it is
made the active response of any jealous woman, that we are led into
the self-apotheosis of an irrepressible pair?

> Eternity was in our lips and eyes,
> Bliss in our brows' bent, none our parts so poor
> But was a race of heaven.
>
> (1.3.35–7)

With such a subject, is it any wonder that Shayk al-Subair reveals again
and again that he cannot wait to escape home from the land of a 'holy,
cold, and still conversation'? In *Antony and Cleopatra*, Shakespeare's borrowed imageries finally come home to roost. That the *terra firma* of his
choice happens to be Egypt may be an accident – it could easily have
been India. It was nearly the Caribbean but Shakespeare chose there
to employ stage effects, deliberately, and thus denied his island that
specific dimension of richness which comes from a physical and human
identity. Moreover, in *The Tempest* Shakespeare is concerned not with
history, but with enchantment. By contrast, Alexandria (or Tripoli in
this case) is the home of that tantalizing glimpse of the topography of
Achilles' frazzled brains, it is the demythologized context of Othello's
romantic yarns, the source of all those secret potions of love or death-
like sleep from *Romeo and Juliet* to *A Midsummer Night's Dream*, the destina-
tion or port-of-call of those rich argosies that billow through the pages
of *The Merchant of Venice*, and even the unseen crusader ship of Shakespeare's history plays.

Only if Ahmad Ba-Kathir, Ahmad Shaqui, Khali Mutran, Gibran
and a host of others had failed to recognize this, would the history of
this relationship have been astonishing. Their fascination with Shakespeare is not in the least surprising after all; the scepticism of some of
their fellow-poets and dramatists about Shakespeare's claim to an English ancestry is simply a passionate compliment to those qualities in
Shakespeare, a few of which we have touched upon, but above all the

paradox of timelessness and history, a realism evoked – simultaneously – of time, place and people – with which he has infused *Antony and Cleopatra* more deeply than any of his plays except perhaps *Macbeth* – which is a horse of an entirely different colour.

Sean O'Casey may be proved only partially right – I return to his rhetorical question, regarding whose answer there is nothing rhetorical in the stance of Shakespeare's Arab co-practitioners in the field of drama. The Shayk was born too early for Philippi, or indeed for the battle of the Nile, but the Nile did course through his veins. Personally, I was left with only one problem to resolve – if the Shayk was indeed an Arab, who was his wife? It seemed to me that we could not dispose of one problem without the other – such being the power of documents in our time. Those documents insist that our William was well and truly wived by someone whose name was recorded as Anne Hathaway. Perhaps there were others, but even Othello had imbibed sufficient European influence to content himself with only one wife, so why not his very creator, Shayk al-Subair? Being a monogamist does not therefore destroy the case for Shakespeare's Arabic origin. Well then, I consulted my colleague in Arabic Studies and our assiduousness was rewarded. Anne Hathaway proved to be none other than an English corruption of Hanna Hathawa. The first name stands for 'to dye red'; the second, Hathawa, means 'to scatter, to disperse', someone who disseminates. The puzzle was resolved. Shayk al-Subair's spouse Hanna Hathawa, a high-coloured lady, came to life in her own right, a little-known theatrical agent whose publicity activities on behalf of her husband will, I hope, provide endless preoccupation for at least a dozen doctoral theses.

In the meantime, one acknowledges with gratitude the subjective relation of other poets and dramatists to the phenomenon of Shakespeare, for even the most esoteric of their claims lead one, invariably, to the productive source itself, and to the gratification of celebrating dramatic poetry anew. That Shakespeare may turn out to be an Arab after all is certainly less alarming a prospect than that he should prove to be Christopher Marlowe. No one has yet begun to ransack the sand-dunes of Arabia, shovelling aside the venerable bones of Bedouins in the hope of disinterring the bones of the author of *Antony and Cleopatra*. By contrast, that talented but junior brother of his genius, the author of *Tamburlaine*, has not been permitted a peaceful sleep in his grave, especially at the hands of yet another group of ex-colonial enthusiasts, this time, the Americans. Happily, for the majority of Shakespeare-lovers, those other secret lives of the Shayk which remain to be uncovered outside *Bingo* or the *Arabian Nights* will just have to wait, until his tomes have yielded up the last of their treasures.

First published in *Shakespeare Survey 36*, 1983

NOTES

1 Quoted in *Sean O'Casey: A Collection of Critical Essays*, ed. Thomas Kilroy (Englewood Cliffs, N.J., 1975), p. 115.
2 A marvellously preserved carving of the Egyptian 'Boat of the Dead' in the Pushkin Museum, Moscow, demonstrates most glaringly the relationship of the transcription to the funerary craft.

CHAPTER 6

Shakespeare in the trenches

Balz Engler

In April 1916 the tercentenary of Shakespeare's death was celebrated both in England and Germany, although the two countries had been at war for almost two years. This may just sound like an intriguing story, but it is also of considerable critical interest, because it illustrates how Shakespeare's international reputation survived under pressure, how conflicting views of him were defined by the political situation, and how these views, in turn, shaped the meaning of Shakespeare's texts, and affected the history of literary studies after the war.

In other words, in tracing these developments here Shakespeare will be considered as a public symbol, as myth.[1] But this will be done in a comparative perspective, which may help to remove the national limitations characteristic of most studies in this area.[2]

In England a committee, with the Prime Minister as its honorary president, had prepared elaborate ceremonies.[3] They could not really include 23 April, the day of Shakespeare's birth and death (and, significantly for many, St George's Day), because, in 1916, it coincided with Easter Sunday. Officially suggesting a parallel between Christ and Shakespeare would have meant taking things too far. Therefore the celebrations concentrated on the first week of May. On four days great institutions did homage to Shakespeare, on Sunday the Church, on Monday politics, on Tuesday the arts, on Wednesday education.

Sunday 30 April was declared Shakespeare Sunday. In many churches Shakespeare sermons were preached.[4] Shakespeare and patriotism was the most frequent subject. At Holy Trinity Church in Stratford, for example, it was about the strength that Shakespeare must have gained from his early experience of the Warwickshire countryside – strength 'which heartens our England to strive and endure'.[5] One sermon noted how the wave of patriotism that had recently passed over the land had made people understand Shakespeare better again, after shameful neglect, due to gross materialism; 'we who think of him, who after three hundred years risen from the dead still lives and moves and speaks to us in his marvellous creations, must needs thank Him Who is the bringer of all that is good and gracious . . .'[6]

On Monday a public meeting was held at Mansion House, with the participation of the Government, the Archbishop of Canterbury, and the diplomatic representatives of the Empire and the allied and neutral, but not the enemy, countries. Lord Crewe (standing in for the Prime Minister), the American ambassador, the representatives of the South African Union and of Sweden, among others, addressed the meeting.

On Tuesday afternoon a special performance took place at Drury Lane, in the words of the organizing committee 'a tribute to the genius of William Shakespeare, humbly offered by the players and their fellow-workers in the kindred arts of music and painting'. It was to be done 'in the spirit of the Bayreuth festivals; and there can be little question but that the audience will find that, as the occasion is worthier, so is the execution finer'.[7] The King and Queen were present; the proceeds went to joint funds of the British Red Cross Society and the Order of St John. A programme of Shakespeare music by living composers was followed by a performance of *Julius Caesar* with Frank Benson as Caesar, and a pageant of Shakespeare figures impersonated by well-known actors and actresses (in the tradition of earlier Shakespeare centenaries).[8] It was after this performance that Frank Benson was knighted – the King borrowed a sword from the property-room.

On this occasion a memorial volume was presented to the public, *A Book of Homage to Shakespeare*, edited again by Israel Gollancz, the indefatigable secretary of the tercentenary. It contained lavish illustrations, the homage of the painters, as well as 166 addresses, poems and critical essays in many languages, from most, but not the enemy, countries.[9]

Wednesday 3 May was declared Shakespeare Day for the schools and training colleges. In the spirit of Empire Day it was to create 'a bond between the English-speaking children in the United Kingdom, the Dominions and the United States of America'.[10] London schoolchildren were given badges with the Droeshout portrait, offered by the British Empire Shakespeare Society.[11]

The celebrations were to begin with a reading from Ecclesiasticus 44 ('Let us now praise famous men'), followed by the singing of Shakespeare songs, a discourse on the poet, the reading of scenes from his plays, and closing with 'God save the King'. The London County Council had also set up a committee to devise a 'Shakespeare prayer', which was said in all London schools.[12] The beautiful memorial programme[13] printed for the occasion contains 'Notes on Shakespeare the Patriot', concerning his views on language, patriotism, the fleet, etc., and illustrating them with passages mainly from *Henry V*.

Theatrical activities were few; in London just one Shakespeare season, at His Majesty's, was announced.[14] In particular, one dream once again did not come true in 1916: the foundation of a National Theatre.[15] This had been discussed in the House of Commons in 1913, appropriately on St George's Day.[16] Among the arguments then used for the establishment of such a theatre, two are of particular interest to us: the need for a place where those plays could be adequately performed whose language constituted a bond among the English-speaking people; and, quite explicitly, the model of rival Germany, where much more was being done for Shakespeare on the stage. H. J. McKinder, who moved the resolution, quoted from advance sheets of the *Shakespeare-Jahrbuch*, indicating the number of Shakespeare performances by professionals in Germany, 1,156 in 1912; and he ventured to think 'that we have nothing in this land of Shakespeare to show which is comparable in the least degree to the facts indicated by these figures'.[17]

By comparison with the official English celebrations in 1916 activities in Germany were modest. Max Reinhardt revived a cycle of Shakespeare plays that he had first put on in 1914. There was nothing like the Shakespeare Week in London. At the meeting of the *Deutsche Shakespeare-Gesellschaft* in Weimar, which was afterwards criticized as dull and uninspiring, Rudolf Brotanek, in his 'Festvortrag', found that Shakespeare's opinions, as expressed in his plays, were in accordance with the German position in the war. He closed by saying:

We are satisfied that we still adhere to notions of duty which Shakespeare laid down three hundred years ago in his works, those statutes of free and noble humanity. We are pleased that in our statesmen the feeling of fellowship with the people and of responsibility towards God is still so strong as in the soul of Henry V, as studied by Shakespeare, that all our leaders may raise their hands and hearts towards the God of battles and may pray, with the victor at Bosworth:

> O thou, whose captain I account myself,
> Look on my forces with a gracious eye. [...]
> Make us thy ministers of chastisement,
> That we may praise thee in the victory.
> (*Richard III*, 5.5.61–7)[18]

There were reasons for this relative neglect in 1916 – and we have to move back two years in history to understand them: in 1914

Shakespeare's 350th birthday had been celebrated extensively.[19] This year had been chosen, because the *Deutsche Shakespeare-Gesellschaft* was then also marking its fiftieth anniversary. The festivities, as always, took place at Weimar, the city of Goethe and Schiller, three months before the beginning of the war. They were internationally oriented, in particular reflecting the anglophile attitude of German Shakespearians: Franz Josef I of Austria and Hungary joined the Gesellschaft, but also King George V (the Kaiser had been a member for a long time); Viscount Haldane, the British Lord Chancellor, was made an honorary member.

In England the mood had been similar in 1914. There were few events to mark Shakespeare's birthday in April. But in June a Shakespeare Association was founded, with the purpose of organizing the 1916 centenary. Its thirteen vice-presidents were to include luminaries in English studies from all over the world, among them three representatives from Germany.[20] Beerbohm Tree proposed that, in 1916, an international production of all the history plays should be put on in London, with a cast including Americans, Frenchmen, Germans and Italians.[21] Shakespeare could still be shared with the world.

The outbreak of the war in August almost immediately called in question the high principles extolled on both sides only a few months earlier. In September Max Reinhardt's Deutsches Theater in Berlin, which had been preparing a grand cycle of Shakespeare plays to mark the anniversary, polled important personalities on whether, under the new circumstances, it was appropriate to perform the works of Shakespeare, a British author. The answers were unanimous: there was no reason to stop performing him: 'Shakespeare gehört der ganzen Welt' (Shakespeare belongs to the whole world), as the Chancellor, Bethmann-Hollweg, put it; moreover, Germany was at war not with the people of Shakespeare's England, but with their mean and degenerated descendants; and finally, in the words of Fürst von Bülow, Bethmann-Hollweg's predecessor, Shakespeare 'is among the oldest and most beautiful conquests of the German mind, which we shall defend against all the world, like our other spiritual and material possessions'.[22]

War imagery became common on both sides in the following years, the imagery of territorial possession and conquest, of asylum and internment. In a prologue to a Shakespeare performance delivered at Leipzig, in the autumn of 1914, Feste was given a provocative message from Shakespeare to the audience. A translation of it was soon printed in *The Times*:

Ye unto him have been until today
His second home; his first and native home
Was England; but this England of the present
Is so contrarious in her acts and feelings,
Yea, so abhorr'd of his pure majesty
And the proud spirit of his free-born being,
That he doth find himself quite homeless there.
A fugitive he seeks his second home,
This Germany, that loves him most of all,
To whom before all others he gives thanks,
And says: Thou wonderful and noble land,
Remain thou Shakespeare's one and only home.[23]

Ernest de Sélincourt commented: 'Poor Shakespeare! If you want to crystallize the pathetic situation in a phrase you might call it "Shakespeare interned" or "Germany the snapper-up of unconsidered trifles"';[24] and Arthur Quiller-Couch's commentary summarizes many of the prejudices on the English side:

These men do honestly believe our Shakespeare . . ., whose language they cannot speak, cannot write, can but imperfectly understand . . . our Shakespeare's spirit – has migrated to a nation whose exploits it benevolently watches in the sack of Louvain, the bestialities of Aerschot, the shelling of Rheims cathedral.[25]

So far I have been anecdotal, and I should now like to bring some order into what I have reported: how does Shakespeare appear in these events on both sides?

In Germany the claim that Shakespeare was *unser*, ours, presented a problem, of course: nobody could seriously deny that Shakespeare was an Englishman. But there were essentially three strategies to deal with this. One could argue that it was mere coincidence that Shakespeare, the poet of all humankind, was born and lived in England.[26] Then there were the climatic and racial theories, which saw Shakespeare as one of the geniuses of the Germanic North, as against those of the Romance South.[27] This opposition goes back to Herder's attempt in the eighteenth century to free German literature from the grip of French classicism, and to create a sense of German nationhood with the help of literature.[28] In this Shakespeare played a crucial role as a genius who, unobstructed by any moral or aesthetic rules, offered direct access to nature.

Finally, one could claim, as Brotanek and many others did, that Shakespeare had been an English patriot, even an exemplary one. However, his values were no longer upheld by his countrymen, but by the Germans, who had naturalized Shakespeare in a long effort of appropriation. This rhetoric reached its apotheosis with the publication of Friedrich Gundolf's *Shakespeare und der deutsche Geist* in 1911, one of the most influential books of literary criticism in German.[29]

As such Shakespeare could come to be considered one of the three greatest German authors, along with Goethe and Schiller; and it was no coincidence that the Shakespeare-Gesellschaft established its seat at Weimar. Hamlet, along with Faust, became one of the great myths of German culture;[30] and phrases from Shakespeare's plays permeate the German language as much as those from Goethe and Schiller.

In England, as the tercentenary celebrations indicate, Shakespeare was closely associated both with the idea of England and that of the Empire, according to which English and the English way of life had spread their beneficial influence all over the world.[31] In fact, the two ideas are difficult to disentangle: the values that constitute Englishness and those of a world-wide Empire are fused in a complex and ambiguous manner, perhaps best summed up by Rupert Brooke's sonnet 'The Soldier';[32] and we know from more recent European history how national consciousness among the English, under the influence of imperialism, has been only imperfectly developed, unlike that of other nations on British soil. Shakespeare then was both universal, and as such representative of what placed England *above* nationalism, and of what made his own country different from others and placed it *beside* them.

There was nothing as formidable as Gundolf's Shakespeare that could be set against what looked like systematic German attempts to requisition Shakespeare. In this situation, the German challenge to the ownership of Shakespeare was met, at first insecurely, with a more narrowly defined nationalist position, emphasizing borders, denying access to Shakespeare, insisting on what made England and her poet different and difficult to master for other nations.

The struggle for Shakespeare during the First World War was to leave deep traces in the history of Shakespeare studies for decades to come; of these I should only like to mention the reception of German Shakespeare criticism and the development of English as a discipline in England. Before the First World War German Shakespeare criticism, within certain limits set by the image of the philologist as pedant, had been taken seriously, especially in the areas of textual, aesthetic and biographical studies.[33] But now the English began to neglect, even to reject German criticism, an attitude that has persisted in many places.

I remember an eminent English Shakespeare scholar advising me not to use Alexander Schmidt's *Shakespeare Lexicon*: 'Schmidt was German and therefore could not understand Shakespeare properly' – clearly an echo of Quiller-Couch's position. He had failed to notice that the *OED* routinely uses Schmidt's definitions where single occurrences of words in Shakespeare are recorded.[34]

In more general terms, one can also see the effects of this struggle for the possession of Shakespeare as a factor in the establishment of English as an academic discipline after the war.[35] Quiller-Couch, in the essay I have already quoted, went as far as blaming the Germans for the neglect of English literature in English schools:

I do not say, nor do I believe for a moment, in spite of a long malignity now unmasked, the Germans have *of set purpose* treated English literature as a thing of the past or imposed that illusion upon our schools, with design to prove that this particular glory of our birth and state is a dead possession of a decadent race. My whole argument is rather that they have set up this illusion, and industriously, because they could not help it; because the illusion is in them: because this lovely and living art which they can never practise nor even see as an art, to them is, has been, must be for ever, a dead science – a *hortus siccus*; to be tabulated, not to be planted or watered. (p. 314)

Such a view, which acknowledges German influence at an unlikely moment, helped to shape the insistence on literature as a vital force, which we associate with the Cambridge tradition of literary studies, as something that may 'once more bring sanctification and joy into the sphere of common life', as the Newbolt Report put it.[36]

What can we learn for Shakespeare criticism from all this? I should like briefly to mention three points that concern related areas of debate. In 1989 there was a controversy in the *TLS* on whether there were any limits to the interpretation of Shakespeare's plays.[37] The evidence of the First World War supports the view that this is not the case. On both sides, soldiers were sent into battle with the same slogans from Shakespeare;[38] the German Chancellor quoted *Henry V* when German troops stood before Calais;[39] the play was performed in Germany in 1917, and criticism concerned the question why it was not part of a cycle of histories,[40] rather than why it should have been done at all.

This leads me to my second point: What I have said makes it clear that it is the context in which we perceive Shakespeare and his works, *how we use them*, that determines their meaning. In other words, we have to acknowledge the primacy of pragmatics in the study of Shakespeare.

And finally: a comparative perspective may be helpful in the study of this – and in giving up entrenched positions.

First published in *Shakespeare Survey 44*, 1992

NOTES

1 Cf. Balz Engler, 'The Classic as a Public Symbol', *REAL: Yearbook of Research in English and American Literature* 6 (1988/9), 217–36, and *Poetry and Community* (Tübingen, 1990); Graham Holderness, ed., *The Shakespeare Myth* (Manchester, 1988); Marion F. O'Connor, 'Theatre of the Empire: "Shakespeare's England" at Earl's Court, 1912', in *Shakespeare Reproduced: The Text in History and Ideology*, ed. Jean E. Howard and Marion F. O'Connor (New York and London, 1987), pp. 68–98.

2 This seems to be a problem with many books on Englishness. Cf. Brian Doyle, *English and Englishness* (London, 1989); Raphael Samuel, ed., *Patriotism: The Making and Unmaking of British National Identity*, 3 vols. (London, 1989), and its review in *TLS*, 22–8 December 1989, pp. 1407–8.

3 *The Times*, 29 January 1916, p. 5.

4 A. J. Carlyle, *The Shakespeare Tercentenary. A Sermon Preached in the City Church of Oxford, April 30th 1916* (Oxford, 1916).

5 Anthony C. Deane, *His own Place. The Tercentenary 'Shakespeare Sermon' preached in the Church of the Holy Trinity, Stratford-on-Avon, April 30th, 1916* (London, 1916), p. 4.

6 H. D. Rawnsley, *Shakespeare: A Tercentenary Sermon* (London, 1916), p. 11. Note also the speech by the Bishop of Birmingham at the Repertory Theatre on 25 April, in which he stated: 'To Shakespeare patriotism and religion were inseparable. Anything less like the real Shakespeare than the one made in Germany had never been seen or dreamed of', *The Times*, 26 April 1916, p. 9.

7 *The Times*, 21 April 1916, p. 7.

8 The plays represented were *Romeo and Juliet*, *The Merchant of Venice*, *The Merry Wives of Windsor*, *Much Ado About Nothing*, *As You Like It*, *Twelfth Night*, *Coriolanus* and *The Winter's Tale*. A cast list is to be found in J. P. Wearing, *The London Stage 1910–1919*, vol. 1 (Metuchen, 1982), pp. 634–5.

9 Among the essays there is a remarkably generous, but untypical one by C. H. Herford on 'The German Contribution to Shakespeare Criticism', pp. 231–5. Herford, Professor of English at Manchester, had studied in Berlin.

10 Sir Israel Gollancz in his evidence to the Newbolt Committee. His proposal was taken up favourably by the committee. See *The Teaching of English in England: Report of the Departmental Committee* (London, 1921), p. 319.

11 The British Empire Shakespeare Society was founded in 1901, with Henry Irving as its first president (Ivor Brown and George Fearon, *Amazing*

Monument: A History of the Shakespeare Industry (New York and London, 1939), p. 317).

12 Unfortunately I have not been able to locate its text. A report in *The Times* on 3 May 1916, p. 7, confirms that such 'a special form of prayer' was indeed used.

13 *Shakespeare Day 1916* (London, 1916).

14 *The Times*, 3 May 1916, p. 7.

15 Such plans were old, of course. Cf. Geoffrey Whitworth, *The Making of a National Theatre* (London, 1951).

16 The debate is well documented in Whitworth, *National Theatre*, pp. 100–13.

17 *Ibid.*, p. 101.

18 'Wir sind es zufrieden, noch immer zu Pflichtbegriffen uns zu bekennen, welche Shakespeare vor dreihundert Jahren in seinen Werken, jenem Gesetzbuch freier und hochgemuter Menschlichkeit niederlegte. Wohl uns, dass in unseren Staatsmänneren das Gefühl der Zusammengehörigkeit mit dem Volke und der Verantwortung vor Gott noch so klar ist wie in der von Shakespeare durchleuchteten Seele Heinrichs V., dass ein jeder unserer Führer Hände und Herz zum Gott der Schlachten erheben und mit dem Sieger von Bosworth flehen darf:' etc. (Rudolf Brotanek, 'Shakespeare über den Krieg', *Shakespeare-Jahrbuch* 52 (1916), xvii–xlviii, p. xlviii). Brotanek quoted Shakespeare in German, of course.

19 Shakespeare had the misfortune to die at fifty-two; for the benefit of future admirers poets should ideally die at twenty-five or at seventy-five.

20 They were Alois Brandl (Berlin), Max Förster (Leipzig) and Josef Schick (Munich), *The Times*, 19 June 1914, p. 13.

21 *The Times*, 19 June 1914, quoted by Carl Grabau, 'Zeitschriftenschau 1914', *Shakespeare-Jahrbuch* 51 (1915), p. 240. Grabau does not always indicate his sources. I have checked these wherever possible, which showed that his reports can be relied on.

22 Grabau, 'Zeitschriftenschau 1914', pp. 242–3. Shakespeare 'gehört zu den ältesten und schönsten Eroberungen des deutschen Geistes, die wir wie un-seren sonstigen geistigen und materiellen Besitz gegen alle Welt behaupten wollen. Wir haben Shakespeare längst annektiert und geben ihn nicht wieder her' (p. 243).

23 Arthur Quiller-Couch, 'Patriotism in English Literature', in his *Studies in Literature* (Cambridge, 1918), pp. 290–322; p. 316. The original runs as follows:

> Ihr wäret ihm bisher die zweite Heimat
> Gewesen, seine erste, angeborne: England!
> Doch dieses England, wie es heute sei,
> Sein Handeln und sein Fühlen, sei ihm so zuwider,
> Ja, so verhasst dem redlichen und reinen,
> Dem Königsgeiste seines freien Wesens,
> Dass er sich dort als heimatlos empfände!
> Als solch ein stolz aus eigner Wahl Verbannter,
> Als Flüchtling käm er heut in seine zweite Heimat,

> Ins deutsche Land, das stets vor allen ihn geliebt,
> Dem dankbar er vor allen andern sei,
> Käm hin und spräche: Treues, tiefes, edles Land,
> Was Du mir warst, das sei mir fürder zwiefach:
> Des Shakespeare einzige und wahre Heimat [.]

(Ernst Hardt, 'Prolog zu einer Shakespeare-Aufführung im Herbste des Jahres 1914', *Shakespeare-Jahrbuch* 52 (1916), p. 2.) The tone of this prologue is typical. Cf. also Gerhart Hauptmann's speech at the meeting of the *Deutsche Shakespeare-Gesellschaft* in 1916: Shakespeare belongs to the whole world, but there is no people in the world, 'auch das englische nicht, das sich ein Anrecht wie das deutsche auf Shakespeare erworben hätte. Shakespeare Gestalten sind ein Teil unserer Welt, seine Seele ist eins mit unserer geworden: und wenn er in England geboren und begraben ist, so ist Deutschland das Land, wo er wahrhaft lebt.' [not even the English, who have earned a right to Shakespeare in the way the Germans have. Shakespeare's figures are part of our world, his soul has merged with ours: and if he was born and buried in England, it is in Germany where he truly lives.] (Gerhart Hauptmann, 'Deutschland und Shakespeare', *Shakespeare-Jahrbuch* 51 (1916), vii–xii; p. xii.)

24 Ernest de Sélincourt, *English Poets and the National Ideal* (London, 1915), p. 13.
25 Quiller-Couch, 'Patriotism', p. 317.
26 See, for example, Franz Kaibel, 'Dichter und Patriotismus: Die Betrachtung eines Deutschen zum dreihundertsten Todestag eines Engländers', *Shakespeare-Jahrbuch* 52 (1916), 36–63.
27 Climatic theories of this kind became accepted also in England, partly under German influence, cf. Carlyle's writings or Hyppolite Taine, *History of English Literature*, trans. H. van Laun, second edn (Edinburgh, 1872).
28 The hidden presence of France also in the early twentieth-century debate is made explicit by Josef Kohler, 'Die Staatsidee Shakespeares in *Richard II*', *Shakespeare-Jahrbuch* 53 (1917), 1–12. Cf. also Jonathan Bate, 'The Politics of Romantic Shakespeare Criticism: Germany, England, France', *European Romantic Review* 1 (1990), 1–26.
29 Eckhard Heftrich, 'Friedrich Gundolfs Shakespeare-Apotheose', *Jahrbuch der Deutschen Shakespeare-Gesellschaft West*, 1988, 85–102; pp. 86–7.
30 In the German Hamlet myth, Hamlet, the northern prince, stands for Germany, brooding and unable to act. In the context of the First World War there were attempts to reinterpret this myth, to turn Hamlet into a warlike hero. See Bernhard Fehr, 'Unser Shakespeare', *Westermanns Monatshefte* 120:1 (May 1916), 348–52, one of the most revealing contributions to the Shakespeare tercentenary.
31 Cf. the Earl's Court exhibition of 1911, as described by O'Connor, 'Theatre of Empire'.
32 Similar ideas were expressed by F. R. Benson at Stratford ('At Shakespeare's Shrine', *The Times*, 20 April 1915, p. 12. 'At the shrine on this day comes knowledge, clear and unmistakable, that there is no proper shrine to

the Shakespeare memory save the hearts of Englishmen. The altar at Stratford is kindled, and again it grows cold; but on Europe's battlefields ten thousand nobler altars enlighten the world with flames which shall not be extinguished. These are Shakespeare's men, though some of them may scarcely be familiar with the name of Shakespeare.') Cf. also the letter from C.L.D., *TLS*, 4 May 1916, quoting J. R. Seeley's essay on 'Milton's Poetry' in his *Lectures and Essays* (London, 1870), pp. 152–3.

33 The account offered by Sidney Lee, *Shakespeare's Life and Work* (London (1900), 1907), pp. 193–6, may be typical: 'During the last half-century textual, aesthetic, and biographical criticism has been pursued in Germany with unflagging industry and energy; and although laboured and supersubtle theorising characterises much German aesthetic criticism, its mass and variety testify to the impressiveness of the appeal that Shakespeare's work has made to the German intellect.' Lee specifically mentions Nicolaus Delius (textual criticism); Karl Elze (biography and stage history); F. A. T. Kreyssig, *Vorlesungen über Shakespeare* (1858 and 1874), *Shakespeare-Fragen* (1871), Otto Ludwig, *Shakespeare-Studien*, E. W. Sievers, Ulrici, *Shakespeare's Dramatic Art* (1839) and Gervinus' commentaries (1848–9).

34 Wolfgang Keller thinks that neglect set in at the time of the Boer War (when the two countries for the first time were on opposite sides), but that it really became serious after the First World War (Wolfgang Keller, 'Shakespeare als Dichter der Deutschen', in *Shakespeare in Europa*, ed. Paul Meissner (Stuttgart, 1944), pp. 1–116).

35 Chris Baldick, *The Social Mission of English Criticism, 1848–1932* (Oxford, 1983), pp. 86–108, 'Literary-Critical Consequences of the War' deals with this topic.

36 *The Teaching of English in England: Report of the Departmental Committee* (London, 1921), p. 258.

37 Cf. Terence Hawkes, 'Wittgenstein's Shakespeare', in *'Bad' Shakespeare*, ed. Maurice Charney (Cranbury, N.J., 1988), reviewed by Robert Hapgood, *TLS*, 25–31 August, p. 927, and Terence Hawkes's letter to the editor (*TLS*, 8–14 September 1989).

38 Cf. Paul Fussell, *The Great War and Modern Memory* (London, 1975, 1977), pp. 198–9; and, for example, Alois Brandl, 'Jahresbericht für 1914/15', *Shakespeare-Jahrbuch* 51 (1915), v, quoting *Henry V*.

39 *The Times*, 24 April 1915, p. 9.

40 Rudolf Raab, '*Heinrich V.* in neuer Bearbeitung am Karlsruher Hoftheater', *Shakespeare-Jahrbuch* 55 (1919), 223–5.

CHAPTER 7

Bowdler and Britannia: Shakespeare and the national libido

Michael Dobson

The inception of the 'Shakespeare industry' during the eighteenth century, with which I shall be largely concerned in this paper,[1] has not always been considered an especially sexy topic, I admit, and it is probably still true that for most historians of Shakespeare criticism the period which gave us the first 'scholarly' edition (Rowe's, 1709), the first public squabble over textual editing (between Alexander Pope and Lewis Theobald, 1725–6), and the first solemn pilgrimage to Stratford (Garrick's Jubilee, 1769) isn't one with any very obvious erotic overtones. Nonetheless, it is precisely the sexual dimension of the Enlightenment's processing of Shakespeare that I mean to sketch here, and especially its inextricable connection with the development of English nationalism. I shall be suggesting that the definition of Shakespeare as an object of nostalgic veneration during the eighteenth century is inseparably bound up with both the construction of modern sexuality and the construction of English national identity; so bound up, in fact, that it would be possible to regard the Enlightenment Shakespeare we still largely inherit as not just the ally but the offspring of Bowdler and Britannia, propriety and nationalism. In the course of this argument I shall be illustrating how in the eighteenth century Shakespeare came to embody the national libido – albeit, paradoxically, at the expense of his own.

Thomas and Henrietta Bowdler, of course, did not publish the Family Shakespeare until 1807 (and it remained anonymous until the second edition of 1814, the title page of which credits Thomas with the entire project so as to preserve the reputation of his unmarried sister), but the name 'Bowdler' provides a convenient shorthand for that normative policing of sexuality which actually begins far earlier, gathering momentum in English culture throughout the eighteenth century. George Mosse, indeed, cites the Bowdlers' Shakespeare as the perfect exemplar of this movement (which he terms 'respectability') as early as the third page of his deservedly influential *Nationalism and Sexuality* (1985).

Although Mosse's study otherwise neglects Shakespeare, and seems to me to date the full emergence of 'respectability' rather late, his argument that nationalism successfully co-opted earlier cultural forms while remaining unshakeably allied to a new model of propriety is one with considerable resonance for the Enlightenment's revaluation and reuse of Shakespeare:

> Nationalism is perhaps the most powerful and effective ideology of modern times, and its alliance with bourgeois morality forged an engine difficult to stop. In its long career, it attempted to co-opt most of the important movements of the age, to absorb all that men thought meaningful and held dear even while holding fast to certain unchanging myths and symbols . . . But however flexible, nationalism hardly wavered in its advocacy of respectability.[2]

The Shakespeare who had survived into the bookstalls and theatres of the early eighteenth century offered these interlinked emerging ideologies of nationalism and respectability both opportunities and challenges. As a relic of the already thoroughly idealized days of Good Queen Bess, his authentic Englishness was not in question; indeed one of the reasons his plays now attracted more attention than those of Jonson or Fletcher was their interest in the national past – paradoxically, the more frequently his histories were rewritten to support different viewpoints during the constitutional crises of the 1680s and 1710s, the more transcendentally valuable they appeared to be. But he certainly wasn't respectable: his texts and his biography alike, as Margreta de Grazia has pointed out in *Shakespeare Verbatim*, were riddled with lowness, 'extravagance', 'licentiousness' and 'irregularity'.[3] De Grazia has brilliantly demonstrated the extent to which the whole enterprise of textual editing, from Rowe through Malone (and indeed the Bowdlers), was established specifically to deal with this embarrassing verbal wantonness: but what she does not point out is the extent to which this policing of Shakespeare's texts often goes hand in hand with the co-opting of their author as himself a policing figure. Jeremy Collier was already displaying this combined strategy of monitoring Shakespeare and then invoking him as a monitor in 1698, in his famous *Short View of the Immorality and Prophaneness of the English Stage*, which at first berates Shakespeare for smuttiness but subsequently congratulates him for making a properly improving example of Falstaff – 'He is thrown out of Favour as being a *Rake*', Collier notes smugly,

> and dies like a Rat behind the Hangings. The Pleasure he had given, would not excuse him. The *Poet* was not so partial, as to let his Humour compound for his Lewdness.[4]

But this double move of at once redeeming Shakespeare for sexual propriety and invoking him as a potential redeemer of the contemporary public is displayed most fully by the cleaned-up version of *The Merchant of Venice* produced by George Granville, Lord Lansdowne in 1701, *The Jew of Venice*. The prologue to this adaptation, contributed by Granville's cousin Bevill Higgons, marks one of Shakespeare's first appearances in person – if that is the word – on the Augustan stage, and he is appropriately ushered on to it by one of his most distinguished polishers; as the curtain goes up, 'The Ghosts of *Shakespear* and *Dryden* arise Crown'd with Lawrel.'[5] The dialogue which ensues is almost obsessively concerned with sexual normality, here equated with both literary and national purity. Dryden reports to his elder colleague on the dismaying state of modern audiences, who, abandoning sterling British drama for foreign ephemera, have concomitantly abandoned heterosexuality:

> [Dryd.] *Their sickly Judgments, what is just, refuse,*
> *And French Grimace, Buffoons, and Mimicks choose;*
> *Our Scenes desert, some wretched Farce to see;*
> *They know not Nature, for they tast not Thee . . .*
> *Thro' Perspectives revers'd they Nature view,*
> *Which give the Passions Images, not true.*
> Strephon *for* Strephon *sighs; and* Sapho *dies,*
> *Shot to the soul by brighter* Sapho's *Eyes:*
> *No Wonder then their wand'ring Passions roam,*
> *And feel not Nature, whom th'have overcome.*
> *For shame let genial Love prevail agen,*
> *You Beaux Love Ladies, and you Ladies Men.*

The creator of the Sonnets, wholly innocent of the homoerotic, is suitably despairing at this news – '*These Crimes, unknown, in our less polisht Age, / Now seem beyond correction of the Stage*' – but he promises to do what he can to remedy the situation, offering his play (now properly '*Adorn'd and rescu'd by a faultless hand*') as a contribution to the internal discipline which is the proper and unique function of literature:

> *The Law's Defect, the juster Muse supplies,*
> *Tis only we, can make you Good or Wise,*
> *Whom Heav'n spares, the Poet will Chastise.*

Granville's adaptation itself faithfully continues Higgons's crusade against 'foreign' sexual deviancy: while the attachment of Antonio to Bassanio is toned down, the attachment of Shylock to his ducats is spiced up into the realms of sexual perversion. In Granville's hands the Jew becomes a fetishistic precursor of Auric Goldfinger who, for once accepting Antonio's invitation to dinner, offers an explicit toast to the sole object of his desires:

> 'I have a Mistress, that out-shines 'em all –
> 'Commanding yours – and yours tho' the whole Sex:
> 'My Money is my Mistress! Here's to
> 'Interest upon Interest.   [*Drinks*
>   (364)[6]

Processing Shakespeare's text for Augustan consumption (notably by quietly excising anything resembling 'French Grimace, Buffoons, and Mimicks', such as the Gobbos), Granville identifies its author as an unswervingly native foe to foreign dramatic genres and unnatural reproductive practices alike.

Given the interconnection already visible in this adaptation between the securing of Shakespeare as a native foe to foreign importations and his promotion as a respectable champion of sexual normality, it is perhaps inevitable that as the level of investment in Shakespeare as a national hero increases over the ensuing decades – notably during the 1730s – the insistence on both his morality and his virility should increase likewise. Between his appearance in effigy in Lord Cobham's Temple of British Worthies at Stowe in 1735 and the unveiling of his monument in Westminster Abbey in 1741, a growing body of panegyric on Shakespeare presents him not just as a patriotic moral exemplar but as a tonic for national potency, in every sense.[7] To the playwright George Lillo, praising the advocacy of Shakespeare's plays carried out from 1737 onwards by the Shakespeare Ladies' Club, the Bard's drama serves as the snake-charming music by which the Ladies are arousing Britain's dormant masculinity: according to Lillo the Ladies' Club '*strove to wake, by* Shakespeare'*s nervous lays, / The manly genius of* Eliza's *days*'.[8] This note is sounded more stridently at the close of the catch-penny playlet *Harlequin Student*, produced at Henry Giffard's unlicensed Goodman's Fields theatre to cash in on the public interest aroused by the unveiling of Shakespeare's monument in the Abbey three years later. The conclusion of what has been for three-quarters of its dura-tion a perfectly orthodox and hedonistic harlequinade is interrupted by a posse of angry gods, who proceed to lecture the audience for having tolerated the show so far. Jupiter, producing a full-size copy of the Abbey statue, suggests that instead they should

> For ever thus th'unequall'd Bard adore,
> Let Mimes and Eunuchs lull the Sense no more,
> But with his Muse, your own lost Fame restore.[9]

In the duet between Minerva and Mars which ensues, Minerva exhorts the audience to

> Banish Foreign Songsters hence,
> Doat on *Shakespear's* manly Sense.
> Send th'Invading Triflers home,
> To lull the Fools of *France* and *Rome!*
>   (p. 24)

Mars, even more anxious about the enervating consequences of Italian opera than Jupiter, warns the audience that 'Eunuchs taint the soundest [heart] / Weaken Man in every Part,' but promises that

> SHAKESPEAR's Soul-exalting Muse
> Will raise your Thoughts to nobler Views,
> Read but o'er his matchless Verse,
> Soon you'll prove the sons of *Mars.*
>   (*Ibid.*)[10]

In an unidentified contemporary poem, preserved in manuscript in the Bodleian Library, this duet is extended to suggest that the power of Shakespearian drama has global as well as physical implications:

> While Britons bow at Shakespear's shrine
> Britannia's sons are sons of mine.
> Like him shou'd Britons scorn the Art
> That binds in chains the human heart
> Like him shou'd still be unconfin'd
> And rule the World as he the mind.[11]

It is worth remembering here that the claim that Britannia rules the waves was first made at exactly the same time as the claim that Shakespeare rules world literature; the latter, as this poem makes exceptionally clear, may indeed simply be a sub-clause of the former. By 1741 the world-beating power of Shakespearian drama is already figuring not just national but imperial potency.

In all these examples of texts in which the disciplining and promotion of Shakespeare seeks to discipline and promote British manhood, it is notable that the figure of Shakespeare, however salutary a force for virility, is represented as himself angelically free from flesh and blood – presented either as a ghost (his dangerous, erring corporeality bowdlerized away) or as a marble statue. The Shakespeare imagined by emergent nationalism, it seems, is the cause that sex is in others, but is not sexy in himself. This seems to be very significant, and I would like in the remainder of this paper to suggest why it might be the case, and with what consequences.

The most obvious reason for this neutering of the Bard is a continuing anxiety about the apparently unexemplary nature of the historical Shakespeare's sex life, as unacceptable, according to most of the traditions and even some of the documentary evidence, as the low puns excised from his texts by the likes of Granville, Pope and Bowdler. In the field of biography proper these moral qualms about the Bard's private life have been amply documented by Samuel Schoenbaum in *Shakespeare's Lives*, but a feeling that Shakespeare is much more convincing as a national icon if his body is left out of the picture entirely pervades a significant proportion of all Enlightenment writing about Shakespeare, in whatever medium. It is very striking, for example, that even when Shakespeare makes his first personal appearance in the novel – a form in which one would expect both intimacy and physical detail – he is still carefully denied a body, and is indeed specifically engaged in monitoring the sexual transgressions of others as a punishment for his own past licentiousness. In *Memoirs of the Shakespear's-Head in Covent-Garden* (1755), Shakespeare's ghost appears to one chosen client of the disreputable pub of the title, and explains miserably that he is undergoing purgatory: for a certain term his soul has been 'fix'd the Guardian of this *Bacchanalian Temple*, a Post alloted to punish me for the Errors of my youthful Conduct'.[12] An Old Hamlet posthumously recruited to the Vice Squad, Shakespeare proceeds temporarily to render his hapless auditor as invisible and ethereal as himself, and spends the rest of the narrative providing a guided tour of the seamy goings-on in progress in the tavern's various private rooms, offering a disgusted, moralistic commentary throughout. Once more, Shakespeare can only function as an adequately respectable figure at the expense of his own historical specificity, his own physicality.

This novel, presenting Shakespeare as the monitory ghost of a more sexually innocent past, is in precisely the tradition of Higgons's prologue to *The Jew of Venice*, a text which initiated other durable traditions too – notably that of Shakespearian homophobia. As Schoenbaum points out, for example, the first sustained biographical reading of the *Sonnets* – offered by George Chalmers in 1797 – insists that the Young Man sonnets are all definitely addressed to a woman. Chalmers confidently identifies the woman in question, too – as Queen Elizabeth I – and it

was here that for some writers one alternative to the representation
of the National Poet's own sexuality, or perhaps one nationalized
sublimation of it, might be found.[13] As early as 1702, John Dennis had
explained away the unclassical imperfections of *The Merry Wives of
Windsor* by claiming it was written in haste at the request of Elizabeth,[14]
and this exculpatory rumour of a personal relationship between Shakespeare and his illustrious sovereign is one which snowballed as Shakespeare's status as a national hero rose. In 1739, Theophilus Cibber could
claim that Shakespeare, although a mere player, was 'beloved by the
Queen',[15] by 1763 the *Biographia Britannica* was insisting that Eliza had
personally forgiven one of Shakespeare's notorious youthful misdemean-
ours, intervening to prevent his punishment for poaching Sir Thomas
Lucy's deer.[16] This particular story, repeated in several subsequent biographies, would be most fully and revealingly developed in two popular
texts of the early nineteenth century. Sir Walter Scott – a writer always
acutely aware of precisely what is at stake in the national legends he
retails – puts it to especially good effect in *Kenilworth* (1821). Conflating
Shakespeare's deer-poaching with more erotic trespasses, Scott, like
Chalmers, has Shakespeare's sexual innocence certified by Elizabeth,
in the course of a dialogue otherwise designed to assure the reader that
the Bard was already recognized by the Crown as his nation's chief
writer even in his own lifetime. Petitioned by bear-baiting impres-
arios to close the theatres, Elizabeth solicits the opinions of her entire
assembled court on the subject of contemporary drama, and especially
requests their views about 'one Will Shakespeare (whom I think, my
lords, we have all heard something of)'.[17] Elizabeth herself declares, with
the special prescience displayed by so many of Scott's more sympathetic
characters, that Shakespeare's history plays will form a permanent part
of Britain's literary heritage; but more striking than this orthodox
opinion of the Bard's professional output is her corresponding insistence on correcting certain details of his biography. When Sussex offers
some personal reminiscences, Elizabeth is quick to delete one particular
detail of the familiar hearsay from the quasi-historical record:

'... [Shakespeare] stood, they say, a tough fight with the rangers of old
Sir Thomas Lucy of Charlecot, when he broke his deerpark and kissed his
keeper's daughter.'
  'I cry you mercy, my Lord of Sussex,' said Queen Elizabeth, interrupting
him; 'that matter was heard in council, and we will not have this fellow's
offence exaggerated – there was no kissing in the matter, and the defendant
hath put the denial on record.' (p. 223)

Usefully guaranteeing Shakespeare's national status and his chastity at once, this imagined relationship between Shakespeare and the Virgin Queen forms the substance of the first English play to feature him as protagonist, Charles Somerset's *Shakspeare's Early Days* (1829), a play even more striking than the Scott novel on which it draws in its bowdlerization of Shakespeare's life. Fleeing Stratford after stealing a deer only in the cause of virtue – for the succour of a starving peasant – Somerset's Shakespeare arrives in London, pursued by Sir Thomas Lucy, where he is not only pardoned by Elizabeth but invested as Poet Laureate immediately after the defeat of the Armada. The tableau with which Somerset closes the play celebrates, in effect, the platonic betrothal of the National Poet to Britannia. Centre stage, Shakespeare kneels while Elizabeth hangs a miniature of herself, framed with diamonds, around his neck, to the accompaniment of a rousing chorus:

> Shakspeare! Shakspeare! none beside!
> Shakspeare is his nation's pride![18]

Although Shakespeare is here represented for once in the flesh, this popular play, remarkably, utterly suppresses his relationship with Anne Hathaway, not to mention any conjectural intrigues with young men or dark ladies. In Somerset's play the youth who leaves Warwickshire for London is not married, still less the father of three children. Once again, the representation of Shakespeare as 'his nation's pride', worthy to be placed at the right hand of Gloriana herself, seems to require the suppression of any actual historical details of his physical life.[19] The ghostly Shakespeare abstracted from his plays – themselves morally pruned for eighteenth-century performance, as Bell's acting edition (1773–4) shows most fully – might be worthy of national veneration, as might the blameless servant of the Virgin Queen imagined by Scott and Somerset – but the Shakespeare of the unexpurgated plays and uncensored biography simply didn't fit the role in which eighteenth-century England nonetheless needed to cast him.[20]

Above and beyond this simple bowdlerization of Shakespeare's life as a motive for these curiously sexless representations of a writer nonetheless charged with embodying his country's libido is the very nature of the nationalist project they serve, as it replaces local and specific allegiances with an internalized loyalty to a generalized national ideal. In resurrecting the Bard as an idealized British ancestor the writers I have quoted find themselves engaged in distilling the virtuous spirit of Shakespeare, independent of the actual details of his work or life, to stand for the virtuous spirit of British national identity, independent of regional, social and historical differences. Alongside a desire to establish the connection between Shakespeare's plays and Shakespeare's body – to demonstrate, to use Margreta de Grazia's term, Shakespeare's 'entitlement' in his own works (*Shakespeare Verbatim*, pp. 177 ff.) – there exists an equally strong current in nascent bardolatry which seeks to deny that connection, to assert that the national poet's genius transcends mere Shakespeare just as the idea of Britain transcends the contingent British Isles. A bodily, specific Shakespeare would for this purpose be a distracting irrelevance anyway, quite apart from his recorded lapses from manly propriety; a bathetic Mr Shakespeare of sixteenth-century Stratford as opposed to the timeless national father invoked by Higgons and co. in the likeness of Old Hamlet. It is notable in this respect that the very investiture of Shakespeare as National Poet, the Stratford Jubilee of 1769, although at first glance a reverent return to Shakespeare's provincial origins, had as its central event Garrick's presentation to the town of an 'official' likeness of Shakespeare-as-National-Poet – a copy of the idealized, metropolitan Abbey statue – to supplement or perhaps supplant the bathetic, archaic bust in Holy Trinity Church of the corpulent local burgher buried there.[21] This separation of the unbounded creative genius of 'Shakespeare' from the merely licentious body of William Shakespeare of course survives today in the form of the Authorship Controversy, the first major contribution to which, Colonel Joseph Hart's now famous digression on the Bard in *The Romance of Yachting* (1848), is motivated by precisely such a refusal to accept that the immoral Shakespeare of the biographies could have contributed anything to the immortal 'Shakespeare' of the Complete Works other than just the pieces which the Bowdlers cut out:

The plays [William Shakespeare] purchased or obtained surreptitiously, which became his 'property', and which are now called his, were never set upon the stage in their original state. They were first spiced with obscenity, blackguardism and impurities, before they were produced; and this business he voluntarily assumed . . .[22]

The strain of sexually normative nationalism in eighteenth-century bardolatry has thus bequeathed us both the national institution of the Shakespeare industry and the heresy which is its most perennially bitter enemy.

I would like to conclude simply by pointing to a text which goes even further in suggesting how far the Enlightenment's deification of Shakespeare occurs at precisely the intersection of the allied imperatives of modern nationalism and modern sexuality, and it too is connected with the Stratford Jubilee. By 1769 Shakespeare was apparently on the point of transcending not only his own body but his own corpus: the celebration of the Jubilee, famously, did not seem to require the performance or even the quotation of any of Shakespeare's plays – just as for the majority of tourists today a reverent visit to Shakespeare's Stratford does not necessarily imply the remotest interest in visiting the Royal Shakespeare Theatre. In fact the Jubilee's invocation of the national spirit of the Bard was so vague that one contemporary wag suggested that Shakespeare was serving primarily as the pretext for a far more useful patriotic exercise. I quote from the *Middlesex Journal* of 10 August 1769:

It has been generally believed, that the institution of the Stratford jubilee was only a matter of taste and amusement; but the more sagacious see a great political view carried on at the bottom of it: this is the population of that manufacturing part of the country, which will be effected by drawing great numbers of people from the neighbouring towns, to repose together on the verdant banks of the Avon. The season seems peculiarly favourable to this important view by its heat, should the same continue.[23]

Shakespeare's Jubilee is here revealed, like the earlier panegyrics I have quoted, as above all a celebration of British productivity. However his involvement with Britannia and Bowdler alike may have mandated the lopping away of his particular textual and sexual lapses, for this commentator Shakespeare is nonetheless helping to populate the Midlands in the cause of England's industrial future. Whatever else the Jubilee did or did not celebrate, it surely marked the climax of the process I have been describing, Shakespeare's triumphant installation as Britain's national Willy.

First published in *Shakespeare Survey 46*, 1994

NOTES

1 Parts of this chapter derive from research undertaken with Dr Nicola Watson (Open University), and I am happy to acknowledge the assistance of my illustrious collaborator at every stage of its conception and development.
2 George L. Mosse, *Nationalism and Sexuality: Middle-Class Morality and Sexual Norms in Modern Europe* (Madison, Wis., 1985), p. 9.
3 '"Extravagance" characterized accounts of Shakespeare's life just as "irregularity" distinguished his works, during the Restoration and beyond.'

Margreta de Grazia, *Shakespeare Verbatim: The Reproduction of Authenticity and the 1790 Apparatus* (Oxford, 1991), pp. 75–7.

4 Jeremy Collier, *A Short View of the Immorality and Prophaneness of the English Stage* (London, 1698), p. 154.

5 George Granville, Lord Lansdowne, *The Jew of Venice* (1701), in Christopher Spencer, *Five Restoration Adaptations of Shakespeare* (Urbana, Ill., 1965), pp. 345–402; 'Prologue', pp. 348–9. 'The Profits of this *Play* were design'd for Mr *Dryden*; but, upon his Death, given to his Son', explains a footnote.

6 I am indebted here to Laura Rosenthal's unpublished paper 'Disembodied Shakespeare: the Author as Ghost' (given at the conference 'Literary Property and the Construction of Authorship', Cleveland, Ohio, April 1990): on Granville's Shylock, see also J. H. Wilson, 'Granville's "Stock-Jobbing Jew"', *Philological Quarterly* 13 (1934), 1–15.

7 For a (much!) more detailed account of the development of nationalist Bardolatry during this crucial period, see Michael Dobson, *The Making of the National Poet: Shakespeare, Adaptation and Authorship, 1660–1769* (Oxford, 1992), pp. 134–64.

8 George Lillo, *Marina*, 'Epilogue', in *The Plays of George Lillo*, ed. Trudy Drucker, 2 vols. (New York and London, 1979), II, 127. Even the Ladies' Club's own poet Mary Cowper sees their crusade as primarily engaged in the improvement of British manhood: see her poem 'On the Revival of Shakespear's Plays by the Ladies in 1738', which concludes by promising the Ladies' Club a bright future in which their activities on behalf of the Bard will have rescued Britain's young men from the pernicious influence of continental culture, thereby securing themselves better lovers. BM Add. MSS. 28101, 93v–94v: printed in Dobson, *Making of the National Poet*, pp. 150–1.

9 [Henry Giffard], *Harlequin Student, or the Fall of Pantomime; With the Restoration of the Drama* (London, 1741), p. 22.

10 Theophilus Cibber, appropriately, had defended Giffard's theatre against closure two years earlier in very similar terms, expressing his horror that

a Freeman of *London*, a Native of *England*, our Fellow-Subject, and our Brother in a Social Tye, shall be denied the Liberty that is allowed *French* Dancers, and Harlequins – to effeminate Eunuchs, and Sod-[omitica]l *Italians*; yet such shall be encouraged, and *Englishmen* despised!

Theophilus Cibber, 'An Address to the *H—ble* Sir *J—B—*' [1739], in *Two Dissertations on Theatrical Subjects* (London, 1755), p. 74.

11 *Ode to Shakespeare*, in Bodleian Library MS. Mus d 14. The poem is set to music, attributed to William Boyce.

12 *Memoirs of the Shakespear's-Head in Covent-Garden. By the Ghost of Shakespear*, 2 vols. (London, 1755), I, 5–6.

13 George Chalmers, *An Apology for the Believers in the Shakespear-Papers* (London, 1797), pp. 51–2, 55: see Samuel Schoenbaum, *Shakespeare's Lives* (Oxford, 1970), pp. 233–5. Despite his acknowledgement that they are fakes, Chalmers retains this idea from the Ireland forgeries, which include a letter from

Elizabeth thanking 'goode Masterre William' for some 'prettye Verses': see Schoenbaum, *Shakespeare's Lives*, pp. 207–8.

14 See his introduction to his adaptation *The Comical Gallant; or the true amours of Sir John Falstaff* (London, 1702). Dennis went on to claim that the libertarian ideals expressed by Shakespeare's Brutus and Cassius provided the principal inspiration for Elizabeth's defiance of Spain: see his 'Prologue to the Subscribers for *Julius Caesar*' (1707) in *A Collection and Selection of English Prologues and Epilogues*, 4 vols. (London, 1779), III, 1–2.

15 Cibber makes this claim in the course of an argument that the British theatre has always been patriotically Anglican, reaching its apogee with Shakespeare: 'the first Traces of it were in *Henry* the VIIIth's time; it sunk with the PROTESTANT RELIGION beneath Queen *Mary*'s Persecution: In Queen *Elizabeth*'s time it flourished again, – and *Shakespear* was a Player, beloved by the Queen' (Cibber, 'An Address to the *H—ble* Sir *J— B—*', p. 78).

16 *Biographica Britannica*, 6 vols. in 7 (London, 1763), 'Shakespeare'.

17 Sir Walter Scott, *Kenilworth* (1821: ed. H. J. C. Grierson, London, 1952), p. 222.

18 Charles A. Somerset, *Shakspeare's Early Days* (London, 1829), p. 48.

19 Cf. Anna Jameson's remarks 'On the Love of Shakespear' in *Memoirs of the Loves of the Poets*, published in the same year: '[T]he workings of his wondrous and all-embracing mind were directed by a higher influence than ever was exercised by a woman, even in the plenitude of her power and her charms. Shakespear's genius waited not on Love and Beauty, but Love and Beauty ministered to *him*; he perceived like a spirit . . .' (Anna Jameson, *Memoirs of the Loves of the Poets: Biographical sketches of women celebrated in ancient and modern poetry* (1829: Boston, Mass., 1857), p. 182).

20 Cf. the debate over Shakespeare's sexuality carried out in Walter Scott's *Woodstock; or, the Cavalier* (1826), in which the tradition that Sir William Davenant may have been Shakespeare's illegitimate son is anxiously countered in a bid to guarantee the morally uplifting status of the Complete Works: see Nicola Watson, 'Kemble, Scott and the Mantle of the Bard', in *The Appropriation of Shakespeare: Post-Renaissance Reconstructions of the Works and the Myth*, ed. Jean Marsden (Hemel Hempstead, 1991), pp. 73–92.

21 On the Jubilee, see especially Christian Deelman, *The Great Shakespeare Jubilee* (London, 1964); Dobson, *Making of the National Poet*, pp. 214–26.

22 Joseph C. Hart, *The Romance of Yachting* (New York, 1848), pp. 211–12.

23 This account of Shakespeare's Jubilee as a nationalized utilitarian love-in chimes well with Henry Abelove's account of a 'change in late eighteenth-century English conceptions of what sex is, what it is for', 'Some Speculations on the History of "Sexual Intercourse" during the "Long Eighteenth Century" in England', in *Nationalisms and Sexualities*, ed. Andrew Parker, Mary Russo, Doris Sommer and Patricia Yaeger (New York, 1992), pp. 335–42.

CHAPTER 8

'Shakespur and the Jewbill'

James Shapiro

In 1769 David Garrick's Stratford Jubilee helped establish Shakespeare as a national poet and as a permanent cultural fixture, one who, in Jane Austen's familiar phrase, would soon enough become part of an Englishman's constitution.[1] Garrick's subsequent play – called *The Jubilee* and written for those unable to attend the celebrations in Stratford – further secured this reputation, while positioning Shakespeare against those at the periphery of English culture. *The Jubilee* includes a bumbling unnamed 'Irishman' who travels from Dublin to witness the festivities only to sleep through them and return, as he says, to 'go home and be nowhere'. The play also contains a comic exchange between Stratford locals, who, when they hear celebratory fireworks, fear that ''Tis certainly a plot of the Jews and Papishes', a confusion no doubt exacerbated by the fact that to them, the word 'ju–bil–ee' sounded a lot like 'Jew Bill'. Sukey, a young woman of Stratford, explains to her friend Nancy (who wonders 'who is this Shakespur, that they make such a rout about 'en?') that had 'you lived at Birmingham or Coventry, or any other polite cities, as I have done, you would have known better than to talk so of Shakespur and the Jewbill'.[2] By framing the Jubilee events with the skewed perspective of these outsiders, incapable of grasping the difference between a local hero and a Jewish threat, Garrick offers up a Shakespeare who cannot possibly belong to Stratford, let alone to the boorish Irish, but is the rightful property of a cultivated London society that can properly know his worth. This essay is about that Jew Bill, formally known as the Jewish Naturalization Act of 1753, and the ways in which Shakespeare, Englishness and Jewishness crossed paths at this historical moment, and in so doing helped illuminate and redefine each other.

The facts of this alien legislation and the ensuing controversy have been well documented.[3] In January 1753, after some debate within the Jewish community in England, a Jewish banker named Joseph

Salvador decided to petition the government to relax restrictions on Jewish naturalization. With the support of the ruling Whig party a bill to this effect was introduced on 3 April into the House of Lords, where it was rapidly approved and soon passed through the Commons as well. Then, unexpectedly, opposition gradually mounted, and then erupted; by autumn, the clamour for repeal reached a deafening roar. Before 15 November, when the Whigs led the way in repealing the bill that they themselves had first advocated, more than sixty pamphlets, endless newspaper columns, various satiric illustrations, sermons, and an assortment of related books had been printed, pro and con, on the Jew Bill. Almost as rapidly, the Jew Bill and the issues circulating around it virtually disappeared from print and public scrutiny.

The flavour of the debate is nicely conveyed in a column by a contemporary polemicist, Arthur Murphy, who writes that:

The English have naturally interwoven in their Constitution a peculiar Kind of national Self-Love, and the least Attempt to dispense a Favour to Foreigners alarms their Fears, and awakens that Jealousy which is natural to their very Frame. It is to this we owe the general Discontent, which has broke out among all Ranks of People upon the late Occasion . . . As it is apparent from what has been observed already, that the Christian Religion has no longer a Footing in this Country, it may not be improper to repeal the sacramental Test, and to substitute in its Room the Act of Circumcision.[4]

A month after the Jew Bill was overturned Murphy wrote on a related topic that 'with us islanders Shakespeare is a kind of established religion in poetry'.[5]

At first glance, the Jew Bill seems harmless enough: a slight alteration or two in the requirements for becoming a naturalized British subject. Considerably more proved to be at stake, however, than updating alien laws that had remained unchanged since the reign of James I.[6] The controversy not only touched upon what legal rights foreigners living in England should be accorded, but also called into question what is 'naturally woven' into what Murphy calls the English 'constitution', for the act of redefining the place of Jews in English society raised some troubling questions about the essential nature of English culture and identity.

While there is little disagreement about *what* happened in the summer and fall of 1753, there is considerable difference of opinion over *why* this controversy occurred. Two main explanations have been offered.[7] The first, that the episode reveals yet another chapter in the history of traditional English anti-Semitism: the legislation thus provided an

opportunity for Jew-baiting that was not to be missed. This position is
lent support by the fact that until recently mainstream British historians
have tended to ignore the episode completely, overlooking in the process
evidence such as the report in the *London Evening Post* from November
1753 that on the previous 'Saturday Night amidst the Rejoicings for the
celebrating his Majesty's Birth-Day in the Borough of Southwark, the
Populace dress'd up the Effigy of a Jew, and burnt him in a large bonfire'.[8]
There is certainly enough evidence in the Jew Bill controversy of the
crudest sort of prejudice. Charges of Jewish ritual murder resurfaced
at this time and the public was reminded of the Jews' 'insatiable thirst
for the blood of Christians, especially of Christian children, which they
often steal and solemnly crucify'.[9] The English Enlightenment was
built on the solid foundations of sixteenth- and seventeenth-century
conceptions of Jewish criminality and racial and national difference,
foundations with a very long half-life.

Mainstream historians, sceptical (and at times dismissive) of this anti-
Semitic explanation, have countered that what was actually at stake
in this conflict was a political struggle in an election year between
entrenched Whigs and the aggressive out-of-power Tories who seized
on this convenient issue to wrest more parliamentary seats.[10] As Thomas
Perry puts it in his book on the Jew Bill, 'the clamor was meant to
prepare the ground not for a pogrom, but for a general election', and
its 'real targets were the Court Whig politicians, not the Jews'.[11]

Problems with each of these interpretations persist, however: why
fight so heatedly over the place of Jews in England if this was merely
partisan political struggle? On the other hand, if this was an unleashing
of anti-Semitic sentiment, why was there almost no physical violence
directed against English Jews? To these binary and partial positions,
both of which contain arguments of considerable merit, I offer a third
and supplementary one that tries to be sensitive to the nuances of
eighteenth-century English politics yet at the same time not too hasty in
reconstruing the substance of the polemical literature as something
other than what the polemicists actually wrote. I'd like to suggest that
the buried threat occasioned by the naturalization of Jews had to do
with the surprising vulnerability of English social and religious identity
at this time: if even a Jew could be English, what could one point to
that defined essential Englishness? The anonymous author of the satiric
tract *The Exclusion of the English*, written five years before the Jew Bill
debate, may well be the first English writer to ask, in print, that most
nagging of questions: 'If You consider rightly, it will be very hard

to answer the question What is an Englishman?'[12] And a poem that appeared in the popular *Gentleman's Magazine* – 'The Jew naturalized, or the English alienated' – makes much the same point in 1753: 'Such actions as these most apparently shews, / That if the Jews are made English, the English are Jews.'[13]

Racial thinking about the Jews was hardly limited to the margins of English political discourse. In fact, it even informed the parliamentary debate during the effort to repeal the Jew Bill. When the Duke of Newcastle, who had initially supported the Bill but recognized the political necessity of its repeal, nonetheless insisted that he 'knew that every Jew born here was, by the common law, a natural born subject', his opponent, the Duke of Bedford, would have none of it: 'whatever opinion the noble Duke may have of our common law, with respect to Jews born in this kingdom . . . no Jew born here can be deemed a natural born subject whilst he continues to be a Jew'. The Jews must 'always continue a people separate and distinct from the people that naturalize them'.[14] Bedford presses this racist line of thought by maintaining that Jewishness was an essence even more ineradicable than the blackness of colonial slaves:

I shall suppose, that for strengthening our sugar colonies, and for peopling them with subjects instead of slaves, a scheme were proposed for naturalizing all the blacks born in any of them without any other condition whatsoever: I will say that our adopting such a scheme would be ridiculous, because their progeny would continue to be a distinct people; but if the conditions were added that no blacks should be naturalized unless they declared themselves Christians, and that no such black man should be naturalized unless he married a white woman, nor any black woman unless she married a white man, the ridicule of the scheme would be very much softened, because their progeny would in time unite and coalesce with the rest of the people: it might a little alter the complexion of the people of these islands; but they would all be the same people and would look upon themselves in no other light then as subjects of Great Britain. This must shew the imprudence, and even the ridiculousness, of our adopting the doctrine, that all Jews born here are to be deemed natural-born subjects, for their latest posterity whilst they continue Jews, will continue to be, and will consider themselves as a people quite distinct and separate from the ancient people of this island.[15]

The Jew Bill controversy clearly needs to be situated within the broader context of a century of English debate over alien immigration and naturalization as well as within emerging notions of racial difference.[16] The kind of incoherent racial ideas found in Bedford's speech had their roots in late sixteenth- and early seventeenth-century English thought.

This is where Shakespeare's play enters the picture, because its exploration of Jews as nation, race and aliens resonated with – and indeed for
many writers at this time, helped identify – inchoate but powerfully felt
anxieties circulating in this 1753 controversy. Historians have scratched
their heads and wondered in footnotes why so many of the polemicists
writing about the Jew Bill simply ignored the political and economic
implications of the legislation and discussed instead the threat of Jews
circumcising Englishmen, taking Christian servants, and racially contaminating the English nation. I'd like to argue here that Shakespeare's
play, with its knife-wielding Jew, its conversion and intermarriage, its
Christian servant, and its disturbing exploration of the Jews as members of an international nation and as political aliens (we might recall
here that it is Shylock's violation of a law against aliens that enables
Portia to trip him up), became a powerful weapon in the arsenal of
those opposed to the naturalization of Jews in England.

The history of *The Merchant of Venice* in the early eighteenth century –
including the success of Granville's revision, *The Jew of Venice*, and
Macklin's impressive revival – is well known,[17] though one feature of its
stage history in these years that has been largely overlooked is *when*
Londoners might have expected to see the play performed. Since
Macklin's production had been staged at the opening of Drury Lane on
15 September 1747 an informal tradition emerged that the play would
be performed near the start of each autumn season at Drury Lane (along
with *The Beggar's Opera*). Thus, after a fairly late appearance in 1748
(3 November), it was the fourth play performed in 1749 (9 September),
the opening play in 1750 (8 September), and the second play in both 1751
(9 September) and 1752 (19 September). In the months leading up to
the Jew Bill debate the play remained in repertory, appearing on 4 January 1753 at Covent Garden, a week later at Drury Lane, once again at
Covent Garden on 26 January, and on Shakespeare's birthday in April
at Covent Garden, before the controversy developed in earnest in May.[18]
    When the autumn season came around once more in early Septem-
ber 1753 the patrons of Drury Lane must have been looking forward
to the return of *The Merchant of Venice* with unusual interest. The controversy over the Jew Bill was reaching the boiling point; another two
months would pass before Parliament would meet and discuss its repeal.
A column in the politically neutral *Cambridge Journal* on 25 August, two
weeks before the theatres reopened in London, reported that: 'We are
credibly informed, that some of the most eminent among the Children

of Israel, have made Interest with the Patentee of Covent Garden Play-house, not to engage Mr Macklin for the ensuing Season, to prevent his playing the Character of Shylock in the *Merchant of Venice*, which it is apprehended will certainly be called for by the Public.'[19] Though perhaps tongue-in-cheek about the Jews' attempts to silence Macklin, the *Cambridge Journal* was correct in reckoning that Shakespeare's play would most assuredly be called for. Yet on opening night, 8 September, the management of Drury Lane refused to stage *The Merchant of Venice*, offering instead *The Beggar's Opera*. The disappointment was palpable enough to elicit protest. We learn from the manuscript diary of the theatre's manager, Richard Cross, that the public clamour for the play was ignored:

Ye Naturalizing Bill having made some Noise against the Jews, some people call'd out for ye *Merch[an]t of Venice*, & a Letter was thrown upon ye Stage desiring that play instead of the Opera, but we took no Notice of it, some little hissing but it dy'd away.[20]

Cross draws the obvious connection between the 'noise' over the 'Naturalization Bill' and the 'hissing' in the theatre, but the call for Shylock was not heeded. There would be no performances of *The Merchant* at either Drury Lane or Covent Garden that autumn. Not until 6 April, months after the bill had been repealed and interest in the controversy had died down, was the play staged again in London. Some form of censorship, or self-censorship, was clearly at work.

A hint as to the source of this censorship can be found in an unusual manuscript note included in the Gabrielle Enthoven Theatre Collection in the Victoria and Albert Museum, placed in the Drury Lane file:

Last Sunday – 8th July. 1753. An Order came from the Lord Chamberlains Office to the Managers of both Theaters, forbidding them under the severst Penalty, to exhibit a certain scandalous Piece, highly injurious to our present happy Establishment, entitled the Merchant of Venice.[21]

Since 26 May marked the end of the 1753 theatre season, and the theatres remained closed until September, why would the Lord Chamberlain send such a note in July? And send it on a Sunday? As L. W. Conolly notes, it turns out that the facetious entry was actually copied from a newspaper column entitled 'News for One Hundred Years hence in the *Hebrew Journal*', which had first appeared in the *Craftsman*. This 'News' column offers a glimpse at life in a future England ruled by Jews, and includes a now Jewish Lord Chamberlain's warning not to stage Shakespeare's 'scandalous Piece, highly injurious to our present happy establishment, entitled, *The Merchant of Venice*'.[22] Clearly, in such a Judaized England, no place could be found for Shakespeare's anti-Jewish play. Capitalizing on how accurate this forecast for a hundred years in the future soon proved, the issue of the *London Evening Post* immediately following the reopening of the theatres in September made much of the suppression of Shakespeare's play: 'It is shrewdly suspected that one Part of the *Hebrew Journal* for One Hundred Years hence, will be fu'filled this Winter, by the Neutrality of both our Theatres, in not obliging the Town with the *Merchant of Venice*.'[23] Of particular interest here is the inference on the part of this pro-Tory newspaper that it was the 'neutrality' and self-censorship of the theatres, rather than bias towards the Jews or the Whigs that had initially supported the Jew Bill, which accounted for the suppression of *The Merchant* at this time. Apparently London's theatres were simply trying to stay out of the political crossfire.

Quite a few of the pamphlets and books published in 1753 illustrate how *The Merchant of Venice* served the ends of those opposed to Jewish naturalization. 'J. E., Gent[leman]', the author of *Some Considerations on the Naturalization of the Jews*, in the midst of a long diatribe against Jewish naturalization, turns to the matter of the Jews' 'exorbitant avarice'. The subject immediately put him 'in mind of a passage in the *Merchant of Venice*', and he begins by citing Shylock's hatred of Antonio: 'I hate him for he is a Christian.' He then proceeds to quote at length from *The Merchant of Venice*, including the lines from the trial scene where Shylock gloats over having been awarded a pound of Antonio's flesh. Shakespeare's play provides for him indisputable evidence of the danger to the English threatened by the Jews. After three uninterrupted pages of quotation from Shakespeare's play, he confidently asks his readers: 'And now, Englishman and countryman, judge ye, what advantage it can be to you to have these Jews naturalized! What can you get by them? They are all griping usurpers. And what can they get out of you, but your very Blood and Vitals? It can never be your temporal interest to see such persons made Englishmen.'[24]

Additional evidence of how Shakespeare's play was invoked in opposition to the Bill also appears in the anonymous *The Repository*, a collection which includes several allusions to Shylock. Thus, we find 'The Prophecies of Shylock', a passage in biblical prose addressed to the Jews about the English, which reads in part: 'Therefore, thus saith the Lord, I will destroy them in mine Anger, . . . give you their Land for a Possession', and 'establish you as their Rulers.'[25] Another allusion

to Shakespeare's protagonist comes near the end of the pamphlet, in
a poetic dialogue between 'Shylock and Zimri'. Shylock's last verses
likewise turn on Jewish revenge against the Christians:

> How sweet are the Thoughts of that glorious Scene,
> When none but a Jew over Jewry shall reign!
> No Ruler, nor King, over Jews shall have Place,
> But who is descended from David's great Race.
> From around all the Globe each Nation shall meet
> And the Gentiles shall lick up the Dust of his Feet.[26]

A similar invocation of Shylock appears during the election campaign
in an attack on one of the supporters of the Jew Bill, Sir William
Calvert. A note in *Gray's Inn Journal* describes an imaginary cabal of
Jewish stock-jobbers and other 'Children of Israel' who support the
candidate 'on account of his attachment to our cause in the last Parliament'. Predictably, one of the signers is 'Josephus Shylock'.[27] Shylock
also appeared in contemporary political cartoons: one of those in circu-
lation at this time – 'Shylock's Race from the Chequer Inn to Paris' –
depicts the Jew Sampson 'Gideon's involvement in the 1753 lottery',
and shows Shylock riding on a pig's back with the devil.[28] And according to John Smith's *Poetical Description* of Hogarth's xenophobic series
of *Election* prints executed at this time, an impatient 'Shylock' – that
'Money-loving Soul' – appears in the service of a corrupt Tory candidate whose subsequent victory precipitates in the final print of the
series a vision of a future Judaized England.[29]

Shylock also emerged as a ringleader in fantasies of Jewish attempts
to take over England. In a column entitled 'The Thirty-fourth Chapter
of Gen[esis]' that first appeared in the *London Evening Post*, Shylock is
introduced along with real figures in the controversy, such as the Pelhams
and Salvador, supplanting Jacob's sons in a parodic version of the rape
of Dinah:

And it came to pass, in the Year Seventeen hundred sixty-three, that the
Daughters of the Britons, which their Wives bear unto them, went into the
Synagogues of the Jews, to see the Daughters of the Israelites.

And when the Sons of Gid—, of Shylock, of Men—, Fran—, and Salv—,
saw them, they took them, and defiled them . . .

And Gid— and Shylock came to the Gate of the Change, and communed
with the Men of their own Nation . . .

And unto Gid— and Shylock hearken'd all the Jews that went unto
the Change; and they told the Pelh—tes, who ordered every male to be
circumcised . . .

And it came to pass on the Third Day, whilst their Private Parts were sore, that the Jews took their Swords, and slew every Male of the Britons.[30]

Here, the biblical and Shakespearian narratives are conflated, with Shylock taking the role of father of the rapists, and then (since the story is reversed with the Jews as both violators and revengers), as one who first arranged for the Britons to be circumcised, then slain.

Recalling Shylock's threat to cut a pound of flesh from the part of Antonio that pleaseth him best, the anonymous author of the satiric tract, *Seasonable Remarks on the Act Lately Pass'd in Favour of the Jews*, offers Shakespeare's play as 'proof' that the Jews 'have not forgot their old practices of circumcising, crucifying, etc.', reminding his readers of 'an instance on record with regard to a Jew at Venice', that 'seems to show that nothing less than our flesh as well as our money will satisfy their unchristian appetites'.[31] Again and again in the literature of 1753, the Jewish threat was imagined in terms of circumcision and emasculation.[32]

The pamphlets and newspaper column also register a shift in Shylock from stage character to one who steps out of the theatre into the daily lives of English men and women and whose influence extended out of the City into the countryside. In the *London Evening Post*, for example, an account appears of 'a Gentleman', who, 'travelling on the Uxbridge Road overtook a Farmer, who look'd very disconsolate; . . . he ask'd him the Matter; when the Farmer replied, Lord, Sir, I have had no Sleep for these three Nights, the Thoughts of the Jews ever running us distracting me; For we hear, in the Country, that the Jews will Circumcise all their Tenants; and my Landlord having ruined himself by Cards and Dice, is about selling my Farm, and several others in the Neighborhood, and we hear to a Jew. For last Week two strange-looking Men (one they called Shylock) came to look at mine.'[33] Further evidence that these examples offer not simply a Shylock abstracted and separate from *The Merchant of Venice*, but one very much based on the character of Shakespeare's play, is apparent from allusions in the pamphlet literature to Lancelot Gobbo, Shylock's servant. One example appears in *Gray's Inn Journal*; following 'More News for One Hundred Years hence, in the Hebrew-Journal' there is an advertisement, dated August 1853 and signed by Lancelot Gobbo, addressed 'To the Gentlemen, Rabbi and Freeholders of the County of Sussex; Gobbo beg[s] the Favour of your Votes and Interest.'[34] The attack is clearly aimed at Prime Minister Henry Pelham, and the joke is straightforward enough: like Gobbo, Pelham is merely a servant – and a lowly one at that – of

Jewish masters. Yet another reference to Shylock, this time as a 'Christian Impostor', immediately follows in the advertisement below the allusion to Gobbo: 'By Desire, At the Theater-Royal in Drury-Lane, on Sunday next, will be presented a COMEDY, called, I believe . . . The Christian Impostor. The Part of Dr Tillotson to be performed by Rubens Shylock.'[35] Shylock's name continued to be invoked long after the furore over the Jew Bill had passed. By 1765 he had become not simply a character but an author, responsible for the second and third books of *The Jew Apologist*. Three years later a defeated Shylock would take up his pen again in defence of Jewish naturalization, this time offering *The Rabbi's Lamentation upon the Repeal of the Jew Act*.

It appears that in 1753 even the English theatres were not immune from expressions of anti-Jewish sentiment. In recounting the 'only instance of actual public unpleasantness towards Jews' that he found 'in any contemporary source' – a definition narrow enough to exclude attacks against itinerant Jewish pedlars, one of whom was slain – Thomas Perry quotes from the following account in the *London Evening Post*: 'After the second musick, some Jewish ladies and gentlemen were noticed in one of the balconies, when the cry immediately began, *No Jews, out with them, circumcise them*, &c. &c. and was followed with showers of apples, &c. with great rudeness, till the company were obliged to leave their seats; but upon remonstrance from a gentleman that sat next to them, to some others in the pit, a loud clap ensued, the company were reinstated, and met with no other molestation.'[36] Why members of the audience would call for the circumcision of Jewish men – or for that matter of Jewish women – is not entirely clear. The incident perhaps cast further light on why London's theatre managers were loath to stage *The Merchant of Venice* or any other plays about Jews at this time.

The popular pressure to see Shylock on-stage and the possibilities of capitalizing on popular interest in the Jew Bill, while resisted in London, did not extend to provincial touring, where self-censorship and a desire to please Whig patrons were not as strong. While standard stage histories of *The Merchant of Venice* and of English provincial touring companies offer no extant records of performances of the play outside London in 1753, I was fortunate to stumble upon an account of just such a touring production, probably staged in late spring or summer of that year, perhaps in the north of England, or perhaps in Edinburgh. The sole evidence of this production survives in John Cunningham's *Poems* (1766). Cunningham was an actor and poet who also penned occasional prologues.[37] Included in his collected verse is one such occasional piece, composed by Cunningham at the age of twenty-four: 'A Prologue, Spoke by Mrs G—, in an itinerant Company, on reviving the MERCHANT of VENICE, at the Time of the Bill passing for naturalizing the Jews.'

We have no other record of the performance or performances. There is little doubt that 'Mrs G—' is Mrs George Anne Bellamy, a leading actress of the 1750s and a friend of Cunningham's. We know from the entries recorded in *The London Stage* that she was in London from February 1753 until at least 7 May, where she played the leading roles in *Lady Jane Gray, The Brothers, Venice Preserved, Othello, The Orphan* and *Macbeth,* all at Drury Lane. She only resumed playing in London, this time for Rich's company at Covent Garden, some time in September or October 1753. In sum, one of the stars of the London theatre apparently went on tour some time between late May and September, at the height of the uproar over the Jew Bill. Presumably, she played the part of Portia, and as befitted the leading performer, recited the twenty-line Prologue that Cunningham wrote for the occasion:

> 'Twixt the sons of the stage, without pensions or places,
> And the vagabond Jews, are some similar cases;
> Since time out of mind, or they're wrong'd much by slander,
> Both lawless, alike, have been sentenc'd to wander;
> Then faith 'tis full time we appeal to the nation,
> To be join'd in this bill for na-tu-ra-li-za-ti-on;
> Lord, that word's so uncouth! – 'tis so irksome to speak it!
> But 'tis Hebrew, I believe, and that taste, as I take it.
> Well – now to the point – I'm sent here with commission,
> To present this fair circle our humble petition:
> But conscious what hopes we should have of succeeding,
> Without (as they phrase it) sufficiently bleeding;
> And convinc'd we've no funds, nor old gold we can rake up,
> Like our good brothers – Abraham, Isaac, and Jacob;
> We must frankly confess we have nought to present ye,
> But Shakespear's old sterling – pray let it content ye.
> Old Shylock, the Jew, whom we mean to restore ye,
> Was naturaliz'd oft by your fathers before ye;
> Then take him to-night to your kindest compassion,
> For to countenance Jews is the pink of the fashion.[38]

This is an unusually rich document, one that powerfully connects the latent anxieties circulating through Shakespeare's play with the cultural dread produced by the Jew Bill. The Prologue also partakes of the self-contradiction characteristic of many of the polemical pamphlets, not least of all in the itinerant actors' simultaneous denigration of and identification with Jews in the opening lines. The legal status first assigned to wandering players in the late sixteenth century – vagabonds – is here applied, as elsewhere in the pamphlet literature of 1753, to the wandering Jews as well. In the witty tone that pervades the entire Prologue, Mrs Bellamy protests that the similarity with the Jews stops there: the actors hope to win audience approval without having to be circumcised, that is, '(as they phrase it) sufficiently bleeding'.

In the most telling lines of the Prologue, Mrs Bellamy recites how 'Old Shylock, the Jew, whom we mean to restore ye, / Was naturaliz'd oft by your fathers before ye.' A remarkable conflation of naturalization and conversion takes place here: for in Shakespeare's original, Shylock is not naturalized, after all, but threatened with conversion to Christianity. Shakespeare's play is reimagined here as one that depicts a legal and political transformation rather than a religious one, a change not all that surprising in an eighteenth-century England in which national and racial affiliations were gradually superseding theological ones. We are nonetheless left with the paradox that despite the fact that he has been 'naturaliz'd oft', Shylock's Jewishness prevents him from being fully English (even as baptism could not fully wash away his essential Jewishness). Cunningham's Prologue, no less than the Duke of Bedford's comparison of Jews and Blacks, calls into question current theories of nationalism that ignore just how racialized nationalism was in eighteenth-century England, a fact that may explain why cultural historians continue to pass over this popular controversy in silence, a silence that extends to the work of recent scholars intent on identifying Shakespeare's place in the formation of British identity.[39]

This story does not end in 1753, for Shakespeare continues to be invoked by those who need to protect Englishness from the potentially contaminating influence of Jewishness. The taboo over dealing with this subject was recently broken by Elliott Baker in his book *Bardolatry*, where in a chapter entitled 'Was Shakespeare Jewish?' Baker describes an international conspiracy in which Jewish scholars have taken over the Shakespeare business and now dare to trespass on the very 'banks of the Avon'. 'Greenblatt and Levi', he laments, was 'once a good masthead for a clothing store.' He even seizes on Peter Levi's self-identification as 'British as opposed to English' as confirmation that this Jewish scholar's 'devotion to Shakespeare' is 'that of an outsider seeking identification with the core of Englishness'.[40] Baker's message is clear: this latest Jewish invasion must be exposed and resisted. It should come as no surprise that precisely the kind of arguments which first circulated in the Jew Bill debate – the inscrutability of the scheming Jews, anxiety over a Jewish presence on hallowed English ground, the idea that Jews could control English religion (this is 'bardolatry' after all), and the identification of Shakespeare with Englishness itself – form the basis of Baker's polemic. Although the irony may be lost on Baker, his book serves to confirm that the Jew Bill, along with Garrick's Jubilee, was instrumental in the creation of a Shakespeare who from that time on would be bound up with fantasies of social exclusion and cultural longing.

First published in *Shakespeare Survey 48*, 1995

NOTES

1 As Jonathan Bate neatly puts it, 'Shakespeare was constituted in England in the eighteenth and early nineteenth century', and 'cultural life during that period was by constitution Shakespearean', *Shakespearean Constitutions: Politics, Theatre, Criticism, 1730–1830* (Oxford, 1989), p. 1. See too, Michael Dobson, *The Making of the National Poet: Shakespeare, Adaptation and Authorship, 1660–1769* (Oxford, 1992).

2 See David Garrick, *The Jubilee* (1769) in *The Plays of David Garrick*, ed. Harry W. Pedicord and Frederick L. Bergmann (Carbondale, 1980), II, 125, 104, 122.

3 See Thomas W. Perry, *Public Opinion, Propaganda, and Politics in Eighteenth-Century England: A Study of the Jew Bill of 1753* (Cambridge, Mass., 1962); Todd Endelman, *The Jews of Georgian England, 1714–1830: Tradition and Change in a Liberal Society* (Philadelphia, 1979), esp. pp. 50–117; and David S. Katz, *The Jews in the History of England 1485–1850* (Oxford, 1994), pp. 240–53.

4 *The Gray's Inn Journal*, 2 vols. (London, 1756), I, 222, 224 (16 June 1753).

5 As cited in Dobson, *Making of the National Poet*, p. 7, from *Gray's Inn Journal*, 15 December 1753.

6 See J. M. Ross, 'Naturalization of Jews in England', *Transactions of the Jewish Historical Society of England* 24 (1975), 59–72.

7 See Robert Liberles, 'The Jews and their Bill; Jewish Motivations in the Controversy of 1753', *Jewish History* 2 (1987), 29–36.

8 *London Evening Post* (13–15 November 1753), p. 4.

9 Anon., *The Rejection and Restoration of the Jews, According to Scripture, Declar'd* (London, 1753), pp. 34–5.

10 See G. A. Cranfield, '*The London Evening Post* and the Jew Bill of 1753', *Historical Journal* 8 (1965), 16–30.

11 Perry, *Public Opinion*, p. 194, See too, Nicholas Rogers, *Whigs and Cities: Popular Politics in the Age of Walpole and Pitt* (Oxford, 1989), pp. 89–93.

12 Anon., *The Exclusion of the English; an Invitation to Foreigners* (London, 1748), p. 10.

13 *Gentleman's Magazine*, July 1753, p. 346.

14 For the 'Debate for the Repeal of the Jewish Naturalization Act, November 1753', see *The Parliamentary History of England*, vol. xv, 1753–65 (London, 1813), p. 92.

15 *Parliamentary History of England*, xv, 106.

16 See, in this regard, John Toland, *Reasons for Naturalizing the Jews in Great Britain, on the Same Foot with All Other Nations. Containing also, a Defence of the Jews against All Vulgar Prejudices in All Countries* (London, 1714). Toland's work was immediately challenged by the anonymous *A Confutation of the Reasons for Naturalizing the Jews* (London, 1715).

17 See Toby Lelyveld, *Shylock on the Stage* (London, 1961); and James C. Bulman, *The Merchant of Venice* (Manchester, 1991).

18 For the record of performances, see George Winchester Stone, Jr, ed., *The London Stage 1660–1800*, part 4: 1747–76 (Carbondale, Ill., 1962).

19 *Cambridge Journal*, 25 August 1753, 1.

20 As cited in Stone, *London Stage*, part 4, I, 377.

21 See L. W. Conolly's fine detective work in '*The Merchant of Venice* and the Jew Bill of 1753', *Shakespeare Quarterly* 25 (1974), 125.

22 As quoted from *The London Magazine, Or Gentleman's Monthly Intelligencer*, July 1753, p. 302, which reprinted the column from the *Craftsman*, 14 July 1753; no copies of the *Craftsman* survive.

23 *London Evening Post*, 11 September 1753, p. 1.

24 J. E., *Some Considerations on the Naturalization of the Jews*, pp. 17–21.

25 Anon., *The Repository: For the Use of the Christian Electors of Great-Britain; In Opposition to All Jews, Turks, and Infidels*, number 2 (London, 1753), p. 33.

26 *The Repository*, number 2, p. 51.

27 As cited in Perry, *Public Opinion*, p. 166, from *Gray's Inn Journal*, 27 April 1754.

28 For a reproduction of this cartoon see Isaiah Shachar, 'The Emergence of the Modern Pictorial Stereotype of "the Jews" in England', in *Studies in the Cultural Life of the Jews in England*. Folklore Research Center Studies 5, ed. Dov Noy and Issachar Ben-Ami (Jerusalem, 1975), p. 346. See too, Israel Salomons, 'Satirical and Political Prints on the Jews' Naturalization Bill, 1753', *Transactions of the Jewish Historical Society of England* 7 (1912), 205–33.

29 John Smith, *A Poetical Description of Mr Hogarth's Election Prints* (London, 1759), p. 9. For a discussion of Hogarth's prints in relation to the Jew Bill, see Ronald Paulson, *Hogarth* (Cambridge, 1993), III, 166–73.

30 *London Evening Post*, 18–20 October 1753.

31 Anon., *Seasonable Remarks on the Act Lately Pass'd in Favour of the Jews*, pp. 27–8.

32 See Roy S. Wolper, 'Circumcision as Polemic in the Jew Bill of 1753: the Cutter Cut?', *Eighteenth-Century Life* 7 (1982), 28–36. And see, for example,

Anon., *The Christian's New Warning Piece: Or, a Full and True Acount of the Circumcision of Sir E. T. Bart.* (London, 1753).

33 *London Evening Post,* 11–14 August, 1753.

34 *Gray's Inn Journal,* 6 October 1753, p. 12.

35 *Ibid.*

36 As cited in Perry, *Public Opinion,* pp. 75–6.

37 According to the *Dictionary of National Biography,* Cunningham, after 'travelling about a great deal as a strolling actor . . . eventually appeared at Edinburgh, where he became a great favourite with the manager, Mr Digges, and the leading lady, Mrs George Anne Bellamy, and wrote many occasional prologues for them'.

38 John Cunningham, *Poems, Chiefly Pastoral* (London, 1766), pp. 165–6.

39 I'm thinking in particular of Linda Colley's influential work, which invites us to look abroad to France to discover Britain's Other rather than to the dark racial and religious currents circulating around marginal groups like England's Jews (*Britons: Forging the Nation 1707–1837* (New Haven and London, 1992)). For an important exception, see Frank Felsenstein, *Anti-Semitic Stereotypes: A Paradigm of Otherness in English Popular Culture, 1660–1830* (Baltimore, 1995). See too, my *Shakespeare and the Jews* (New York, 1996). For a critique of class-based theories of nationalism that occlude race, see David Theo Goldberg, *Racist Culture: Philosophy and the Politics of Meaning* (Oxford, 1993), esp. pp. 78–80.

40 Elliott Baker, *Bardolatry* (London, 1992), pp. 30–3.

CHAPTER 9

Wilhelm S and Shylock

Laurence Lerner

Who is the mysterious dramatist who has shot to world-wide fame in our century because of his political relevance? His plays were performed before the incipiently fascist public in France and the actually fascist public in Germany during the 1930s,[1] and he was acclaimed for his vigorous portrayal of the dangers of mob rule and the need for strong leadership, as well as for his awareness of the ineradicable enmity between Christian generosity and the Jewish fixation on money. At some point during the war he appears to have moved to England, since he wrote a film script for Laurence Olivier depicting the courage and resourcefulness of the English when fighting on the continent, and was much praised for his patriotism. After the war, his series of plays on English history showed the desirability of hereditary monarchy and the dangers of civil war; but after the student uprisings of 1968 he appears to have treated revolution much more sympathetically. His taste for a deliberately antiquated style and archaic diction lends (paradoxically) a sharpness to his critique of contemporary politics; his passion for anonymity and seclusion has kept biographers guessing, and has fascinated the public; and his obvious wanderlust has enabled him to exert an influence in every major country in the world.

There is some uncertainty even about his name: it has come to us in various spellings, and there are even theories that this was not his name at all, but that of an actor whom the dramatist used to disguise his true identity. Since in this essay I intend to discuss the anti-Semitic play he wrote when in Nazi Germany, I shall use the German form of his given name, and avoid all orthographical controversy by abbreviating his surname: I shall call him Wilhelm S. Although we cannot be sure that he was actually German, there is no doubt about the great success he enjoyed there. He was congratulated for his awareness of Nordic profundity, and for the Nordic traits in the characterization of Hamlet: the tendency to muse about life and its meaning, and the melancholy with which he responds to the death of his father and the marriage of his mother. One critic saw these Nordic traits as interacting with other, more Latinate ('westisch') traits in Hamlet, and attributed the mixture to a corresponding interaction in the dramatist himself. Since biographical information about S is so hard to come by, this claim can hardly be tested.[2]

But the play which particularly led Nazi Germany to congratulate S for his understanding of racial psychology was *The Merchant of Venice*, in which he rewrote the old folk-tale of the Jew who lent three thousand ducats to a Christian merchant in return for a 'merry bond' by which, if the money was not repaid in time, he would be entitled to a pound of the debtor's flesh. The grotesque power of this anti-Semitic story obviously appealed to the German audience because of its brilliant portrayal of the racial characteristics of the Eastern Jew, and the contrast with the nobility of the Christian merchant, 'the royal merchant who loved money not for its own sake but in order to help his friends, who in order to put it in the service of life is willing to renounce everything. He keeps his word and is ready to carry it out to the bitter end.'[3]

That the play contains one apparently philosemitic speech, the well-known self-defence 'Hath not a Jew eyes . . .', need not worry us: the Nordic reader, who shares S's insights into racial psychology, will not err in reading the play, but will realize that this torrent of words is judged and refuted by Antonio, who expresses the poet's own opinion in his speech in the trial scene asserting that reasoning with the Jew is as futile as trying to alter nature:

> You may as well do anything most hard
> As seek to soften that – than which what's harder? –
> His Jewish heart.
>
> (4.1.77–9)

We know today, in the light of racial biology, that Shylock is mistaken in his claim that a Jew is human like the rest of us (or them), since 'der Jude eben rassenbiologisch ein anderer, artfremder Mensch für uns ist': that is, he is 'biologically distinct' and so alienated from us – a point made by the Duke when he speaks of 'the difference of our spirit'.[4]

There is an ideological as well as a racial dimension to the contrast between Shylock and the Christians, which can be interestingly formulated as that between justice and the rule of law:

Rationalism and technical formalism are constitutive elements of every modern system of law. S's parody is not quite directed at these, but should be seen rather as an attack on that ideology of the rule (or the reliability) of law which submits so fully to these technical elements in law that it allows the just decision to yield without struggle to the calculable one. It justifies itself by claiming that it is more important to put an end to struggle than to put a just end to it; that the existence of a legal system is more important than its justice; and that the rule of law has as its prime duty the bringing about of peace. According to this concept (which, I add in parenthesis, is very like the rules by which the police work in our society) peace depends on security and is independent of justice. One only needs to attend to the meaning of these words in terms of foreign politics and national rights to realise what view of law is here in question: it is that of western positivism, the politics of the status quo, or bourgeois security . . . in the legal consciousness of the Old Testament and of Jewry the element of security is of special importance. In the figure of Shylock this connexion is vividly expressed.[5]

This seems a very perceptive reading of *The Merchant of Venice*: precisely this contrast is dealt with in the exchange between Bassanio and 'Balthazar', in which Bassanio begs:

> Wrest once the law to your authority.
> To do a great right, do a little wrong,
> And curb this cruel devil of his will.
>
> (4.1.212–14)

– and Portia, as Balthazar, replies:

> It must not be. There is no power in Venice
> Can alter a decree establishèd:
> 'Twill be recorded for a precedent,
> And many an error by the same example
> Will rush into the state. It cannot be.
>
> (4.1.215–19)

– asserting in other words that the most important thing in law is its reliability, that the rule of law must not be overturned in the interests of justice ('a great right') because – the classic objection of the legalist – it would set a precedent. Shylock too asserted the same contrast:

> The pound of flesh which I demand of him
> Is dearly bought. 'Tis mine, and I will have it.
> If you deny me, fie upon your law:
> There is no force in the decree of Venice.
>
> (4.1.98–101)

That is to say, it is not the task of the court to pass judgement on the law, but to enforce it. And Shylock sees too that this conception of law is the basis of property: that is why he draws the parallel with slavery.

His sarcastic suggestion about the 'purchased slaves' – 'Let them be free, marry them to your heirs' – could be paraphrased (if we remove the sarcasm) as 'let justice override legality', and he correctly indicates that this is out of the question by giving the conventional reply: 'The slaves are ours.' Is it not therefore correct to describe Shylock's view of law as positivist, as based on bourgeois security and the status quo?

Even the love story of S's play can be given a racial interpretation. The annual lecture for 1937 to the German Association for the study of Wilhelm S (yes, he was sufficiently celebrated to have his own Association) was delivered by a Eugenicist, 'someone who has inquired what conception of love and marriage will be suitable or necessary to improve the stock of a people, someone who has further inquired what kind of girls and women the young men of a people ought to incline to in order to beget a more effective, more handsome and nobler posterity'. The lecturer concluded that Portia was just the ticket: she shows the needed 'mixture of reserve, strong feeling and clarity of mind, along with a talent for the masterful assurance that belongs to an inherently aristocratic being. We cannot doubt that she will develop into a truly Germanic mistress of the house (Hausherrin germanischer Prägung).'[6]

It is hard to believe, after all this, that *The Merchant of Venice* has also been performed in Israel (though we must add that it has not always been popular there). Did the Israelis not realize what they were doing, when they put on this anti-Semitic play before their own people? Or were they so committed to a non-political aestheticism that they allowed the dramatic genius of S to override his ideology?

Particularly interesting is the production in 1936, when Israel was still Palestine, because after it took place the theatre organized a public debate, in which author, theatre and director were put on trial, accused of producing 'a play in which [they] involved an anti-Jewish theme without being informed enough to treat the subject'.[7]

I can find no evidence that Wilhelm S, world traveller though he has since become, came to Palestine for this 'trial', so he was no doubt represented by proxy. Play and production were attacked both for what they said and for what they did not say: for attributing to Shylock a spirit of revenge wholly alien to the Jews, 'in whom an ancient spiritual culture is coupled with the long experience of humiliation and suffering', and for not admitting that the responsibility for turning Jews into usurers rested with Christian society, 'because you never let us survive in any other way: you have turned us into usurers and profiteers'. I shall return shortly to this objection.

But first I wish to perform a thought-experiment. Let us imagine that so little is known about S not because he has kept himself hidden but because he lived a long time ago; that he did not write *The Merchant of Venice* as an act of homage to Nazi ideology, but that it was written in a quite different time and place, and was appropriated by the Nazis. What difference would this make? Obviously it would introduce a historical factor. It would enable us to ask whether the Nazi interpreters were distorting the play to fit their own ideology, or whether the distant age in which S wrote (say three or four centuries ago) shared their anti-Semitic assumption.

And instead of being impressed with the enterprise shown by S in writing in so many countries and so many different political situations, we shall now say that it was the various countries and societies that were enterprising, helping themselves to his plays and interpreting them as they wished or felt compelled to. We shall then find ourselves asking whether interpreting an old play is fundamentally different from writing a new one. To some the difference will seem obvious; but to some schools of criticism now flourishing (represented, say, by Stanley Fish or Terence Hawkes) there will be no significant difference: for if the meaning of a text is constituted entirely by an interpretive community, if we can attribute no qualities to the text itself but only to the way it is read, then there can be no appeal to an author living in the past, outside of the community of readers. This view is now so influential that it is worth pausing to discuss it, since it is central to my thought experiment.

I choose Terence Hawkes as the representative of this position, which he sets forth with great vigour in *That Shakespeherian Rag* and *Meaning by Shakespeare*. The two books maintain that 'great' works of art have 'no claim to existence "in themselves"', and that we should study the ways in which they have been 'worked upon . . . as part of the struggle for cultural meaning'.[8] As an example of how he applies his claim that 'meaning is made rather than found' we can look at his discussion of Nedar, a character who is mentioned but does not appear in *A Midsummer Night's Dream* (Helena is Nedar's daughter). The witty changes that Hawkes rings on Nedar's name culminate in the claim that she should be regarded as a woman, Helena's mother rather than her father, 'not because Nedar necessarily *is* female, but because, in twentieth-century terms, the suggestion that she could be unseats a number of presuppositions investing the play, and demonstrates an indeterminacy, an undecidability, that is a feature of all texts'.[9]

Now since we do not know whether Nedar is male or female (the phrase 'old Nedar's daughter' allows, as Hawkes rightly points out, either meaning) the play can be said to license the claim that she is female, and the fact that previous commentators have seen 'her' as male certainly confirms the view that we have here 'a struggle for cultural meaning'. But that kind of indeterminacy cannot possibly be seen as 'a feature of all texts'. The existence of some indeterminate elements does not show that all elements are indeterminate, it rather reminds us how determinate others are. To claim that 'in twentieth-century terms' Shylock should be turned into a woman would raise very different issues – and much more resistance.

The twentieth-century issue I am here concerned with, however, is not gender but prejudice. Wilhelm S offers us an anti-Semitic *Merchant of Venice*, and we, reacting like good liberals, are upset by it. My 'thought-experiment' was a way of asking how important is the difference between writing an anti-Semitic play, and offering an anti-Semitic interpretation of a play written in 1597. According to the theory that meaning is made rather than found, there can be no difference; and in that case, treating *The Merchant of Venice* as if it was written by Wilhelm S in Nazi Germany is not the (ingenious or tiresome) gimmick which my readers have no doubt assumed it to be, but indistinguishable from the normal study of Shakespeare.

It will now be clear that I believe they *are* distinguishable, and appealing to history is the obvious way to distinguish them. But, as we are all aware nowadays, to appeal to the thought system of sixteenth-century England as a guide to correct understanding of S's plays soon raises problems. The appeal to history can alter our reading of a text only if some kind of direct access to the past is possible; if it produces the same kind of arguments as already rage about the plays, we may find ourselves reasoning in a circle.

And if we do appeal to history we shall soon find that German critics in the 1930s anticipated us, and were prepared to defend *their* reading on historical grounds:

The Merchant of Venice is not the tragedy of Shylock, as was believed by the sentimental sympathy of the 19th Century, which, closely related to semitic ways of thinking, thought that higher justice sided with the Jew, downtrodden and spat upon, and wanted to reopen the trial to Shylock and decide it in favour of the enemy of the Christians. The play begins with Antonio's puzzling and unhealthy melancholy, and ends in complete serenity. The concluding scene in Belmont follows consistently from the preceding struggles and decisions, as the Empire is the consequence of the return of the Jews to the Church. The so-called Jewish tragedy is an enchanting comedy of incomparable political power and beauty, transfigured by theology. The prominent use of music should be explained by the fact that great music is to be seen as part of a great political system. The final scene is not to be understood as lyrical in the way bourgeois moonlight romanticism is lyrical, but in its connexion with heavenly matters and eternal glory, with peace as the final goal of all politics in accordance with essential human nature, with the libera securitas et secura tranquillitas, the union of nature and grace symbolised by the wedding of Portia and Bassanio, the transfiguration of the body and the harmony of blessed spirits.[10]

Clemens Lang here is (almost) impeccably historical. He abuses the sentimental sympathy of the nineteenth century in a way that has been a commonplace since Irving Babbitt and T. S. Eliot, adding, however, one detail that sticks out like a sore thumb: the assertion that this sentimentality is closely related to a Jewish way of thinking ('semitische Geistesart'). If, as his hostile critics have sometimes suggested, Eliot would have liked to say that too, at least he never did; but it is not difficult to guess where Lang got the idea. The view that *The Merchant of Venice* is the tragedy of Shylock was put forward by Heine in *Shakespeares Mädchen und Frauen* in a memorable and eloquent paragraph:

When I saw this play produced in Drury Lane, there was a beautiful pale British woman standing behind me in the box, who wept copiously at the end of the fourth act, and cried out several times 'The poor man is wronged!' [The exclamation is in English in the original]. She had a face of the noblest Grecian profile, and her eyes were large and black. I have never been able to forget them, those large black eyes which wept over Shylock!

And when I think about those tears, I have to count *The Merchant of Venice* among the tragedies, although the framework of the play is decorated with the liveliest masques, images of satyrs and cupids, and although the poet actually wanted to give us a comedy . . .[11]

Even though Heine, in an elegant touch, is careful to attribute the exclamation to a pale and beautiful young woman 'vom edelsten griechischen Schnitt', the conclusion that the play is the tragedy of Shylock belongs to Heine himself, and to Clemens Lang, writing in the 1930s, it is an example of the 'semitische Geistesart'. Of course Lang has generalized wildly in attributing not just this interpretation of *The Merchant of Venice* but the whole of the 'sentimentalisches Mitleid des neunzehnten Jahrhunderts' to the Jewish way of thinking; and each of the passages I have quoted from the Nazi critics contains a similar touch of wanton anti-Semitic generalization that can be removed with greater or less damage to the main argument. In the case of Günther's lecture, for instance, the restatement of the wedding celebrations that normally end a romantic comedy in terms of eugenics is merely quaint to the Shakespeare critic, but alarmingly important to the historian of Nazism. In the case of Lang, the damage done by removing the anti-Semitic digression is negligible, and his main argument is an account of Renaissance political thinking that the majority of historical scholars would find quite acceptable, even perceptive. 'Shakespeare carries on tiptoe his burden of Renaissance thought', says Philip Brockbank of this play,[12] and though Lang's formulation ('Die angebliche jüdische Tragödie ist eine bezaubernde Komödie von unvergleichlicher politischer Kraft und theologisch verlkärter Schönheit') may be less elegant, his point is essentially the same. The analogy with music (seeing both human society and God's universe as a harmony), and the claim that the play is a romantic comedy whose conclusion is meant to emerge from the resolution of earlier conflicts: all this is what any responsible literary historian would tell us. S is a playwright who loves to build wholes out of contrasting and interrelating parts, and Heine's humane and sympathetic interpretation would make nonsense of the whole of the last act: to attribute a sour taste to the serene ending of this enchanting comedy would be merely perverse.

Does this mean that the W S of our thought-experiment, who wrote 400 years ago, clearly wrote an anti-Semitic play? If we can establish that Elizabethan society was anti-Semitic, then since the play is by an Elizabethan it too must be anti-Semitic. That is precisely the kind of simplistic argument that the New Historicism has set out to subvert. If historical scholarship is a matter of uncovering the tensions and contradictions of past societies, then literary history must expect to find these tensions reproduced in the texts produced by those societies. And even if we claim to find in the homilies and sermons of Renaissance England a clear attempt to pin down these shifting contradictions in unambiguous assertions, we can still say (with the New Historicism) that to read such homilies in depth is to see that the pinning down does not ever quite succeed, or (with the more traditional literary critic) that whatever may happen in sermons, drama does not pin down, and to reduce *The Merchant of Venice* (or any other play by W S) to a homily is to ignore what makes it a great play, even what makes it a play.

I return now to the 'trial' of the play after it was produced in Palestine in 1936. The prosecution charged that the play failed to admit that the responsibility for turning Jews into usurers rested with Christian society 'because you never let us survive in any other way: you have turned us into usurers and profiteers'. This is the most interesting form of the indictment I have come across, since it raises the question of what a play can and cannot say. Certainly there is no awareness *in Shylock* that Christian society is responsible for forcing him into a degrading profession; on the contrary, he seems to embrace it with gusto, citing his Old Testament precedents for 'thrift' with a chuckle of pleasure:

> When Jacob grazed his uncle Laban's sheep –
> This Jacob from our holy Abram was,
> As his wise mother wrought in his behalf,
> The third possessor; ay, he was the third –
>
> (1.3.70–3)

Shylock is pleased both at his own knowledge of Scripture and at the way it confirms him in his profession; and he then proceeds to tell a story that demonstrates Jacob's thrift and shrewdness, concluding, in reply to Antonio's objection (a medieval commonplace) 'Is your gold and silver ewes and rams?', with a further chuckle at his own financial acumen: 'I cannot tell, I make it breed as fast.' Shylock, clearly, is a money-lender to the core.

But is that incompatible with the view that society is responsible? Once the Jews have been driven into money-lending, there is no reason why they shouldn't do it well, and even enjoy doing it. Awareness of the social explanation does not need to be part of the consciousness of the individual money-lender.

Does it then need to be part of the consciousness of the play? That is trickier. Certainly it does not need to be explicitly said in the play: for that purpose we would need a chorus, or a perceptive observer among the characters who would point out (cynically or sorrowfully or even appreciatively) the mechanisms in Venetian society that were keeping Shylock down. That would be one kind of play, but not the only kind, and not the kind that S writes.

But are there not subtler ways of conveying such awareness? One suggestion that has often been popular with directors and critics is that Shylock really meant the bond to be a merry one, and was only goaded into revenge by his daughter's elopement. Tyrone Guthrie, who also (in 1959) produced the play in Israel, held this view: 'It is my view that Shakespeare's portrait is not anti-semitic, that the pound of flesh wager was entered upon as a jest, and only turns to vengeance after Shylock has been robbed and his daughter abducted by young Venetians of Antonio's set.'[13]

This is attractive, not only to liberal critics but also to directors, since it suggests a tableau that was introduced notably by Henry Irving in his Lyceum production, and has often been repeated, the return of Shylock at the end of act 2, scene 6 to find the house empty, his daughter gone, and (perhaps) the shutters flapping in mockery.[14] But attractive as it is, this interpretation seems refuted by the text for two reasons: first, that Shylock's aside on his first appearance ('I hate him for he is a Christian') suggests that the bitter hostility to Antonio was there from the beginning, and second that Jessica tells us quite explicitly 'When I was with him' (that is, before the elopement)

> I have heard him swear
> To Tubal and to Cush, his countrymen,
> That he would rather have Antonio's flesh
> Than twenty times the value of the sum . . .
>
> (3.2.282–5)

Yet although this disposes of Guthrie's reading, it does contain a tiny verbal detail that reveals a good deal about how Venetian society treated Shylock: that is Jessica's use of 'his'. Tubal and Cush were, after all, her countrymen too, but she has now identified herself completely with the Christian shutting out of Shylock. The ease with which Jessica changes sides, like her stealing of his ring and selling it for a monkey, aligns her with Christian exclusiveness and frivolity, and if we had pointed it out to Heine's 'schöne blasse Brittin' it would surely have strengthened her feeling that the poor man is wronged.

Not of course that we need hunt for such tiny verbal details in order to see how Venetian society excluded Shylock. It mocked him, cruelly and grossly, most famously in the parody by Solanio and Salerio of his grief when his daughter has run away:

> I never heard a passion so confused,
> So strange, outrageous, and so variable
> As the dog Jew did utter in the streets.
> 'My daughter! O, my ducats! O, my daughter!
> Fled with a Christian! O, my Christian ducats!
> A sealèd bag, two sealèd bags of ducats,
> Of double ducats, stol'n from me by my daughter!'
>
> (2.8.12–18)

Mockery as crude as this would goad anyone to wanting his pound of flesh. It does not matter that Shylock doesn't hear this speech, just as it doesn't matter that he doesn't hear his daughter say 'his countrymen':

he must have caught that tone in her voice when she was still with him, and he must have heard mockery like Solanio's a hundred times ('Many a time and oft / On the Rialto you have rated me'). This is a glimpse of the endemic anti-Semitism of the Venetians, and can easily be interpreted as an explanation for Shylock's lodged hate and certain loathing of Antonio.

But it is also a comic speech, which must have been thoroughly enjoyed by the original audience. The alliteration of ducats and daughter is brilliant: the two losses are, to him, equivalent, and the equivalence is reproduced in the signifiers. The same effect recurs in more complex form in 'double ducats', where the relation between form and meaning becomes a kind of tautology: money is twice as important as people realize, and to express this we use both the word 'double', and an act of doubling. The speech is a perfect mimesis of the fury of the comic villain whose thoughts are fixated on money.

Mimesis? Or caricature? A representation of the crude greed of the Jewish usurer, or of the crudity with which the Venetians perceive him? Is the speech anti-Semitic, or a representation of anti-Semitism? Again, this raises the question of what dramatic representation can and cannot do. The question whether the play shows any awareness of the social explanation for Shylock's greed is unanswerable, because plays do not show that kind of awareness directly. A play is a representation of social behaviour, not an explanation of it. Of course representation can imply explanation (ideology, as the point might now be put, is unavoidable), but not in any simple, monocausal fashion: explanation results from the interaction between play and audience, and the audience will decide whether anti-Semitism is being expressed or caricatured – not because all meaning is indeterminate, but because audiences fit meaning into an ideological framework. The original audience may have identified with Solanio and roared with delight – both original audiences, Shakespeare's Elizabethans and Wilhelm S's Nazis. But a different audience (you and I, reader) will laugh uneasily, or feel indignant, or praise the author for his exposure of Solanio's crude mockery. And audiences are not uniform: there could have been someone in 1597, and there almost certainly was someone in 1939, who had a Jewish friend, or for any reason felt uneasy about the ideological demands made on him, who did not laugh either. It is even possible that Shakespeare did not laugh.

First published in *Shakespeare Survey 48*, 1995

NOTES

1 For a valuable bibliography of discussions of S in Germany in the 1930s, see Ruth Freifrau von Ledebuhr, 'Der deutsche Geist und S: Anmerkungen zur S-Rezeption 1933–45' in *Wissenschaft und Nazionalsozialismus* (Herausgeber, 1988). I have also used Werner Habicht, 'S and Theatre Politics in the Third Reich', in *The Play out of Context*, ed. Scolnicov and Holland (1989); and *S im dritten Reich* by Georg Zähringer (Magisterarbeit, 1988).

2 Alex Niederstenbruch, 'Einige Gedanken zur rassischen Betrachtung von S's Hamlet', *Zeitschrift für neusprachlichen Unterricht* 41 (1942): 31–3. This and all other German passages are translated by me.

3 Dr Karl Pempelfort, 'Er besteht auf seinem Schein', *Königsberger Tageblatt*, 31 March 1935; reprinted in Joseph Wulf, *Theater und Film im dritten Reich* (Gutersloh: Mohn, 1964), p. 257.

4 Gregor Schwartz-Bostunitsch, 'Shylock und wir', *Der Weltkampf* 17 (1940), 17.

5 Wilhelm Grewe, 'Shylock, oder die Parodie der Rechtssicherheit', *Deutsche Volkstum* 18 (1936), 77–9.

6 Hans F. K. Günther, 'S's Mädchen und Frauen' (Vortrag vor der deutschen S-Gesellschaft), *S-Jahrbuch* 75 (1937) 85, 104.

7 Ya'akov Fikhman, quoted in Avraham Oz, 'Transformations of Authenticity', *S-Jahrbuch* (1983), 169.

8 Terence Hawkes, *That Shakespeherian Rag: Essays on a Critical Process* (London, 1986), p. 123.

9 Terence Hawkes, *Meaning by Shakespeare* (London and New York, 1992), p. 39.

10 Clemens Lang, 'S's Kaufmann von Venedig – die Tragödie des Juden Shylock', *Deutsches Volkstum* (1933), 962–5.

11 Heinrich Heine, 'S's Mädchen und Frauen' (1838), *Sämtliche Werke* (Munich, 1972), III, 652.

12 Philip Brockbank, 'S and the Fashion of these Times', *Shakespeare Survey 16* (1963), p. 40.

13 Tyrone Guthrie, *In Various Directions: A View of Theatre* (1965); quoted by Oz, 'Transformations of Authenticity', p. 172.

14 John Gross, *Shylock: Four Hundred Years in the Life of a Legend* (London, 1992), discusses this, amid much else of relevance to the present essay.

CHAPTER 10

Cruelty, 'King Lear' and the South African Land Act 1913

Martin Orkin

Present-day South Africans read Shakespeare in a semi-industrialized, capitalist, *apartheid* state located in a condition of advanced crisis.[1] This may prove to be a period of transition or collapse, but it is one that remains, as has been the case in the last fifty years and longer, characterized by brutal exploitation and repression. The Land Act of 1913, for instance, was one of the crucial pieces of legislation in the formation of what subsequently became the *apartheid* state. It distinguished different groups within the population of South Africa and purported to divide the land between them. In fact, as political commentators have underlined, it was to reserve less than 10 per cent of the total land surface of what was then the Union of South Africa for the black inhabitants of the country. Thus the Act, in responding to the demands of white farmers to convert sharecroppers on their land into farm labourers or servants, dispossessed many black landowners and outlawed, as well, leasing or tenant farming. Commentators recognize that this Act, which came about partly as a result of the sustained thrust of mining as well as farming capital, together with other laws, ostensibly protecting black rights, actually eroded them. It destroyed 'a whole class of peasant producers, forcing them into already crowded reserves or driving them into new and arduous social relationships – as farm workers, as mine labourers, and later in the least skilled and most badly paid positions in urban industrial, municipal, and domestic employment'.[2]

Perhaps the most famous of the individual reactions to this Act was from Solomon Plaatje.[3] He recognized the extent to which loss of land ownership and land tenancy would lead to complete political subjugation. Others then and since have recorded the reaction to the passing of the Act by large numbers of the affected population. Thus Bessie Head writes that 'rather than lose their last shred of independence . . . black people, tenants on the land, took to the road with their dying stock'.[4] And Plaatje describes in detail the subsequent misery and hardship thousands of old as well as young people experienced along the open road because of their refusal to stay on the now white-owned farms as servants.[5]

For the South African critic, to recall such facts as one takes up *King Lear*, a play that is in part about land, is not an indulgence. Historians working on late feudal and early capitalist England emphasize the importance of land – G. R. Elton observes that in the seventeenth-century English world the 'economic centre of gravity' was land and he stresses the extent to which status was dependent upon possession of land.[6] Society 'regarded only land and landed wealth as ultimately acceptable in creating status. True, there was wealth of other kinds . . . mercantile and banking fortunes . . . lawyers' incomes . . . but the only form of wealth which could gain you social recognition was land, possession of land.'[7]

More important for *King Lear*, Jonathan Dollimore has demonstrated the concern in the play with the connection between possession of land, property and power.[8] And Robert Weimann reminds us that we are all characters in history – 'our own points of reference are, like our predecessors', products of history'.[9] He emphasizes that to recreate the mimetic and expressive dimensions of the plays is not only 'impossible without reference to Shakespeare's world . . . to reassess their affective and moral effects is impossible without reference to our audience and our world'.[10]

It is not merely the question of acquisition or possession of land which might encourage in the South African audience or reader particular recognitions in the text. The apparent awareness in the play of the impact upon the poor of the sixteenth- and seventeenth-century economy, with its systems of enclosures and vagrancy laws, must be, in South Africa, still with its notorious pass laws and influx control – albeit in new and disguised forms – of pressing interest. We know that the displacement of the poor during the enclosure movement increased the already serious problem of poverty and hardship caused in Shakespeare's day by poor harvests, the aftermath of war, and the population explosion.[11] There was a ' "savage depression of the living standard of the lower half of the population" in Shakespeare's time, a depression created by an 800 per cent increase in the value of land, an overall inflation rate of 500 per cent . . . and a fall in real wages by half'.[12] Moreover, vagrancy laws enabled the gentry, when they had a full labour supply, to remove the remainder of the poor back to the villages of their birth.[13] These villages more often than not were poverty-stricken as a result of enclosures. And enclosures, we should remember, in a rather crude way also converted a tenant labour system into a wage labour system – the latter, as the South African state understands only too well, is easier to control and much cheaper.

When Shakespeare wrote *King Lear*, historians tell us, pressure against enclosures was building up in the Midlands, including Warwickshire, to break out a year or so later in rioting which was in turn brutally suppressed by the gentry. Laws to control beggars were another way in which vagrancy, a continued problematic consequence of the flux in economic conditions, was handled. When he joins that class persecuted and hounded by the state apparatus, Edgar speaks not only of Bedlam beggars and their sufferings but of that countryside through which they roam, which includes low farms, poor pelting villages, sheep-cotes and mills. The sense of the impact of the Elizabethan and Jacobean economic system upon the powerless and landless resonates when Lear speaks of 'Poor naked wretches' (3.4.28), and Gloucester, too, gives his purse to Poor Tom, as many critics note, recognizing that 'distribution should undo excess, / And each man have enough' (4.1.70–1).[14]

The ambiguities surrounding the shift of power that takes place in the play and the political cruelty that accompanies it are especially important to South Africans. Just before he has his eyes put out – in the scene which Dr Johnson described as 'too horrid to be endured in dramatick exhibition' and which even so recent a critic as Harry Levin can describe as having only a 'certain propriety as a literal climax to a whole train of metaphors involving eyesight and suggesting moral perception' – Gloucester, in reply to Regan's demand that he explain why he has sent King Lear to Dover, declares:

> Because I would not see
> Thy cruel nails pluck out his poor old eyes;
> Nor thy fierce sister in his anointed flesh
> Rash boarish fangs.
>
> (3.7.54–7)[15]

At this moment Gloucester ceases completely to deal with the *de facto* power faction or group within the ruling class. His direct statement of defiance aligns him with the hunted victims of that power – King Lear, without protection or shelter on the heath, and Edgar, proclaimed an outlaw throughout the land and disguised as Poor Tom. But the propriety of this scene to the concerns of *King Lear* is more extensive than Levin's comment admits. He in fact also remarks that the scene presents a 'deliberate and definitive' breach of classical decorum – the Greeks

preferred to have Oedipus' eyes put out off stage.[16] He does not indicate that this 'breach' of decorum illustrates and embodies – in what
we might call a terrifying emblematic way – one aspect of the political
thrust of the play. For in this scene the whole nexus of emerging
relationships that *King Lear* explores, which begins in the opening scene
with a shift of power and which intensifies relentlessly in the scenes and
acts to follow, comes to a point of awful clarity. Moreover, the inter-
rogation and torture it presents set a seal on this process of change,
identifying for the audience at the same time the essential nature of the
de facto ruling power.

The phrase *de facto* is, however, in part inappropriate for the power
which Goneril, Regan, and Edmund acquire in the first three acts. The
text invests their possession of power with elements of legality: the
daughters of the King have each received formally from their father
control of most of the kingdom, the fugitive Edgar has been defined as
an enemy of the state, and even the 'kangaroo' court that tries Gloucester
is prompted by the Duke's communication with an invading army –
foreign intruders whom he has also helped the King to join. Yet although
we might note these facts we recoil from the suggestion of legitimacy;
King Lear stresses the extent to which the shift of power within the
dominant order initiated in act 1, scene 1 becomes at once also a *seizure*
of power. It is sometimes forgotten that if Lear makes an appalling
decision which proves to be mistaken, what follows is only possible
because the connative dissembling of his two daughters enables them to
acquire for themselves most of his domain. By the end of the first scene,
furthermore, they indicate their determination to deprive him of the
remaining material evidence of his authority. In the acts that follow,
this arrogation of power is complemented by Edmund's own frenetic
activity in the displacement of brother and then father. When, then,
ignoring the Fool's plea for compromise and submission to the authorities, Lear chooses the open heath he does not merely cease to be the
de facto representative of the system of government and justice, which
makes its claims for hierarchy and custom, to become its victim. He
becomes also to a large degree that system's opponent and critic.

By means of this strategy the text is able to pursue the disturbing
recognitions it makes from the beginning, when land is shared out with
such catastrophic results, about the actual system of domination and
subordination within the social order. In support of this contention,
Gary Taylor's discussion of 1.4.142–66, originally in the quarto but
which does not appear in the Folio, may be cited.[17] He argues that the

censor omitted the passage from the Folio because of the hints of criticism in it linking aspects of Lear's behaviour with that of James. What we know of the start of James's reign and of James personally suggests that such criticism was merited although any connection between stage and audience monarch should not be understood in a reductive way that insists upon a one-to-one equivalence, but rather in a suggestive way and one that, presumably, might have prompted reflections in Shakespeare's contemporary audience about tendencies in the court of James and its administration.[18] Furthermore, we should recall that if the text, in certain of its parallels in the first two acts, implies criticism of James, this is balanced by other factors which, by the time the King has been removed from the ruling class, encourage in the audience an increasingly sympathetic attitude. Thus the mistake which Lear commits at the beginning of the play is presented as the result partly of faulty perception, and not the consequence of the conscious self-interest displayed by Edmund, Goneril and Regan. Lear, furthermore, understands his mistake by the end of act 1; his later realizations may be seen as amplification of this. After the end of the second act, too, the impulse to criticism of the King is eclipsed by the presence in the text of language that directs the audience to the enormity of what is done to him.[19]

This view of Lear's role is supported as well by some suggestions Leonard Tennenhouse makes in a discussion of *Measure for Measure*.[20] He observes that at this time several comedies use a common device – 'a trickster figure, who is often but not always a monarch . . . from disguise . . . observes the state and witnesses both sexual misconduct and the abuses of political power'.[21] Tennenhouse points out that one of the effects of this technique of removing the ruler figure from his world to enable him to observe it is that 'being thus conceived as something separate from the monarch, the state and not the monarch becomes the object to which our attention is turned'.[22] The Duke's deputies have his authority and they represent his rule. In the same way, *King Lear* ensures that those who remain in control when Lear has been removed from power retain the aura of legitimacy. Through the vehicle of the behaviour of Edmund, Goneril and Regan (and not through the presence of the one dramatic character who suggests the English King himself) the text may safely pursue the problems it has posed from the start of the play about the operation of state power within the dominant order. And, we may add, recent study of Elizabethan and Jacobean censorship confirms the necessity of such a tactic.[23]

For the play's depiction of an apparently legitimate but actually ruthless and cruel ruling class, the image of old age with which it begins proves especially appropriate – old age with its suggestion of the need for love, its intractability and its fallibility, presents a condition of vulnerability. But when Regan says to Lear, 'I pray you, father, being weak, seem so' (2.4.203), she voices a different demand. A great divide opens at once between those who from the beginning of the play are indifferent and cruel towards this condition in human experience, and those who offer throughout a more compassionate response. The human faculty for exploitation and persecution is registered in the language of the Fool, in the image of Poor Tom as innocent fugitive from hostile authority, in the continuing spectacle of Lear himself on the heath. Early in act 3 Lear begins to realize that power, its manifestation in land and wealth, does not automatically denote morality – beneath the semblance of order there often lies criminality. Lear's desire to plumb the depths of Regan's cruelty, find out what breeds about her heart, emerges as hopeless: the participants in the search for absolute justice in the mock-trial scene are the outcasts of the social order – a mad old King, his Fool, an exile in disguise. Against the acknowledged impotence of the seekers of absolute justice the final scene of act 3 demonstrates the extent to which the dominant order, which controls the real apparatus of justice, may operate lawlessly when it chooses, to preserve its position: the putting out of Gloucester's eyes underlines the potential ruthlessness of rulers. The Duke too cries out for a form of providential justice, but his cries are also impotent. Instead, expelled from the dominant order and redefined as masterless, he becomes for the rulers subhuman – 'let him', says Regan, 'smell / His way to Dover' (3.7.92–3).

The treatment of Gloucester suggests the readiness of the dominant order not merely to coerce but, when faced with difference that cannot be contained, to create subversion in order to destroy it. But much earlier in the play, Gloucester's own response to an allegedly traitorous son – whom the audience knows to be innocent – has been disastrously precipitous. In an age troubled by mutinies in cities, discord in countries, and treason in palaces, Gloucester's behaviour evokes that urgent reflex in the dominant order to act punitively in order to contain possible subversion. Precisely as he acts against Edgar, Gloucester recalls the King's behaviour in the previous scene. There, Cordelia's failure to use the code her father demanded, her emphasis instead upon the contractual nature of her relationship with him, prompted the King to make an example of *her* – in his case too, anger led swiftly to fierce

rejection and punishment. Lear follows the same pattern in his treatment of Kent. This suggests how, in contexts of change or uncertainty,
the ruling class may move swiftly, even vindictively, ignoring its own
complicity in or production of disorder (Lear's own culpability in his
treatment of Cordelia and Kent, Gloucester's casual promiscuity, the
implicit, more general responsibility of these two powerful members
of the dominant order for a society apparently bedevilled by mutiny,
discord and treason) to create its enemies (Cordelia, Kent, Edgar) in
order to assert, through punishment (deprivation of inheritance, ban-
ishment, the outlawed target of state persecution and oppression), its
own authority. In the present state of emergency in South Africa, the
government and its class, primarily responsible for the misery and
suffering in the state, nevertheless denies this whilst reacting punitively
against a wide range of individuals it chooses to redefine as subversive
and worthy of severe punishment. Through such persecution too, its
power may be entrenched. In *King Lear* these instances in the first two
scenes are as disturbingly interrogative of the dominant order, of traditional notions of hierarchy and justice, as the image of Kent later in the
stocks emblematically suggests, or as Regan's readiness to eliminate
Gloucester blatantly illustrates.

Such episodes and language contest those episodes and that language in the play, especially in act 4, that suggest a powerful longing for
the validity of a view of the human subject drawn from Christian
discourse. Yet it is precisely readings of the text of this kind that
traditional critics in South Africa avoid. It should be remembered that
the education system in South Africa, subject to censorship and the
demonizing of all forms of dissenting or alternative discourse, works
to legitimate the present South African social order. Such a system not
only deprives its inhabitants of an awareness of alternatives; the very
capacity to analyse or envisage enabling as well as limiting counter-
possibilities is severely inhibited. A use made of the Shakespeare text
which encourages thoughts about the tale – generalized moral abstractions about the story of old King Lear – and thoughts about, indeed
fixation upon, character, human nature, interiority, in the South African
situation has a clear political consequence in assisting in the reproduction of dominant social relations.[24] The participants in such an activity
are encouraged in the belief that they too, like the text, are independent
of social process. Essential truths cease to have any connection with
material reality, and not yet, in South Africa, very much a matter of
intertextuality – except of the most depoliticized kind – they remain

other-worldly. In this, the traditionalist approach to the Shakespeare text actively reinforces in its adherents the tendency to submission.

One other aspect of traditionalist practice with the Shakespeare text in South Africa may be noted. South Africa has been perceived by English affiliated South Africans, or British academics who have always been part of the university establishment in South Africa, as an outpost on the periphery of British influence. This mental set survived long after the British empire went into decline and even after 1960 when South Africa was more or less expelled from the Commonwealth. Literary critics saw themselves as bearers of high culture to the African subcontinent. But after 1948, their struggle was not simply that of an English group within the dominant order that longed for connection with the 'mother country' and that came into contact with subordinate orders imbued with alien and what it therefore defined as inferior cultures. It was also a struggle with the emergence of a new Calvinist (Afrikaner) power group within the dominant order, one that increasingly asserted its own hegemony. Feeling doubly under attack, the bearers of civility find pluralism of meaning in any text even more unpalatable. In a world of 'racism' as well as 'savagism', in which their own participation in the existing relations of domination and subordination is totally ignored, such critics turn to the Shakespeare text as a refuge and a retreat, as a means of personal growth, as the survival line to the metropolis.[25] As recently as 1985 one such critic offers *King Lear* as an example of a 'life-enhancing' text that communicates a 'rich social identity' and one which he contrasts with the Roman plays where the characters 'do not learn, they do not truly suffer, they do not repent, they cannot utter sentiments of human communality'.[26]

Stephen Greenblatt, noting 'the impossibility of fully reconstructing and re-entering the culture of the sixteenth century, of leaving behind one's own situation', observes that 'the questions I ask of my material and the very nature of this material are shaped by the questions I ask of myself'.[27] The study of the Shakespeare text in South Africa in one way or another reflects this fact. Significantly perhaps, the plays most frequently chosen for discussion are those likely to have been written in the period 1599–1606, and most often the tragedies. I would argue then, especially in the context of these texts, that at this moment the study of the Shakespeare text in South Africa is best assisted by the work of those critics who, engaged in recovering the political dimension of Shakespearian drama, recognize that signifying practices are located within the material struggles taking place in the social order.

From this point of view the deaths of Cordelia and Lear, despite the fact that they cherish certain traditional values, are not merely or even primarily the result of accident. What Lear and his daughter experience is the consequence not only of the acquisition and loss of power, but of political cruelty and oppression. Moreover, victims of a dominant class to which they no longer belong – one which operates as it always seems to have done, in its own interest, and which uses state power to preserve its hegemony – defeated in civil war, they face incarceration. Lear says to his daughter of their coming imprisonment, 'We two alone will sing like birds i' th' cage' (5.3.9), and his mind, broken by persecution, envisages in the context of imprisonment a child-like fantasy of escape. His language however is no less located in the hard context of political reality. We'll 'Talk', he says, 'of court news', of

> Who loses and who wins; who's in, who's out;
> And take upon 's the mystery of things,
> As if we were God's spies
>
> (5.3.14–17)

even as his mind comes back to the fact of oppression, the state's exercise of control through spying, he attempts to flee again. They will be the spies of God, he dreams, possessors of an omnipotent detachment free from the pressures of polity, though still, ironically, practising a form of divine surveillance. But yet again, his mind returns once more, and finally, to the 'wall'd prison' (5.3.18) around them.

It is that dominant class of which Lear was once himself part that is, then, primarily responsible for the two deaths at the play's end. When Lear re-enters the stage, we might, merely in one sense fancifully, suggest that he carries not simply the innocent murdered Cordelia, but all of those, not only in Shakespeare's day, who have died similarly. This is ostensibly the last thrust of a power group within the dominant order which ends with Edmund's death. In another sense the tendencies and characteristics the play has recognized continue beyond the last words of the text, in Shakespeare's own world and beyond that too. Dollimore observes, in this connection, that 'far from transcending in the name of an essential humanity the gulf which separates the privileged from the deprived, the play insists on it'.[28] Lear is only able to learn anything once he has lost power totally; rulers in power, the play acknowledges, never do expose themselves to 'feel what wretches feel' (3.4.34).[29] The image of Lear carrying the dead Cordelia, the image too of the powers-that-be crying, at the hint of danger, at the sound of an agonized, opposing voice, 'Shut up your doors . . . 'tis a wild night . . . come out o' th' storm' (2.4.310–11), and the image of that angry old man himself, deprived of power, realizing, in part confusedly, the real nature of its operation, set against the continuing indifference of that domin- ant class in its assertion of hegemony, perhaps more than the images in any other of Shakespeare's plays, have resonance for those of us living in South Africa.

Such realizations seem inescapable. In the same way if certain critics have found evidence in the tragedies of the assertion of bourgeois indi- vidualism, or anxiety about the ways in which traditional signifiers seem to be floating away from the signified, South Africans are located in particularly chilling versions of such processes at an advanced, critical stage. I would then, finally, also argue that many of the young men and women in South Africa, both in the townships and elsewhere, hearing Lear's identification of the materialist basis to power and justice:

> Plate sin with gold,
> And the strong lance of Justice hurtless breaks;
> Arm it in rags, a pigmy's straw does pierce it
> (4.6.167–9)

may be invited – without our betraying the Shakespeare text – to juxta- pose against this, say, Solomon Plaatje's remarks about the passing of the Land Act of 1913:

Well we knew that this law was as harsh as its instigators were callous . . . Lord Gladstone signed no fewer than sixteen new Acts of Parliament – some of them rather voluminous – while three days earlier, his excellency signed another batch of eight, of which the bulk was beyond the capability of any mortal to read and digest in four days . . . The gods are cruel. They might have warned us that Englishmen would agree with Dutchmen to make it unlawful for black men to keep milk cows of their own . . . render many poor homeless (and produce) such a rapid and widespread crash as it caused.[30]

NOTES

1 This essay was first published in *Shakespeare Survey 40*, 1988.
2 Tom Lodge, *Black Politics in South Africa since 1945* (Johannesburg, 1983), p. 2.
3 Solomon T. Plaatje, *Native Life in South Africa* (1916), (Cape Town, 1982), p. 72.
4 Bessie Head, Foreword to Plaatje, *Native Life in South Africa*, p. xi.
5 Plaatje, *Native Life in South Africa*, pp. 78 ff.

6 G. R. Elton, *Studies in Tudor and Stuart Politics and Government*, vol. III, Papers and Reviews 1973–1981 (Cambridge, 1983), p. 340.

7 *Ibid.*

8 Jonathan Dollimore, *Radical Tragedy* (Brighton, 1984), pp. 189–203. My indebtedness to Dollimore is everywhere evident in this article.

9 Robert Weimann, *Structure and Society in Literary History* (Baltimore, 1984), p. 54.

10 *Ibid.*, p. 53.

11 Lawrence Stone, *The Causes of the English Revolution, 1529–1642* (London, 1972), writes: 'In the sixteenth century the combination of rapidly rising food prices and stagnant rents shifted the distribution of agricultural profits away from the landlord and towards the tenant. In the early seventeenth century rents increased more rapidly than prices and profits flowed back to the landlord and away from the tenant. This shift to economic rents was accompanied by a reorganisation of property rights by which more and more land fell into private control through enclosures of both waste and common fields. As a result of this process and of the engrossing of farms into larger units of production, there began to emerge the tripartite pattern of later English rural society, landlord, prosperous tenant farmer, and landless labourer. These changes were essential to feed the additional mouths, but tens of thousands of small-holders were driven off the land or reduced to wage labourers while others found their economic position undermined by encroachment on, or over-stocking of, the common lands by the big farmers and the landlords. The enclosure became a popular scapegoat for the dislocations inevitable in so major a redistribution and reallocation of the land, but there can be no doubt that the extra millions of Englishmen were only fed at the cost of much individual hardship suffered by many of the small peasantry' (p. 68).

12 Alvin B. Kernan, '*King Lear* and the Shakespearean Pageant of History', in *On King Lear*, ed. Lawrence Danson (Princeton, N.J., 1981), p. 11. Carl Bridenbaugh, *Vexed and Troubled Englishmen 1590–1642* (Oxford, 1968), observes: 'the half-century after 1590 was a time of profound unprecedented and often frightening social ferment for the people of England. During these years nearly every member of the lower orders in the countryside and in the towns knew deprivation and genuinely feared insecurity; and well he might, for close to a majority of the population found themselves living perilously near the level of bare subsistence . . .' (p. 355). Christopher Hill, *The Century of Revolution 1603–1714* (Edinburgh, 1961), writes: 'To contemporaries struck by poverty and vagabondage, the overpopulation seemed absolute . . . Wage labourers did not share in the profits of industrial expansion. As prices rose during the sixteenth century, the purchasing power of wages had fallen by something like two thirds. Since the numbers of those permanently dependent on wages was increasing, the number of those on the margin of starving was increasing too. This fall in real wages was catastrophic for those who sold or were evicted from their plots of land and became entirely dependent on earnings . . .' (p. 24).

13 Hill, *Century of Revolution*, writes: 'The harsh Poor Law was breaking up
the bands of roaming vagabonds which had terrorised Elizabethan England; but it could not prevent London attracting an underworld of casual
labourers, unemployables, beggars and criminals. The prescribed penalty
of whipping home unlicensed beggars checked freedom of movement, and
detained a surplus of cheap labour in many rural areas' (p. 26). Keith
Wrightson, *English Society 1580–1680* (London, 1982), notes: 'Poverty, of
course, was nothing new . . . Yet the later sixteenth and early seventeenth
centuries saw the growth of a poverty which was different in both its nature
and extent from that which had been known earlier . . . By the end of the
sixteenth century . . . the poor were no longer the destitute victims of misfortune or old age, but a substantial proportion of the population living in
constant danger of destitution, many of them full-time waged
labourers . . . the extent of the problem was frightening though it varied
from area to area . . . the settled poor (were) relatively fortunate in that
they had a recognised place in society and were eligible for parish relief
under the Elizabethan Poor Law . . . Beyond them and well outside the
charitable consideration of the authorities, were the vagrant poor . . . How
many of them wandered the roads of the period it is impossible to say,
though their numbers were undoubtedly high' (p. 141). Finally, we may
note Hill again: 'although it would be wrong to think of any body of
organised discontent, there is a permanent background of potential unrest
throughout these decades. Given a crisis – a famine, large-scale unemploy-
ment, a breakdown of government – disorder might occur . . . The preven-
tion of peasant revolt was the monarchy's job; in this it had the support of
the propertied class' (pp. 27–8).

14 All references are to *King Lear*, ed. Kenneth Muir, in the new Arden
Shakespeare (1952).

15 *Johnson on Shakespeare*, ed. Arthur Sherbo (New Haven and London, 1968),
p. 703; Harry Levin, *Shakespeare and the Revolution of the Times* (Oxford, 1976),
p. 165.

16 Levin, *Shakespeare and the Revolution of the Times*, p. 165.

17 Gary Taylor, 'Monopolies, Show Trials, Disaster and Invasion: *King Lear*
and Censorship', in *The Division of the Kingdoms*, ed. Gary Taylor and Michael
Warren (Oxford, 1983), pp. 75–119.

18 Taylor, 'Monopolies', cites c4^v–d1; 1.4.136–59. He argues that the passage
refers to James's granting of monopolies, the incredible gluttony which had
become a feature of the banquets at James's court, the King's wholesale
dispensation of titles and his love of hunting (pp. 101–9). G. R. Elton,
Studies in Tudor and Stuart Politics and Government, vol. II, Papers and Reviews
1946–1972 (Cambridge, 1974) summarizes the difficulties when James came
to power in this way: 'When Queen Elizabeth died, she left a system of
government much debilitated by recent change. A price inflation had
seriously weakened the Crown; the Church faced an insidious and fundamental attack from the Puritan party; the House of Commons had recently

grown in power and independence; the ambitions of rising classes (the gentry, the bourgeoisie) were threatening the ascendancy of the monarch and aristocracy. Altogether the traditional power of the Crown was failing in the face of a variety of discontent and criticism. All these strains became increasingly obvious in the reign of James I' (p. 157). Elton cites the inadequacy of the Stuart government as one of the main reasons why these many and varied problems intensified under James. The 'early Stuart governments . . . were incompetent, sometimes corrupt, and frequently just ignorant of what was going on or needed doing . . . What matters is their repeated inability, for reasons also often factious, bigoted and ill-conceived, to find a way through their problems' (p. 161). Of James's reign, particularly, Elton observes that it was 'a reign which was marked even more than any other you could name in (English) history as an age in which nothing happened, in which nothing was done, in which government neglected all its duties' (*Studies*, III, 282). See also J. W. Lever, *The Tragedy of State* (London, 1971), pp. 3–4, for the series of blows which the monarchy sustained at the end of Elizabeth's reign and during the beginning of James's reign. James's task as monarch was not made easier because of his lack of personal charisma – and he had no hope of competing with the great propaganda machine that had presented 'Gloriana' to her public. See Stephen Greenblatt, *Renaissance Self-Fashioning* (Chicago, 1980), pp. 166–9; Stone, *Causes of the English Revolution*, p. 89.

19 Kent, who was not slow to criticize the King earlier, recognizes at the start of act 3 the 'hard rein' (3.1.27) which the King's daughters 'have borne / Against the old kind King' (3.1.27–8) and acknowledges that of 'unnatural and bemadding sorrow / The King hath cause to plain' (3.1.38–9) while Lear himself asserts 'I am a man / More sinn'd against than sinning' (3.2.59–60). The King's madness provides the opportunity for satire too. Maynard Mack, 'The Jacobean Shakespeare', *Jacobean Theatre*, Stratford-upon-Avon Studies 1 (1960), notes: 'Both (Lear) and Hamlet can be privileged in madness to say things – Hamlet about the corruption of human nature, and Lear about the corruption of the Jacobean social system . . . which Shakespeare could hardly have risked apart from this licence' (p. 39).

20 Leonard Tennenhouse, 'Representing Power: *Measure for Measure* in its Time', in *The Power of Forms in the English Renaissance*, ed. Stephen Greenblatt (Oklahoma, 1982), pp. 139–56.

21 Tennenhouse, 'Representing Power', p. 139.

22 *Ibid.*, p. 141.

23 See Margot Heinemann, *Puritanism and the Theatre* (Cambridge, 1980), esp. pp. 36–8; Dollimore, *Radical Tragedy*, pp. 22 ff; Lever, *Tragedy of State*, pp. 1–17; Taylor, 'Monopolies' pp. 75–119. I have not been able to examine Janet Clare, 'Art Made Tongue-tied by Authority: a Study of the Relationship between Elizabethan and Jacobean Drama and Authority and the Effect of Censorship on the Plays of the Period', unpublished PhD thesis,

University of Birmingham, 1981 [since published as *'Art Made Tongue-tied by Authority': Elizabethan and Jacobean Dramatic Censorship* (Manchester and New York, 1990).]

24 Cf. Kenneth Muir, 'The Betrayal of Shakespeare', *Shakespeare: Contrasts and Controversies* (Brighton, 1985), esp. p. 90.

25 B. D. Cheadle, 'Hamlet at the Graveside: a Leap into Hermeneutics', *English Studies in Africa* 22: 2 (1979), 83–90, remarks in the course of his discussion: 'we read literature, presumably at least in part, to grow: by entering into a vision of life that is not our own we extend our awareness and our capacity and a commitment to a particular approach should not be such as to preclude the possibility of literature changing us' (p. 87). C. O. Gardner, 'Tragic Fission in *Othello*', *English Studies in Africa* 20:1 (1977), 11–25, finds at the end of the play a 'loss of harmony' and 'balance' to which, he recommends, we should react with 'recognition, wonder, fear and awe . . . we must learn all that we can from tragic events, we must love and admire all that is generous in thought, in feeling and in deed, but above all or beneath all we must be humble'. This final sentence strikingly suggests the use to which Shakespeare has been put in encouraging certain attitudes – a longing for instruction in particular abstractions about human behaviour, a pseudo-fatalistic or stoic resignation about the frailties of this world, acceptance of the status quo.

26 Geoffrey Hughes, 'A World Elsewhere: Romanitas and its Limitations in Shakespeare', *English Studies in Africa* 28:1 (1985), 1–19; p. 18.

27 Greenblatt, *Renaissance Self-Fashioning*, p. 5.

28 Dollimore, *Radical Tragedy*, p. 192.

29 *Ibid.*, pp. 191–2.

30 Plaatje, *Native Life in South Africa*, pp. 81, 82, 22.

CHAPTER 11

Caliban and Ariel write back

Jonathan Bate

It is no coincidence that the now hugely influential reading of *The Tempest* in the context of 'the discourse of colonialism' began for the purposes of the Anglo-American academy with Stephen Greenblatt's essay 'Learning to Curse', published in 1976, in a book called *First Images of America: The Impact of the New World on the Old* which explicitly marked – in troubled fashion – the bicentenary of the American Declaration of Independence. As was the case more recently in Australia, official celebrations of a young nation's coming to the age of two hundred released an anguished cry from the liberal intelligentsia as they came to full realization of the exploitation and oppression on which their nation was built. Fashionable criticism is interested in assuaging the guilt of empire by making the author of *The Tempest* a scapegoat. But I find it mildly ironic that very few of the 'radical' critics of the 1970s and 1980s have acknowledged that a revisionary reading of *The Tempest* had already been undertaken in the 1950s and 1960s by non-white non-Europeans. I have to admit to my shame that I have been much longer familiar with the 'New Historicist' readings of anguished Stefanos like Stephen Greenblatt, Stephen Orgel and Steven Mullaney than with the remarkable creative work done a generation before them by self-proclaimed Calibans like George Lamming, Edward Kamau Brathwaite, Aimé Césaire and Roberto Fernández Retamar.

The introduction to Stephen Orgel's 1987 Oxford edition of the play, which has already become as influential for its generation as Frank Kermode's Arden edition was for the previous one, is typical. It twice mentions Mannoni's pioneering interpretation of the play in relation to colonialism, but on each occasion passes straight from it to a liberal white interpreter. First: 'The most important treatments of the relevance of colonialism to the play are Octave Mannoni's *Psychologie de la colonisation* (1950), published in England as *Prospero and Caliban*; Stephen J. Greenblatt's brilliant "Learning to Curse" . . .". And secondly:

'[Jonathan] Miller, in a 1970 production at the Mermaid, based his view of the relation of Prospero to Caliban and Ariel on Octave Mannoni's metaphorical use of these figures in his analysis of the revolt of Madagascar in 1947, *La Psychologie de la colonisation*' (p. 83). For a good liberal who is manifestly troubled by the white tradition's silencing and marginalization of blacks, Orgel is here remarkably adept in his own silencing of the major – 'brilliant' indeed – black interpretations of the two decades between the publication of Mannoni's book and the readings of Miller and Greenblatt. Typical, too, is Eric Cheyfitz's *The Poetics of Imperialism: Translation and Colonization from 'The Tempest' to 'Tarzan'*: the author claims that Frantz Fanon is his 'immediate inspiration for reading *The Tempest*', then remarks that 'his name should remind us that Shakespeare's play is the possible prologue not only for the literature of the United States, but for a significant body of Caribbean literature'[2] – yet the rest of the book has nothing to say about that body of literature.

A handful of articles by less well-known critics, together with some pages in the Vaughans' book on the cultural history of Caliban, have begun to break this silence, but the Caribbean appropriation of *The Tempest* still remains unknown to many. The first part of this paper is accordingly devoted to a fine example of it.

Edward Brathwaite, who was born in Barbados in 1930, went to university at Cambridge and is published by Oxford. His work is written in a distinctively Caribbean voice, but it reconfigures rather than entirely rejects the 'high' English cultural tradition that is epitomized by Oxbridge. Unlike certain younger black poets, such as Michael Smith and Linton Kwesi Johnson, whose work relies entirely on the oral and vernacular traditions of reggae and rap, Brathwaite moves between jazz or folk rhythms on the one hand and 'traditional' allusion and diction on the other. His work thus enacts a passage between the old world and the new; his own passage into the tradition is a sometimes liberated, sometimes uneasy, reversal of the 'middle passage' of his forebears into slavery. The three volumes of his 'New World Trilogy' are called *Rights of Passage* (1967), *Masks* (1968) and *Islands* (1969).[3] They are triangulated upon the Atlantic slave trade: in both style and reference they move between England, Africa and the Caribbean. The overall structure of the trilogy proposes that after the passage to slavery in the plantations, it becomes essential for the black to wear masks. To begin with, he or she will inherit alienated western man's mask-making, inauthentic and associated with social roles (the black personae such as

Uncle Tom being subservient). But by making the passage in reverse, returning to Africa and recovering its traditions – the animism, the rituals and the rhythms of the Ashanti nation – a more creative, spiritual use of masks can emerge. The mask becomes that of the god. It is then possible to make the islands of the Antilles a place of grace and beauty, not of oppression.

The classic literary–dramatic role for Brathwaite, as for Fanon and Lamming before him, is Caliban. His poem of this title occupies a pivotal position in the collection *Islands*, which itself works through a development similar to that of the trilogy as a whole – its five sections are entitled New World, Limbo, Rebellion, Possession and Beginning. 'Caliban' is in the middle of Limbo, but within the poem 'limbo' brings a glimpse of freedom.

My description of *Islands* is misleading, insofar as it implies a sequential, historical narrative. Part of Brathwaite's project is to collapse different historical moments, to read the present by making the past simultaneous with it:

> It was December second, nineteen fifty-six.
> It was the first of August eighteen thirty-eight.
> It was the twelfth October fourteen ninety-two.
>
> How many bangs how many revolutions?

The poem begins in Castro's Havana, but it views modern Cuban history through the longer perspective that reaches back to Columbus' first sighting of land on his voyage in 1492. Brathwaite is himself a learned historian of the Caribbean, and such elisions are marks of an historical–artistic technique and attitude remarkably similar to those of Renaissance humanism. So too is the opening stanza of 'Caliban', with its holding together of prophets past and present, its sense that everything is already known but is always having to be learned again:

> Ninety-five per cent of my people poor
> ninety-five per cent of my people black
> ninety-five per cent of my people dead
> you have heard it all before O Leviticus O
>   Jeremiah O Jean-Paul Sartre

Sartre is there because he wrote the preface to Fanon's *Wretched of the Earth*, but the voice who is speaking these lines is not that of the European prophet. The latter's empathetic voicing with the wretched could not but itself be a form of colonialism, of Prospering – I, Jean-Paul Sartre, great white French intellectual, speak with and hence for the Other. But when Brathwaite replies, the white man is not the subject: he is addressed with an 'O', he becomes the other. This change from object to subject is crucial to the creative renewal of the once oppressed – hence the witty title of the New Accent study of postcolonial writing, *The Empire Writes Back*.[4]

When it is Caliban who writes back, as in this poem, the voice is multiple. 'Caliban', after all, is the creation of another great white European. The Cuban revolutionary writer Roberto Fernández Retamar argued that the position of Caliban is the only available one for the 'New World' writer: he has no choice but to use the tool – the language – bequeathed to him by Prospero. At school in Barbados, Brathwaite had to read Shakespeare, Jane Austen and George Eliot: 'British literature and literary forms, the models which had very little to do, really, with the environment and the reality of non-Europe.'[5] He seized on Caliban because Caliban *could* be read as having a great deal to do with his own environment and reality, because (as Lamming did) he found in Caliban a prophecy of his own historical situation. It is a usable prophecy exactly because – unlike Sartre's – it is not directly couched as such. There is a certain scepticism in the attitude to Jean-Paul Sartre since he comes, as Retamar puts it, from the 'elsewhere' of the European metropolis, 'the colonizing centers, whose "right wings" have exploited us and whose supposed "left wings" have pretended and continue to pretend to guide us with pious solicitude'.[6] It is different with Shakespeare. Because of what Keats called his negative capability, because he was not trying to guide Retamar's and Brathwaite's 'us' with pious solicitude, they have no compunction about adopting one of his voices.

The process of writing back necessitates the creation of a new style, and here too Caliban can help. Brathwaite says of the English poetic mainstream: 'the pentameter remained, and it carries with it a certain kind of experience, which is not the experience of a hurricane. The hurricane does not roar in pentameters. And that's the problem: how do you get a rhythm which approximates the *natural* experience, the *environmental* experience?' The answer is in '*nation language*, which is the kind of English spoken by the people who were brought to the Caribbean, not the official English now, but the language of slaves and labourers'. The language, that is to say, which binds, indeed works to create, the black nation; this language and this nation initially cannot help but be parasitic upon the colonizing language and nation, as Caliban is upon Prospero, yet as they develop they take on their own identity, their own freedom.

How does nation language sound? It is 'the *submerged* area of that dialect which is much more closely allied to the African aspect of experience in the Caribbean. It may be in English: but often it is an English which is like a howl, or a shout or a machine-gun or the wind or a wave.' Many of Brathwaite's poems move between the voices of the English tradition and of nation. In his lecture *History of the Voice*, from which I have been quoting this account of nation language, Brathwaite cites John Figueroa's 'Portrait of a Woman' as an example of double-voiced West Indian poetry: 'the "classical", even *Prosperian element* – the *most* part of the poem – is in English. The marginal bit, that of the voice and status of the domestic helper, Caliban's sister, is in a nation but a nation still sticky and wet with the interposition of dialect.'[7] Section one of 'Caliban' is in traditional English: 'Ninety-five per cent of my people poor' is a pentameter. But in sections two and three Caliban speaks in the rhythms of nation:

>   And
>   Ban
>   Ban
>   Cal-
>   iban
>   like to play
>   pan
>   at the Car-
>   nival;
>   pran-
>   cing up to the lim-
>   bo silence
>   down
>   down
>   down
>   so the god won't drown
>   him
>   down
>   down
>   down
>   to the is-
>   land town

The allusion here is of course to 'Ban, Ban, Ca-Caliban' in *The Tempest*'s song of rebellion, 'No more dams I'll make for fish'. Caliban expresses his freedom by deconstructing the name that Prospero has given him; the vigorous rhythm of his song is an affront to Prospero's rod-like pentameter world. It may be imagined as a rudimentary form of nation language. For Shakespeare's Caliban, 'Freedom, high-day!' is an illusion: he has merely exchanged one master, one god, for another. Brathwaite revises the situation by combining Caliban's anthem of freedom with Ariel's song of watery metamorphosis, 'Full fathom five'. When the Caribbean Caliban bends his back and passes beneath the limbo stick, the music and dance transform him: because he has gone

> down
> down
> down

he can rise

> up
> up
> up

A note in Brathwaite's glossary reminds us that 'limbo' is not only a state of spiritual darkness and exclusion, it is also

a dance in which the participants have to move, with their bodies thrown backwards and without any aid whatsoever under a stick which is lowered at every successfully completed passage under it, until the stick is practically touching the ground. It is said to have originated – a necessary therapy – after the experience of the cramped conditions between the slaveship decks of the Middle Passage.[8]

The limbo is first performed with

> eyes
> shut tight
> and the whip light
> crawl-
> ing round the ship
> where his free-
> dom drowns.

But it becomes a means to freedom and celebration:

> sun coming up
> and the drummers are praising me
>
> out of the dark
> and the dumb gods are raising me
>
> up
> up
> up
>
> and the music is saving me

In Ariel's song, Alonso has gone down, down, down, but as the play unfolds we watch his soul rise up, up, up. From recognition of sin in act 3,

> Methought the billows spoke and told me of it,
> The winds did sing it to me, and the thunder,
> That deep and dreadful organ-pipe, pronounced
> The name of Prosper. It did bass my trespass.
>
> (3.3.96–9)

he passes to penitence in act 5: 'Thy dukedom I resign, and do entreat / Thou pardon me my wrongs' (5.1.120–1). In Brathwaite's poem, Caliban follows a similar course – down, then up – by means of the limbo dance.

The key difference is in the kind of god. Alonso's is a high Renaissance Christian God, reached through the linguistic formality of confession. The Caribbean Caliban is raised by gods who are dumb save in the music; as Brathwaite puts it in 'The Making of the Drum', a poem of great importance in *Masks*:

> God is dumb
> until the drum
> speaks

In each case, human art – Prospero's magic, the drummer and the dancer – brings about a perception of something named as divine. But where the hurricane of Alonso's god roars in pentameters, Brathwaite's Caliban finds a god of his own environment and culture. It is a defining characteristic of Shakespeare's Caliban that he hears the music of the isle, and that Prospero's failure to understand this must vitiate any monovocal Prosperian reading of the play; the music of the isle is the key to Brathwaite's poetry too. But he makes a different music, that of his own isles, of Afro-Caribbean culture.

That culture is seen to be close to nature in a way that has been renounced by western man. The 'modernization' (westernization, Americanization) of Havana described in the first part of 'Caliban' is decadent ('the police toured the gambling houses / wearing their dark glasses / and collected tribute'). That modernization is also an assault on nature. Where Ariel's song imagines a creative transformation from dead bone to living coral, economic progress is conceived here as the destructive transformation of living coral into dead concrete:

out of the living stone, out of the living bone
or coral, these dead
towers; out of the coney
islands of our mind-

less architects, this death
of sons, of songs, of sunshine;
out of this dearth of coo ru coos, home-
less pigeons, this perturbation that does not signal health.

When Caliban finds the god in the dance, what he is really achieving is
a reunification with nature. The movement is the same as that in Aimé
Césaire's adaptation *Une tempête*, where Prospero is anti-nature and
Caliban's freedom means a unification of his voice with those of the
birds and the surf. For Brathwaite, the legacy of European and American empire in the Antilles is the death not only of sons of Africa, but
also of songs, of sunshine, of birds, of coral.

The hyphen across the stanza ending passes judgement on western
man. Economic development, high-rise apartments resembling rabbit
hutches, come 'out of the coney / islands of our mind' – but the 'mind'
is transformed into 'our mindless architects'. As Robert Pogue Harrison
has demonstrated in his remarkable book, *Forests*, imperialism has
always brought with it deforestation and the consuming of natural
resources. Since the Enlightenment privileging of 'mind', western man
has mapped his own place in the world so as to justify this:

In his *Discourse on Method* Descartes compares the authority of tradition to a
forest of error, beyond which lies the promised land of reason. Once he arrives
in that promised land, Descartes redefines his relation not only to tradition but
also to nature in its totality. The new Cartesian distinction between the *res
cogitans*, or thinking self, and the *res extensa*, or embodied substance, sets up the
terms for the objectivity of science and the abstraction from historicity, location, nature, and culture. What interests us about Descartes in this context is
the fact that he sought to empower the subject of knowledge in such a way
that, through its application of mathematical method, humanity could achieve
what he called 'mastery and possession of nature'.[9]

Brathwaite's turn of 'mind' to 'mindless' is a rebuke to the *res cogitans* for
its quest to master nature.

The poem 'Caliban', then, is not only about culture against culture,
white against black, European against African ways of seeing; it is
also about culture against nature. This raises doubts about the New
Iconoclast assumption that *The Tempest* must be read only in terms of
cultural confrontation. Readers of the play in relation to the 'discourse

of colonialism' focus on Prospero and Caliban because their troubled relationship seems to encourage talk of hostile exchange between culture and culture. Such readers have political reasons for denying the possibility of exchange between culture and nature; nature, they say, is just someone else's culture. Eric Cheyfitz is typical when he writes in *The Poetics of Imperialism*: 'In *The Tempest* nature is not nature but culture.'[10] Césaire's and Brathwaite's linking of Caliban with nature proposes something very different. It seems to me that in our current ecological crisis, questions of culture's relationship to nature are of as great importance as questions of 'multiculturalism'. There are, however, problems with a model which praises black culture for being in touch with nature in a way that white culture isn't, for if imported into 'our' way of thinking it runs the risk of retaining the image of black traditions as 'other' – only this time a desirably primal, earth-true other. So in thinking about a rereading of *The Tempest* in terms of culture and nature, I shall follow an alternative track and consider an improvisation on the voice of Ariel – a voice which has been oddly silenced by recent criticism's obsession with Caliban.

In 1822, the last year of his life, Percy Bysshe Shelley wrote a group of lyric poems to his friend Jane Williams. One of them is called 'With a Guitar. To Jane'. It begins:

> Ariel to Miranda; – Take
> This slave of music for the sake
> Of him who is the slave of thee.[11]

Written in the same tetrameter as Prospero's epilogue, it is a kind of second epilogue to *The Tempest* from Ariel's point of view. Jane is Miranda, her husband Edward Williams is Ferdinand, and Shelley himself, Ariel. The poem is a 'token / Of more than ever can be spoken'; it lightly and touchingly mediates Shelley's admiration for Jane through the fantasy of Ariel being silently and unrequitedly in love with Miranda. Shelley's ideal or intellectual love finds its analogy in Ariel's nature as a disembodied spirit of fire and air; the impossibility of that love's realization in the material world is expressed in an image suggestive of Ariel's fate at the hands of Sycorax: 'And now, alas! the poor sprite is / Imprisoned for some fault of his / In a body like a grave.' The elegant conceit which allows the poet/lover out of his bind is that the spirit of his art will be held in the guitar which he gives Jane together with the poem, and that when she plays it he will be able to continue serving her as she makes music out of him.

But where does the guitar come from?

> The artist who this idol wrought
> To echo all harmonious thought
> Felled a tree, while on the steep
> The woods were in their winter sleep
> Rocked in that repose divine
> On the wind-swept Apennine.

To make a guitar, you must fell a tree; to harness the power of Ariel, you must split open a pine. Shelley's poem claims that because it was felled while sleeping in winter, the tree 'felt no pain' and that now it is a guitar it is living 'in happier form again'. In the light of Shelley's neo-platonism, the latter phrase may be presumed to imply that in its guitar-form the tree transcends its original particular Apennine hill-side and makes a music which holds together

> all harmonies
> Of the plains and of the skies,
> Of the forests and the mountains,
> And the many-voiced fountains,
> The clearest echoes of the hills,
> The softest notes of falling rills,
> The melodies of birds and bees,
> The murmuring of summer seas,
> And pattering rain and breathing dew
> And airs of evening.

In this account, art – the music of the guitar which is metonymic of the poem itself – offers the ideal or intellectual form of nature. In *The Tempest*, it is in response to Stefano and Trinculo's hearing of Ariel's music that Caliban speaks of how he has sometimes heard something which a Renaissance audience would have thought of as approximating to the music of the spheres. So here, the Ariel music of the guitar knows

> That seldom heard mysterious sound,
> Which, driven on its diurnal round
> As it floats through boundless day
> Our world enkindles on its way.

In another sense, however, this music does not constitute nature perfected. Early in each of the poem's two verse-paragraphs there is a noun which questions the status of the guitar. In the first, it is a 'slave': Prospero uses that word of Ariel, but does so more frequently of Caliban. In the first chapter of *A Philosophical View of Reform*, Shelley had described the struggle for liberty in terms of the abolition of slavery and the enfranchisement of poetry; the presence of the word 'slave' here, with its Calibanesque undertow, suggests that poetry may nevertheless be dependent on certain enslavements of its own. And in the second verse-paragraph there is a suggestion of Bacon's term for false mental images: 'The artist who this *idol* wrought'. The apparently ideal may in fact be an idol. The premise of Ariel's unrequited love for Miranda and the positioning of the poem as a second epilogue to *The Tempest* establish a sense of loss, an elegiac tone, that cannot be unwritten by the gift of the guitar. 'Slave', 'idol' and 'felled' break up the harmonious movement of the couplets; 'wrought', twice used of the making of the guitar, suggests a beating into shape, the hard working of iron as well as wood. If something has to be wrought, resistance is implied:

>   – and so this tree –
> O that such our death may be –
> Died in sleep, and felt no pain.

That the tree died in sleep and felt no pain implies that a tree might be killed while awake and feel pain; an optative like the parenthetic 'may' in these lines is always provoked by fear of its forceful opposite.

The price of art is the destruction of a living tree. You can't have music without dead wood; you can't have poetry without paper. You create culture by enslaving nature. Prospero makes gape a pine and threatens to rend an oak in order to display his power; in this, he is anti-nature. His technology is an image of that 'mastery and possession of nature' which Descartes believed was within the grasp of *res cogitans*, the mind of man. Shelley was an inheritor of Cartesian dualism – his neo-platonism was an attempt to get round it – and it does seem to me that at a profound level his poem registers the irony of our post-Cartesian condition. What are the highest things that the guitar tells of? They are *res extensa*: plains, skies, forests, mountains, birds, bees, seas, rain and dew. Art is an attempt to recover the very thing which has been destroyed so that art can be made.

Nevertheless, the end of *The Tempest* is still there as an image of the possibility of renunciation of the claim to mastery and possession of nature. We don't know where Caliban goes at the end of the play, but we do know that Ariel is free and that the island will be his again. In a general sense, *The Tempest* continues to function as an exemplary humanist text because it is a vehicle through which later cultures can reflect on pressing contemporary concerns. Formally speaking, it achieves this through its multivocality: it does not offer the sole voice of Prospero, it also enables poets like Browning, Brathwaite and Césaire to think as Caliban, Shelley to think as Ariel and even as the tree in which Ariel was confined. In a particular sense, *The Tempest* was and remains an exemplary humanist text because it is set on an island that is its own place. In the sixteenth century, the imaginary island was a place in which one could reflect upon the ideal society in the manner of More's *Utopia*. In the twenty-first century, we will need to imagine an island which Prospero has left, an ecosystem which man must be content to leave alone. We have gone quite a long way towards recognizing the rights of Caliban. Next we will need to set Ariel free.

First published in *Shakespeare Survey 48*, 1995

NOTES

1 *The Tempest*, ed. Stephen Orgel (Oxford, 1987), p. 24 n.
2 Eric Cheyfitz, *The Poetics of Imperialism: Translation and Colonization from 'The Tempest' to 'Tarzan'* (New York and Oxford, 1991), p. 23.
3 Published together as *The Arrivants* (Oxford, 1973).
4 Bill Ashcroft, Gareth Griffiths and Helen Tiffin, *The Empire Writes Back: Theory and Practice in Post-colonial Literatures* (London and New York, 1989).
5 Edward Brathwaite, *History of the Voice: The Development of Nation Language in Anglophone Caribbean Poetry* (London and Port of Spain, 1984), p. 8.
6 Roberto Fernández Retamar, 'Caliban', *Massachusetts Review* 15 (1974), 7.
7 *History of the Voice*, p. 38. Previous quotations from pp. 10, 5, 13.
8 *The Arrivants*, p. 274.
9 Robert Pogue Harrison, *Forests: The Shadow of Civilization* (Chicago and London, 1992), pp. 107–8.
10 Cheyfitz, *Poetics of Imperialism*, p. 26.
11 The poem was first published in 1832; I quote the text based on the original manuscript, repr. in *Shelley's Poetry and Prose*, ed. Donald H. Reiman and Sharon B. Powers (New York, 1977), pp. 449–51.

CHAPTER 12

Casting black actors: beyond Othellophilia

Celia R. Daileader

If you have seen Kenneth Branagh's *Hamlet*, you might recall the opening shot of a black soldier framed by snowfall, keeping watch outside Elsinore. The role of Francisco – the guard who ends his shift as the play begins – is only remarkable for the ominous line, "Tis bitter cold, / And I am sick at heart' (1.1.8–9),[1] but Branagh has made this minor part more memorable by way of several directorial flourishes, not the least of which is the race of the actor. And indeed the phrase 'out in the cold' might seem to apply to any Shakespearian actor of colour – particularly one trying to make his mark in the historically white Royal Shakespeare Company. But in fact the year 1996, in which Ray Fearon appeared in Branagh's *Hamlet*, was indeed a turning-point for the actor who had made his RSC debut as the scorned 'blackamoor' suitor in *The Merchant of Venice* (1993). First winning acclaim as Brachiano in John Webster's *The White Devil*, Fearon then took on another RSC role usually reserved for whites: Paris in *Troilus and Cressida*. From here it was a short leap to stardom in an unprecedented cross-racial *Romeo and Juliet* (1997).

On one level, Fearon's role as Romeo did support Peter Holland's statement that 'companies like the RSC now regularly include black actors and are developing the practice of . . . "non-traditional" . . . [or] "colour-blind casting"'.[2] But a shadow hung over this production, manifested most tangibly in the racially motivated assault on three of the actors in the streets of Brussels, an incident which left Fearon's hand in a cast when I saw the play.[3] Not that it was his cast alone – both a reminder of those realities we attend theatre to escape, and ironically suiting the character whom one critic dubbed a 'street-fighting' Romeo[4] – which dampened my enthusiasm for this visually stunning and critically acclaimed multiracial production. Having followed Fearon's history with the RSC, I was haunted by the sense that he was being groomed for one role alone. If he was lucky, very lucky, he would get to play Othello next.

In fact, Fearon did next play Othello – in 1999, as I completed this essay – and alongside the same actress who played Juliet, a point whose significance I hope eventually to make clear. To understand this turn in a seemingly direct trajectory from margin to centre, we will need to go back to its point of origin, the year 1996. Fearon's roles in *Troilus* and in *White Devil* appear, at first glance, to represent non-traditional casting on the part of their directors, Ian Judge and Gale Edwards, respectively. However, the similarities between Fearon's Paris and his Brachiano reveal racial stereotypes operating on (at least) a subliminal level in both productions. In this essay, I will argue that these breakthrough performances did not, in fact, result from colour-blind casting, though reviews of both plays turned a blind eye to the fact. Indeed, the sexual politics of each play so similarly positions Fearon's character that he seemed to be playing the same character in both – and the more one looks at that character, the more he looks like Othello.

This phenomenon I call 'Othellophilia' has disturbing implications for black actors with Shakespearian aspirations. Equally urgent, however, are the feminist implications of this dramaturgical and political problem, for *Othello*'s racialist rhetoric hinges upon the pairing of a black man and a white woman in such a way as to render the former a vehicle for misogynist figurations of a woman's sexual besmirching or 'blackening', with all the voyeuristic (and potentially racist) titillation such a spectacle provides. Kim Hall has demonstrated the overlap between racism and misogyny in early modern representations of gender and racial difference;[5] I contend that the modern Anglo-American myth of the sexually potent black male and his morally dubious white female target can be traced to the discourses analysed by Hall and in particular to *Othello*. Moreover, the fascination with this theatrical fable of 'black on white' sex virtually ensures its repetition on the classical stage – whether conscious or unconscious on the part of the director and of the audience he or she aims to please.

Because directors and audience create the feedback loop which vitalizes theatre, reviews of a production can open a window into the cultural forces shaping it. This is not, of course, a simple dynamic of mirroring or symbiosis: reviews of a play are almost never uniform, and any one review may as easily reflect the director's worst nightmare as his or her best intentions. Still, the critics are, if not representative of the audience, at least the most vocal segment of it, and reviews, as the most widely disseminated record of specific theatrical productions, do go on to constitute cultural memory. Barbara Hodgdon instructs us to study not only 'director–*auteurs* and the ideo-texts of their *mise-en-scènes*', but also 'the point of historical reception, where "theatre" collides with spectators who may transform it into "a strange, eventful history"'.[6] Thus, in comparing these two cross-racial RSC productions, the critics' polite silence on the matter of race will have to be circumvented. This will prove easier than one might expect, for the sexual politics of the two plays – enhanced by each director's erotic choreography – turns out to have been deeply bound up with the cross-racial casting of Shakespeare's and Webster's adulterous couples. And the critics had much to say about sex in these very *racy* productions.

Given the complicated relations among the dramatic text, its production on stage and its reception by the critics, this chapter will proceed in four stages: one, reviewing the history of the RSC in its casting of black males;[7] two, a comparison of *Troilus* and *White Devil* with regard to their treatment of adultery and related patterns of black/white imagery; three, a discussion of reviews of these two productions and the ways in which the critics unconsciously replicated the texts' racialized language; and finally, four, which examines a photograph from *Troilus* and observes the way the camera captured these undercurrents. At this stage, I hope we can reconstruct the scene of the casting crime in *Troilus*, and see the way Othellophilia, with its attendant opportunities for something approaching biracial porn, functions to exploit both white women *and* black men. With this critical lens in place, we can go forth equipped to examine future cases of cross-racial casting, and to measure our progress towards a more egalitarian classical theatre.

I have focused exclusively on the RSC because it is the world's most prominent theatre company devoted to Shakespeare and his contemporaries: the sheer numbers attending its productions, its high visibility and cultural clout encourage other Shakespeare companies to follow where it leads. Needless to say, the form of stereotyping discussed in this essay is pandemic to Anglo-American culture and not unique to a handful of British directors. In fact, it could be argued that Othellophilia is a positive sign; its very presence indicates some effort at more inclusive casting, however mixed the results. In contrast to the RSC, its Canadian counterpart, the Stratford Festival, has cast few black actors in *any* non-traditional Shakespearian roles, no less in roles as substantial and as 'white' as that of Romeo or Paris. On the other hand, the RSC's casting record after 1962 quite literally pales when compared to the records of, respectively, Joseph Papp, the Shakespeare Festival in Stratford, Connecticut, or the Alabama Shakespeare Festival, during

the same decades.[8] This observation highlights a curious reversal in the
history of black Shakespearian performance, as pointed out by Errol
Hill: the British theatre, which in 1930 launched Paul Robeson's Shakespearian career in casting him as one of the earliest black Othellos,
became after the Second World War less accommodating of black
Shakespearians than the traditionally racist American theatres which
had initially driven Robeson to London, as it had his predecessors,
Ira Aldridge and Morgan Smith.[9] The reversal might, ironically, have
something to do with desegregation, posing the painful necessity that
America confront its racial problems. In the same way, my experience
teaching Shakespeare to black and white students at the University of
Alabama, and viewing mixed-race performances before mixed-race
audiences at our own ASF, has brought to my attention the heightened
awareness which may arise in response to the stigma of racism:
Alabamians – like, to a lesser degree, all Americans – cannot afford
to be complacent. So I hope my British readers will forgive a scholar
from the American South for taking up the topic of racial stereotypes
in their theatres and in their theatre reviews. As the proverb goes, the
old offender is the best keeper.

But perhaps my anxieties are groundless. Perhaps playing Othello
will prove, not the apotheosis of Fearon's RSC career, but merely a
stepping-stone to bigger, 'whiter' tragic roles like Hamlet or Coriolanus.
This season, in fact, the company has taken in a wealth of non-white
actors – comprising some 25 per cent of their ranks – in order to stage
Oroonoko; this cast could also change the face of their Shakespeare.
Either way, the RSC is at a crossroads. What better time to look back
and take stock?

BLACK MALES IN THE RSC: A BRIEF OVERVIEW

Shakespeare penned only three racially marked adult male roles: Aaron
in *Titus Andronicus*, the Prince of Morocco in *The Merchant of Venice* and
Othello. That amounts to three out of some 1,100 total dramatis personae, or approximately one quarter of 1 per cent. The RSC, in the early
modern plays which constitute the bulk of its repertoire, has tended to
confine black actors to these three roles or to servant figures and other
minor characters. The exceptions to this rule, over the past two decades,
arise mainly in relation to the accomplishments of Hugh Quarshie,
who joined the company in the early 1980s to play Shakespeare's demonic
Moor, Aaron (in a double-billing which also cast him as an outlaw in

2 Hugh Quarshie as Aaron in *Titus Andronicus*, Royal Shakespeare Company, 1982

3 Hugh Quarshie as Tybalt in *Romeo and Juliet*, Royal Shakespeare Company, 1986

The Two Gentlemen of Verona), but who made his big break in 1982 when he took over, after opening night, the role of Hotspur in *1 Henry IV*.[10] Other triumphs against tradition followed: all in one year, 1986, Quarshie played Tybalt in *Romeo*, Arcite in *The Two Noble Kinsmen*, and Banquo in *Macbeth*. In time, Quarshie went on to play Mark Antony in *Julius Caesar* (1995), as well as two other classic, white roles: Belville in Aphra Behn's *The Rover* (1986) and Loveless in Sir John Vanbrugh's *The Relapse* (1995).

Although Quarshie's classical credentials are impressive, many of these seeming breaks with tradition, upon closer examination, show that race did matter in dramaturgy – and whether or not race mattered in casting, it clearly had an impact on the reviews. Let us take, for instance, Quarshie's Arcite, whose pairing with a white Palamon added a contemporary political dimension to their quarrel, as well as preventing the audience from confusing the two cousins. Here is one reviewer's mode of contrasting the men: 'Murphy speaks his lines heroically . . . and Quarshie looks the handsome part.'[11] Other productions required the actor, while not playing a 'blackamoor', to play a more contemporary racial stereotype. In the modernized 1986 *Romeo*, for instance, Quarshie's Tybalt donned black leather and wielded a chain (replaced, at the

Capulet ball, by a saxophone). The critics ate it up. Exclamations like 'Wow! Shakespeare swings!'[12] were prompted by the sensational opening sequence, but perhaps most of all by Quarshie's variously described 'black thug of a Tybalt',[13] his 'flash-grinning, leather-trim, chain-wielding Tybalt',[14] his 'chain-wielding black Tybalt in matching leather',[15] his 'black Tybalt in black leather',[16] or what you will. Indeed, the role made such an impression that one critic could not resist bringing it up months later in reference to Quarshie's Banquo, one of the few genuinely colour-blind roles the actor has played for the RSC, here inexplicably inspiring the most overtly racist remark that I have come across during this study: 'Hugh Quarshie plays Banquo as Harry Belafonte. Mr Quarshie is an actor of very precise gifts; he has only two expressions: the first is "menace" and largely consists in wearing black leather . . . ; the second is "decency" and involves smiling for no apparent reason.'[17]

And this quote may indeed touch upon the Catch-22 of colour-blind casting: even when the director is 'blind' to 'colour', the audience often will not be. With the exception of the critic quoted above, Quarshie's 'amiable' Banquo was commended;[18] not so his Mark Antony, whose performance in the funeral oration – perhaps haunted by memories of Martin Luther King – was almost universally deemed 'lacking . . . electricity'.[19] Again, though, I would not harbour such suspicions if the critics had proven themselves truly colour-blind. One critic (raising, again, the spectre of that renowned Calypso-singing Shakespearian) wondered 'why Mark Antony swans around with his robe flapping open, unless it is to emphasize [the fact that] Hugh Quarshie is as handsome as Harry Belafonte'. The gratuitous nudity is something I too found alarming, for reasons which will later be discussed, but the same critic then linked this flash of skin to 'the moral dilemma that caused the collapse of Rome'.[20] No other critic commented on this 'moral . . . collapse', though others did note Quarshie's bare chest, 'skimpy briefs',[21] and 'becoming nappy and nightshirt'.[22]

And speaking of moral decay, I have yet to mention Quarshie's role as Mephistopheles in Goethe's *Faust*, which, though technically a modern play and therefore outside the scope of this essay, warrants consideration due to the legend's medieval origin, first dramatized in the Renaissance as Christopher Marlowe's *Doctor Faustus*. Also worthy of note is the casting of two separate RSC productions of Marlowe's version, in the light of which a striking pattern emerges. Given Quarshie's role as Mephistopheles in 1995, it seems too strange a coincidence that an earlier *Faustus* (1989) had cast black actor Dhobi Oparei as Lucifer, and that a later *Faustus* (1997) cast Joseph Mydell as yet another black Mephistopheles.[23] But let us stick to Quarshie, for the sake of argument. Interestingly, by 1995 the critics had grown reluctant to comment on race; this is a pattern which clearly separates the eighties' reviews from those of the nineties. Nonetheless, Quarshie – who appeared in one scene in dark shades and a leopard-skin jacket – was universally praised as a 'coolest of cool' Mephistopheles;[24] indeed, in a pattern which is already growing familiar, critics dwelt on the 'smart suits' and 'smooth' charm of this 'cool dude' of a devil.[25] Strangely enough, no one brought up the fact that in the Renaissance, the devil was described as black – a notion which makes possible Webster's oxymoron, *White Devil*. But Webster's eponymous devil, and the demonic in general, will be given fuller treatment below.

Also relevant are Quarshie's roles in non-Shakespearian seventeenth-century plays. As a 'black soldier of fortune'[26] in a 1987 production of *The Rover* – aptly described by one critic as 'sheer sexual adventure'[27] – Quarshie drew high praise, and perhaps paved the way for his eventual stardom in another Restoration sex-comedy, *The Relapse*. Far from merely swanning about in an open robe, Quarshie's Loveless, in Ian Judge's 1995 production, was wheeled onstage in a rumpled bed, naked from (as it turns out) the waist up (fig. 4). When eventually a woman emerged from under the blankets, dressed in a prudish white nightie and bonnet, it was not her presence in bed which startled me so much as the sartorial contrast, which in fact set the tone for this very be-ribboned and be-powdered production. Quarshie's nudity, in the first scene, may have suited his role as the hypersexual adulterer-to-be whose 'relapse' into debauchery drives the main plot – but the fact that his was the *only* exposed torso, in a production which literally revolved around an onstage bed, seemed odd. Fortunately, by this point in Quarshie's career the critics had ceased comparing him to Harry Belafonte, but nonetheless, the bed, and Quarshie's chest, attracted much attention. And if one or two critics found the production, and Quarshie's Loveless, strangely *not* sexy, I am not terribly surprised.[28] In retrospect it looks as though Judge was simply warming up. He had yet to get his hands on Ray Fearon.

WHAT THE TEXTS SAY

Errol Hill has argued that success in the role of Othello is 'necessary to legitimize the black performer's admission to the professional ranks of

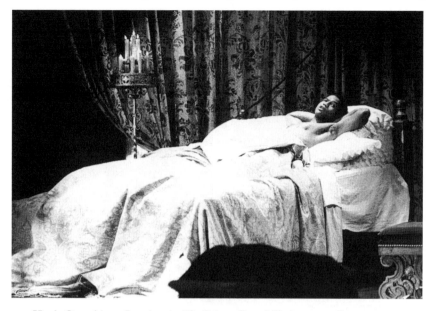

4 Hugh Quarshie as Loveless in *The Relapse*, Royal Shakespeare Company, 1995

the Western dramatic stage'.[29] The good news is that Quarshie seems to have broken this norm, thus setting the precedent for Fearon: by 1998, both actors had achieved a measure of success in the RSC *without* playing Othello. In fact, the more senior actor has recently made known his resistance to the role, which he sees as reinforcing racist stereotypes.[30] On the other hand, the above overview of Quarshie's career has brought certain recurrent themes to light, all of which come into play in *Othello* and hence in Othellophilia: violence, physicality, sexuality, the demonic; black leather, leopard skin, black nudity against white dishabille. These elements are not the *whole* picture, but they are a prominent part of the picture. Now we must ask whether Fearon's work fits within this frame.

As Fearon's first two major RSC roles, Webster's Duke and Shakespeare's Prince in *Troilus and Cressida* share one important trait: adulterous, lawless, all-consuming lust. Both stop at nothing in their pursuit of a woman, Brachiano plotting murder and Paris starting a war. Paris and Helen, though not the protagonists of the play, nonetheless constitute the erotic centre of the narrative: their adultery both generates and saturates the plot ('All the argument is a whore and a cuckold', as Thersites puts it (2.3.72)), and their affair both predates and outlives the titular relationship. Thus, in both productions, the transgressive nature

5 Ray Fearon as Brachiano in *The White Devil*, Royal Shakespeare Company, 1996

of the central, tragic coupling was reiterated in its cross-racial casting, just as the cross-racial nature of *Othello*'s central coupling renders it transgressive even in marriage. Miscegenation, after all, is adultery writ large.

Both Brachiano and Paris are, like Othello, thieves of women: in their case, the woman is stolen from her husband, not her father, but Shakespeare often blurs the distinction, as in Brabanzio's warning to Othello: 'She has deceived her father, and may thee' (1.3.292). Both men's sexuality, hence, is linked with aggression, with breached boundaries and anti-social, animalistic drives. Whether Helen ran off or was abducted, whether Desdemona eloped or was bewitched actually makes little difference to the position of her lover *vis-à-vis* the power structure he has defied. This may be why both Paris' and Brachiano's sexual relationships require a (white) male voyeuristic commentator/pimp who is as vital as an Iago in tickling (or enraging) the audience. As James Andreas notes, 'sexual encounters between the races are not private moments', but 'represent a public shattering of the racist taboo and as such demand an audience'.[31]

Both Brachiano and Paris – whatever the race of the actor – also require a white mistress, in ways that call attention to the nexus of race and gender in the uses of the black/white binarism. Both texts – from Webster's oxymoronic title to Shakespeare's harping on Helen's 'marvellous white' (1.2.132) skin – inscribe 'whiteness' as an essential feature of these heroines, a feature crucial in creating the irony of their moral or sexual 'soiling'. Prefigured in the 'fair devil' (3.3.479) Othello sees in his bride, these white sinners are Desdemonas that *did*. As Ania Loomba notes, 'In *The White Devil*, "blackness" is a signifier for various forms of socially unacceptable behavior', not the least of which is female sexual transgression, metaphorized in Vittoria's 'Moorish' servant, Zanche, the 'black fury' to her mistress's 'devil in crystal'.[32] Kim Hall has analysed at length the implications for black/feminist criticism of these popular early modern skin-tone tropes; she notes that 'Frequently, "black" in Renaissance discourses is opposed not to "white" but to "beauty" or "fairness", and these terms most often refer to the appearance or moral states of women . . .' Hence, 'the polarity of dark and light is most often worked out in representations of black men and white women'.[33] In these two plays, though, the visual polarity indicates a hidden moral parity: the point is the possibility of finding, inside a white woman, 'a soul so black' (3.2.183–4).[34]

In the case of the 1996 production of *White Devil*, the heroine's moral 'blackness' is explicit in the programme illustration, wherein a darkly lipsticked and very pale Vittoria, photographed only from nose to hip-level, suggestively grips her own low-cut, white bodice with hands gloved in black. This gloved self-caress, and the *trompe-l'œil* by which the hands may not initially seem to belong to Vittoria, implies that the black Brachiano is a part of her, the personification of her 'black deeds' (5.6.300), the object of her 'black lust' (2.2.7).

Hall's exploration of the early modern cult of 'fairness' in its relationship to racial anxieties invites us to pay closer attention to beauty tropes which might otherwise be dismissed as trivial – for instance, references to sunburn and cosmetic use, and the recurrent trope of whitewashing, or 'washing the Ethiope'.[35] Along these lines, *Troilus and Cressida*'s treatment of pigmentation, especially with regard to Helen, takes on certain racist overtones which become even more pronounced in the light of Judge's casting. Helen's hair-colour is mentioned in the very first scene, introducing an on-going discussion of beauty and complexion which allows Pandarus to compare Helen and Paris to the titular couple.[36] By the same token, the sexual sullying of the 'fair . . . , fair' Helen (3.1.45) is a matter of great concern in the play. Troilus, in urging the Trojans to continue keeping her, insists, 'We turn not back the silks upon the merchant / When we have soiled them' (2.2.69–70) – a statement echoed almost verbatim in *The White Devil* ('Will any mercer take another's ware / When once 'tis tous'd and sullied?' (4.2.156–7)). Diomed gives the cuckolded Menelaus credit for his willingness to have his wife back, 'Not making any scruple of her soil' (4.1.53–7). Paris, on the other hand, believes they can 'have the soil of her fair rape / Wiped off in honourable keeping her' (2.2.148–9).

The oxymoronic 'fair rape' (like that of 'white devil') is ideologically loaded – as is evident in the awkward treatment of the phrase by the Riverside editors, who (speaking of whitewashing) provide the unhelpful gloss, 'the abduction of her fair self'.[37] I grant that sources disagree on Helen's role in her own *raptus*, and Shakespeare hardly portrays her as suffering, but nonetheless, as Suzanne Gossett points out, to Jacobean culture it was not inconceivable that a woman might marry her rapist.[38] To conclude that Shakespeare did not mean to describe the rape itself as 'fair' is to slight both syntax and historical context, and to elide the play's complicated sexual politics. Although my primary concern here is not the problem of Helen's consent, but rather the structural similarities between Paris, Brachiano and Othello, the editorial obfuscation required to rescue the concept of fairness from contact with a polluted noun has wider ideological implications. But we will soon view a picture of this 'fair rape', and decide for ourselves whether that's what it is.

I have tried to suggest, above, that the pairing of Helen and Vittoria with a black lover in these two RSC productions simply carried through – in metadramatical fashion – the logic of the sexual allegory embedded in each text. Once again, though, the critics' attempts at what a cynic might call 'nineties' sensitivity' occluded their perception of this racial dynamic, even while their language, in many ways, reinforced it. Both productions enjoyed, on the whole, favourable reviews, as did Fearon's performances in each. Both productions were described in similar terms, with critics emphasizing three particular qualities: sex, gore and 'darkness'.

'Full-blooded, unequivocally erotic', remarked one rave review of Webster's play; [39] that first modifier was a favourite, appearing in three out of the ten reviews I studied. The relationship between Vittoria and Brachiano was described as 'not so much a love-affair as a lust-affair, intensely and ruthlessly erotic'.[40] 'The stage steams with lust', declared another (in his excitement neglecting his Shakespearian glossary), 'Bodices are unlaced, bodkins bared and codpieces set a-quivering!'[41] Two reviews brought home the 'goriness' of the production by making much of the fact that a 'schoolgirl . . . fainted during the last act'.[42] Similarly, reviews of *Troilus* stressed sex and violence, describing it as an 'awesome bloodbath',[43] as 'bloody and . . . magnificent',[44] and almost without exception, dwelling on the amount of 'flesh on view'.[45] Indeed, of the two plays, *Troilus* drew more negative criticism, with five out of fifteen reviews either lukewarm or scathing, and I suspect that the nudity may be partially responsible: one of the mere two reviews which avoided the subject of nudity happened to be the most shrill, with moral outrage all but seething through the print in sputtering repetitions of 'slick, slick, slick' and 'cheapened', 'cheapen', and 'cheapminded', not to mention those vaguely homophobic references to 'pretty boys' (absurd, considering the importance of pretty boys in Shakespeare's own theatre).[46] Of the overwhelming majority who mentioned the nudity, six did so in disapproving tones – though one male seemed disappointed that Helen was *only* 'briefly naked'.[47]

Fearon's contribution to the much-noted eroticism of both productions was indisputably vital. Descriptions of the two roles, at times, echoed one another: 'Fearon's swaggering Duke' and his 'languid Paris'[48] were noted for their febrile sensuousness, for the way they enfleshed the obsessive and amoral sexuality of the play's universe. Another seized-upon aspect of Fearon's Brachiano was the believability and sensationalism of his death by way of the poisoned visor – it was this which seemed to precipitate the swoon of the 'schoolgirl' in the audience.

For all the attention paid to Fearon's body, though, no direct reference was made to his race. Rather, in a curious displacement, the adjective 'black' was repeatedly applied to each production overall. One critic praised *The White Devil* as 'relentlessly bloody, blackly comic',[49] his uncannily Jacobean-sounding, alliterative comment fusing two prominent themes in the reviews. Along the same lines, *Troilus* was seen as 'dark' and 'disillusioned',[50] as a 'dark and difficult play',[51] as 'black night-of-the-soul comedy'.[52] And in the most telling of all intersections, both plays were likened – by separate critics – to Joseph Conrad's *Heart of Darkness*.[53]

There is no telling whether the two critics who referred to Conrad's colonialist narrative were any more conscious of Fearon's role in the association than was a third critic who referred to Webster's 'gleefully savage vision',[54] but there is evidence enough that the critics noticed Fearon's race, despite the very loud silence surrounding it. The closest any of the reviews came to acknowledging Fearon as a black actor was when one critic, in the midst of praising his 'leathery Brachiano', made the parenthetical suggestion 'Fearon (a future Othello?) . . .'[55] The *Othello* reference speaks for itself – and my point is that the role still in some ways constitutes the glass ceiling for black male Shakespearians – but I am also intrigued by the modifier 'leathery'. In fact, Fearon did wear leather in this production; he wore a near duplicate of the toe-to-collar black leather worn by Quarshie's Tybalt in the 1986 *Romeo*. However, the adjective, leather-*y*, not leather-*clad*, might as easily refer to skin as to clothes, and I suspect that the author liked this ambiguity, just as a previous critic clearly enjoyed his description of 'a black Tybalt in matching leather'.

In short, we should not be fooled by the critics' efforts to ignore Fearon's race. In one particularly embarrassing case, a reviewer described Helen and Paris, in the love scene which is the subject of figure 6, as 'less a golden than a gilded couple, down to the weird glittering crewcut that substitutes for his hair'.[56] I confess to finding the metallic sheen of Paris' and Helen's hair one of the most arresting details in the scene, but the simple truth is that the glittering locks

6 Ray Fearon as Paris in *Troilus and Cressida*, Royal Shakespeare Company, 1996

– artificial on both actors – only looked 'weird' on the black actor, and no aestheticizing of the skin/hair contrast can claim freedom from the cultural encoding of 'black' and 'gold'. Indeed, Helen's hair only literalized the tropic quintessence of European beauty. Moreover, this image insists that whatever moral failing the reviewer implied by the modifier 'gilded' must be considered alongside its unspoken partner, 'black'.

On the other hand, 'gilded' is one of the more polite modifiers applied by critics to, in particular, the women in these two plays; one critic, for instance, called Cressida 'a wonderfully impassioned slut'.[57] And lest we assume that the rhetoric of 'black lust' has lost its misogynistic utility, I cite a review of *The White Devil* which complained that Lisa Jardine's programme note '*whitewashes* Vittoria as a powerless victim of male power' (emphasis added).[58] The comment is forgivable enough in the light of the pervasiveness of the whitewashing idiom in modern English, but a glance at the short text which provoked it reveals a dubious chain of associations. Jardine's two-page feminist reading includes the following lengthy quotation from Joseph Swetnam's *The arraignment of lewd, idle, froward and unconstant women* (1615): 'Woe be unto that unfortunate man that matcheth himself with a widow . . . For thou must . . . make her forget her former corrupt and disordered beha-viour; the which if thou take upon thee to do, *thou hadst even as good undertake to wash a Blackamoor white*' (emphasis mine). The intersection of misogyny and racism is troubling enough in a Renaissance text; when echoes of this racialized language appear in a contemporary (male) critic's complaint about 'wrongheaded' feminist readings which obscure a female character's 'brutality' and 'artfulness', it is clearly time to put Othellophilia on the couch.

WHAT THE PICTURES SAY

The racialized sexual politics of Judge's casting may be ignored in reviews, but cannot be ignored in this photograph (fig. 6) – which my students invariably mistake for a still from *Othello*. The contrasting complexions, the profusion of bed-clothes and leopard skins, and the passive position of the white female all remind one, at first glance, of Desdemona's murder, with its suggestions of a barbaric male sexuality unleashed on a loving victim. Even the presence of the white male observer/abettor seems appropriate, given Iago's symbolic – if not actual – presence during the sexualized murder. And in fact the syphil-itic whiteness of Pandarus' face is a necessary component to the visual allegory, serving to comment on the polluting and destructive nature of the biracial coupling he applauds. His whiteness closes the colour-frame while also, paradoxically, devaluing the whiteness of Helen in the manner of the juxtapositional death's head in a *memento mori* image. (Interestingly, the same critics who refused to comment on Paris' com-plexion did mull over the significance of Pandarus' make-up.) More-over, Pandarus' quasi-sodomitical position behind Paris suggests the kind of homosocial triangle, theorized by Eve Kosofsky Sedgwick,[59] which threatens female agency.

I would also point out that the three-way banter in 3.1 to which Judge added this orgiastic physicality (not to mention Pandarus' mock orgasm) has no obvious purpose in the narrative. The scene merely allows Pandarus to repeat the word 'fair' ten times in seven lines, to flirt with the 'fair queen' (punning on 'quean', or whore, as Jardine's pro-gramme note emphasizes), and to sing a bawdy song. In other words, the interaction merely serves to advance the ironic treatment of Helen's 'fairness', and to intensify the atmosphere of promiscuity and perver-sion surrounding the royal adulterers. Throw in a leopard skin and some black/white sex, and few will miss the point.

Thus, the image announces what the critics kept mum – that Fearon's race was a fundamental element in the transgressive and spectacular eroticism of Judge's production. Perhaps the reviewers' self-censorship is not a bad sign; it is certainly preferable to racist outrage. Nonetheless, we all notice skin-colour, we cannot help but notice skin-colour, and an artistic medium which works with bodies will not only notice, but make use of skin-colour. Indeed, my response, as an artist and a non-black woman, to the *Troilus* triad was a complicated mixture of astonishment, pleasure and racial guilt. The combination of textures, the intertwining of two beautiful bodies, the contrasts of light and dark, and yes, the delicious surprise of Fearon's aureole, all afford immense pleasure: yet I was irked by the indispensable role, in creating these effects, of the half-nude black male, especially when I brought into my aesthetic ruminations a consideration of the larger position of black actors in Shakespearian theatre.

On the other hand, the position of *women* in Shakespearian theatre, and more specifically in this production, was hardly comfortable either: in this sequence Helen was lifted up, once, in her lover's arms – but she still spent much of the scene on the bottom layer of this man sandwich, and she wound up, as the lights faded, flat on her back under Paris. Might one not, thus, reconsider the *Troilus* triad from a feminist point of view? To return to my students' misattribution of the image, it is obvious that, as an isolated moment, the photo *could* depict a rape (albeit a 'fair' one): aside from being pinned under not one, but two men, Helen has one hand restrained, the other ambiguously free, in a gesture which only appears 'languid' in context. And whether or not Helen is having a good time here, the one 'on top' is, nonetheless, a white male – and a *very* white male at that. Susan Griffin argues that 'At the heart of the racist imagination we discover a pornographic fantasy: the spectre of miscegenation. The image of a dark man raping a fair woman embodies all that the racist fears' (and, I would add, all that he fantasizes).[60] Moreover, early modern texts such as Shakespeare's *The Rape of Lucrece* describe rape as 'so black a deed' (226) that it can *literally* turn 'pure' blood to 'black' (1742–3). And though the photo's captured moment may not constitute rape as it is currently defined, we recall Brabanzio's incredulity at the thought of his daughter's *consenting* to the Moor: miscegeny, to a racist, is always, at some level, rape.

And if it isn't rape, if she 'wanted it', it is not miscegenation, but rather proof that a woman is not truly white, but white*washed*. Judge declares in the programme, 'About the women in this play there's an *exotic*, flaming brilliance, and Shakespeare uses them to remarkable effect. It's very much a man's world but when a beautiful *creature* comes into it, there's a sudden rush of release because *not only is it seductive it's also destructive, this curious siren, witch-like quality that they all have*' (emphases mine). The stark misogyny of these statements requires little comment – the only question is whether the misogyny originates in the text or in Judge's interpretation. Clearly, though, nothing in Shakespeare's Prologue compares to the stupefying oversimplification of Judge's statement, 'There is nothing more destructive than Cressida's sexuality'; or, perhaps in response to an anticipated rebuttal like *what about the war?*, his follow-up statement, 'Helen destroys the world by being desirable.' This director is not, of course, the first male to lay the blame on Helen, but here, again, these introductory comments are at odds with the Prologue, which presents the famous adulterers as 'ravished Helen' and 'wanton Paris', and overall emphasizes the war as a male endeavour, the aim 'To ransack Troy', an act of phallic retribution, a rape for a rape (lines 7–10). Also unsettling in Judge's remarks are the pronouns: the ambiguously-placed 'it', and worse still, the alarmingly general 'they all'. Out of twenty-six characters, there are, after all, *only four women* in this play, two of whom speak just a handful of lines. Cassandra and Andromache, though possessed of a certain foresight, are anything but siren-like: their sole purpose is to prophesy disaster and *to be ignored*. And if Judge's sweeping 'they all', in conjunction with the modifier 'exotic', smacks of ethnic stereotyping (one review mentioned the *Kama Sutra* in reference to the biracial embrace in question),[61] I can hardly resist offering the cynical observation that prejudices (and fetishes) tend to travel in packs.

In Judge's case, the evidence is mounting: who can forget his use of Quarshie in *The Relapse*, produced just one year earlier? And there is more evidence than the one bare-chest scene: in the light of the feminist questions posed above, the production's central seduction scene ought also to be re-considered. Here, Loveless began undressing (a charged moment, given the earlier nudity) as he chased a willing but coy sexual prospect around that ubiquitous on-stage bed. Though he never did get his shirt off (Restoration fashions were a lecher's nightmare), Loveless nonetheless concluded the scene, as did Paris in the *Troilus* orgy, in bed atop the blazing-blonde vixen, who weakly called for help, then succumbed with a giggling, 'I'm ravished, ruined, undone!' (4.4.68).[62] The scene was then played out in an inverted fashion between Loveless' wife and a considerably paler aspirant to adultery, who posed the same sexual imperatives but met with genuine and successful opposition; in other words, this scene involved a 'real' rape attempt, as distinct from the former scene, in which the victim wanted to be raped. Given the racial politics Judge cast (in both senses) into the juxtaposition, it is hard to say whether women or blacks fared worse.

That the visual effect of this double marginalization can be, to many viewers, more seductive than disturbing only brings home its propagandistic potential. Judge himself nearly admits as much when he comments, in the programme for *Troilus*, on the play's incitement to voyeurism, and here what emerges is the way in which he mirrors Pandarus, who 'says the most shockingly wonderful things and we are delighted until we are horrified'. If Judge is a kind of pander, then, to what or whom is he pandering? To Othellophilia and to Othellophiles.

Though tempting, it may nonetheless be misguided to lay all the blame on this particular director. After all, one cannot pander where there is no appetite for the product – and if the critics are at all representative of audiences in general, there is evidence enough that these appetites are out there, resulting in murmurs of 'Fearon (a future Othello?)'. And unfortunately Judge is not the only such pander associated with the company; he has earned his place at the centre of this critique for sprinkling his biracial porn with just enough misogyny. And if this judgement seems harsh, I will modify it by way of the dubious compliment that at least Judge's production did not aspire to anti-racist 'brownie-points', unlike a more recent instance of allegedly colour-blind casting, which I have hitherto excluded out of reluctance to grant it that status. I speak of Adrian Noble's 1998 *Tempest*, in which a black actor played Ferdinand while a white actor played Caliban – casting clearly designed to foreclose the colonialist interpretation of the play. Noble went so far as to drive home the point by literalizing Ferdinand's 'servitude' to Prospero, presenting the prince bare-chested and chained; in so doing, he recast Prospero as the benevolent white master manumitting his slaves – indeed, throwing his own daughter into the bargain, with far more paternal warmth than Brabanzio shows *his* black son-in-law.

The work of Judge and Noble, however, may be unique in the degree of calculation behind their use of stereotypes: in most cases, I believe, Othellophilia is not consciously perpetuated, but rather simply 'happens'. And, as in any counter-hegemonic move, a director with truly liberal intentions in casting a black actor will have to work hard to surmount audience preconceptions. Michael Attenborough's 1997 *Romeo*, for instance, struck me as politically innocuous and a superb production to boot, casting a number of excellent, non-white performers on both sides of the feud; as a result, the variety of complexions seemed merely to enhance the set's rich texture, rather than offering some sort of racial allegory. Nonetheless, only one critic applauded Attenborough's 'achievement' in ethnic casting which rendered race 'an irrelevance';[63] another critic directly contradicted this interpretation, finding in the director's choice of Fearon a subtle (albeit liberal) 'point' about race relations.[64] More disturbing than these benign, if contradictory remarks, however, were the frequent echoes, in responses to Fearon, of responses to his black predecessor, Quarshie: twelve out of sixteen critics directly mentioned Romeo's 'virile' physique or 'full-blooded' sexiness;[65] the remaining four mentioned his 'flashing grin',[66] his 'swaggering' and sweating,[67] or dwelt on the 'raw, earthy vigour' of the production generally.[68] And this is without taking into account the highly erotic, biracial images used to promote the play – images which appeared not only in programmes and on posters, but alongside reviews as well (one such review featured a shirtless, reclining Fearon, and the headline, 'Never mind the poetry. He's a good kisser.').[69] Overall, I counted forty-nine explicit responses to the sex appeal of a black actor (what leading actor does not have sex appeal?) in the above-mentioned reviews; this figure by far outnumbered such comments on the white female co-star.

My point is not, of course, that there is anything inherently wrong with the appreciation of black male beauty, or with the kind of display which leads to such appreciation: these attitudes are clearly an improvement over the Renaissance English equation of 'black' with 'ugly'. And a stage whereon black actors go shirtless is by far preferable to a stage whereon whites in blackface play black roles. Nonetheless, there is something unsettling about this parade of black pectorals – framed by white cloth or a white woman's arms (fig. 6); strapped in black leather (figs. 2, 3 and 5), stretched across leopard-skin (fig. 7), even, in the case of Noble's *Tempest*, festooned in chains (fig. 8) – this pageant of black fantasy-flesh, the fruits of allegedly colour-blind casting. Where, for instance, are the actors whose biceps don't make the grade? Not in leading roles, certainly. And lest we forget: these men are the lucky ones. Look at the standard profile of a black actor in the RSC, count up all the blackamoors, servants, outlaws, bastards (literal, as in Edmund, or figurative, as in Oswald), throw in the occasional soldier, policeman, or executioner, and the picture is not so pretty. The choices for a black actor are limited indeed. It's almost as bad as being a woman.

7 Ray Fearon as Paris in *Troilus and Cressida*, Royal Shakespeare Company, 1996

8 Evroy Dear as Ferdinand in *The Tempest*, Royal Shakespeare Company, 1998

CONCLUSION

I return to my opening anecdote about Fearon's brief appearance,
framed by snowfall, at the beginning, and again at the end, of Branagh's
Hamlet. The racial encoding of the image – though not, strictly speaking, Shakespearian – invites comparison with some of the figurations
analysed by Toni Morrison's *Playing in the Dark*, wherein she argues that
'encounters with Africanism' in American literature (though also, I
would emphasize, in imperialist English literature) are necessary to the
self-definition of the white protagonist, and thereby of the culture he
reifies and reflects: 'Images of blackness can be evil *and* protective,
rebellious *and* forgiving, fearful *and* desirable – all of the self-contradictory
features of the self. Whiteness alone is mute, meaningless, unfathom-
able, pointless, frozen, veiled, curtained, dreaded, senseless, implacable.'[70]
Branagh's use of Fearon may be entirely arbitrary; there are, in fact,
black people *inside* Branagh's Elsinore as well, and moreover, Branagh's
casting of Denzel Washington as Don Pedro in *Much Ado About Nothing*
seems sufficient evidence against directorial prejudice. And yet, this
shot of a dark-skinned figure in the snow seems calculated to produce a
kind of pathos, for the opening scene, that would not have been afforded
by one of the three white actors who played the arriving watchmen.
Significantly, Branagh's screenplay first identifies Fearon's character
as 'the lonely FRANCISCO' (not just 'bitter cold and sick at heart') and
later as 'Poor FRANCISCO'.[71] Simply put, a black man positioned outside
the gate will appear more *shut out* than a white, more cold than a white,
more alone than a white – in sum, more '*poor*' than a white. And not
only because whites have been shutting out blacks in Anglo-American
culture for as long as they have known them, but also because 'blackness',
through the same binary logic that designates 'darkness' as 'female' and
as 'matter' (versus 'light' as 'male', as 'spirit', etc.), metaphorizes the
embodied selfhood which has baffled and intrigued, disgusted and
inspired, repelled and compelled western thought from at least the
Roman Empire on. As Hélène Cixous says of all women, 'We are "black"
and we are beautiful.'[72] To return to Morrison: why is 'whiteness
alone . . . meaningless'? The question may occur to Hamlet himself, as
he strives to make his 'inky cloak . . . denote (him) truly' (1.2.76–83).
Whiteness alone is meaningless because it is – in a way blackness,
despite its bad name, is not – nullity, absence, void. Whiteness unframed
has no body, no voice; it is antithetical to art.

Feminists, black and non-black, have good reason to be wary of the idealization of this whiteness. Othello ponders his bride's face, and asks, 'Was this fair paper, this most goodly book, / Made to write "whore" upon?' (4.2.73–4). Just one of many deadly masculinist tropes, the blank page represents the sexual purity a woman must, but really never can, embody. In passing, I should point out that in coining the term Othellophilia, I was not initially conscious of the fact that it ended in a homophone for Shakespeare's famous female suicide. But now the feminizing and self-destructive suffix seems appropriate. For the methods by which black actors are Othellofied inevitably complement the way their co-stars are Des/demonized. And lest the danger of these roles be viewed as purely theatrical, I would only point out one real-life case of Othellofication, set just outside Hollywood: the media drama surrounding the arrest and trial of O. J. Simpson.[73] Sometimes the world *is* a stage, and sometimes that is a tragedy.

NOTES

1 All quotations are from William Shakespeare, *The Complete Works*, gen. eds. Stanley Wells and Gary Taylor (Oxford, 1986).

2 Peter Holland, *English Shakespeares: Shakespeare on the English Stage in the 1990s* (Cambridge, 1997), p. 181.

3 Ben Dowell, 'RSC Actors Assaulted', *The Stage*, 21 May 1998.

4 Bill Hagerty, *News of the World*, 9 November 1997.

5 Kim Hall, *Things of Darkness: Economies of Race and Gender in Early Modern England* (Ithaca, 1995), *passim*.

6 Barbara Hodgdon, 'Looking for Mr Shakespeare after "The Revolution": Robert Lepage's Intercultural *Dream* Machine', in *Shakespeare, Theory and Performance*, ed. James Bulman (London, 1996), pp. 68–91. Hodgdon's study of this multiracial production at London's Royal National Theatre quotes some of the same reviewers as I do, highlighting similar patterns of response. One notable distinction between Hodgdon's project and my own is the former's focus on a foreign (French-Canadian) director whose intentions in multicultural casting and iconography were largely lost on his xenophobic reviewers; my analysis, however, takes up the work of British directors whose artistic vision and politics in most cases do not seem widely at variance with the sensibilities of their reviewers.

7 Because it is even harder to find black females in major Shakespearian roles (even the self-described 'black' Cleopatra tends to be played by whites), and because this kind of casting would involve a different sexual dynamic, I have not undertaken an account of this minority, who deserve an essay of their own.

8 Errol Hill, *Shakespeare in Sable: A History of Black Shakespearian Actors* (Amherst, 1984), pp. 137 and 144–74.
9 *Ibid.*, pp. xv and 140.
10 Because Quarshie did not play the role on the opening night, his perform-ance largely escaped the notice of critics.
11 Giles Gordon, *London Daily News*, 27 May 1987.
12 Michael Ratcliffe, *Observer*, 13 April 1986.
13 John Barber, *Daily Telegraph*, 10 April 1986.
14 Ratcliffe, *Observer*, 13 April 1986.
15 Michael Coveney, *Financial Times*, 9 April 1986.
16 Sheridan Morley, *Punch*, 16 April 1986.
17 Eric Griffiths, *Listener*, 20 November 1986.
18 Lyn Gardner, *City Limits*, 20 November 1986. See also Steve Grant, *Time Out*, 19 November 1986; Christopher Edwards, *Spectator*, 22 November 1986; Dan Jones, *Sunday Telegraph*, 16 November 1986; and Coveney, *Financial Times*, 12 November 1986.
19 Charles Spencer, *Daily Telegraph*, 7 July 1995. See also Jack Tinker, *Daily Mail*, 6 July 1995; Carole Woddis, *What's On*, 12 July 1995; and John Gross, *Independent on Sunday*, 9 July 1995.
20 Hagerty, *Today*, 6 July 1995.
21 Nicholas de Jongh, *Evening Standard*, 6 July 1995. Coveney also notes Quarshie's 'strange underpants' (*Observer*, 9 July 1998).
22 Tinker, *Daily Mail*, 6 July 1995.
23 The role actually seems to have a tradition of 'non-traditional' casting, as evidenced by Jack Carter's playing the role opposite Orson Welles in the 1930s (Hill, *Shakespeare in Sable*, p. xv).
24 Paul Taylor, *Independent*, 11 September 1995.
25 Benedict Nightingale, *The Times*, 11 September 1995; Jane Edwardes, *Time Out*, 20 September 1995; Michael Billington, *Guardian*, 11 September 1995. Similar remarks were made by Sarah Hemming (*Financial Times*, 12 Sep-tember 1995), John Peter (*Sunday Times*, 17 September 1995), Spencer (*Daily Telegraph*, 11 September 1995), Gross (*Sunday Telegraph*, 17 September 1995) and Woddis (*What's On*, 20 September 1995).
26 Edwards, *Spectator*, 19 July 1986; and de Jongh, *Guardian*, 12 July 1986.
27 Morley, *Punch*, 23 July 1986.
28 Peter, *Sunday Times*, 30 April 1995; Coveney, *Observer*, 23 April 1995.
29 Hill, *Shakespeare in Sable*, p. 40.
30 Hugh Quarshie, 'Hesitations on Othello', International Shakespeare Asso-ciation Occasional Papers, no. 7, 1999.
31 James Andreas, 'Othello's African-American Progeny', *South Atlantic Review* 57 (1992), 39–57; p. 47.
32 Ania Loomba, 'The Colour of Patriarchy: Critical Difference, Cultural Difference, and Renaissance Drama', in *Women, 'Race', and Writing in the Early Modern Period*, ed. Margo Hendricks and Patricia Parker (Manchester, 1994), pp. 27–8. Loomba quotes 4.6.224 and 4.2.85.

33 Hall, *Things of Darkness*, p. 9.

34 John Webster, *The White Devil*, ed. John Russell Brown, Revels Plays (Manchester, 1966).

35 Hall, *Things of Darkness*, pp. 62–122.

36 Cressida's hair is 'darker than Helen's', says Pandarus; Troilus insists that Cressida's hand is so white that by 'comparison all whites are ink' (1.1.41–56). Pandarus grants her 'as fair o' Friday as Helen is on Sunday', then interrupts himself, curiously, with 'I care not an she were a blackamoor' (77–8). Troilus dismisses the comparison: 'Helen must needs be fair, / When' the men of Troy 'paint her thus' in their blood (90–1). Pandarus continues the banter in the next scene, this time with Cressida; they debate whether Troilus is 'brown', or whether he or Paris 'hath colour enough' (1.2.88–102), and so on, down to a 'white hair' on Troilus' chin (132–6).

37 G. Blakemore Evans, gen. ed., *The Riverside Shakespeare* (Boston, 1974), p. 462, n. to 2.2.148.

38 Suzanne Gossett, '"Best Men are Molded Out of Faults": Marrying the Rapist in Jacobean Drama', *English Literary Renaissance* 14.3 (1984), 305–27.

39 Maureen Paton, *Daily Express*, 3 May 1996.

40 Peter, *Sunday Times*, 5 May 1996.

41 Coveney, *Observer*, 28 April 1996.

42 Edwardes, *Time Out*, 1 May 1996; Coveney, *Observer*, 28 April 1996.

43 Tinker, *Daily Mail*, 25 July 1996.

44 Hagerty, *News of the World*, 28 July 1996.

45 Gross, *Sunday Telegraph*, 28 July 1996.

46 Alastair Macaulay, *Financial Times*, 26 July 1996.

47 David Hughes, *Mail on Sunday*, 4 August 1996.

48 Coveney, *Observer*, 28 April and 4 August 1996, respectively.

49 Spencer, *Daily Telegraph*, 27 April 1996.

50 de Jongh, *Evening Standard*, 25 July 1996.

51 Robert Gore-Langton, *Daily Telegraph*, 26 July 1996.

52 de Jongh, *Evening Standard*, 25 July 1996.

53 Coveney, *Observer*, 28 April; Steve Grant, *Time Out*, 31 July 1996.

54 David Murray, *Financial Times*, 29 April 1996.

55 de Jongh, *Evening Standard*, 29 April 1996.

56 Nightingale, *The Times*, 26 July 1996.

57 Gore-Langton, *Daily Telegraph*, 26 July 1996.

58 de Jongh, *Evening Standard*, 29 April 1996.

59 Eve Kofosky Sedgwick, *Between Men: English Literature and Male Homosocial Desire* (New York, 1985), *passim*.

60 Susan Griffin, 'The Sacrificial Lamb', in *Racism and Sexism: An Integrated Study*, ed. Paula S. Rothenberg (New York, 1988), pp. 296–305; p. 298.

61 Nightingale, *The Times*, 26 July 1996.

62 Sir John Vanbrugh, *The Relapse,* in *Restoration Comedies*, ed. Dennis Davidson (Oxford, 1970).

63 Robert Butler, *Independent on Sunday*, 9 November 1997.

64 Spencer, *Daily Telegraph*, 7 November 1997.

65 Nick Curtis, *Evening Standard*, 6 November 1997; Macaulay, *Financial Times*, 10 November 1997; Gore-Langton, *Express*, 7 November 1997; Spencer, *Daily Telegraph*, 7 November 1997; Hagerty, *News of the World*, 9 November 1997; Coveney, *Daily Mail*, 14 November 1997; Georgina Brown, *Mail on Sunday*, 16 November 1997; Edwardes, *Time Out*, 12 November 1997; Neil Smith, *What's On*, 12 November 1997; David Benedict, *Independent*, 8 November 1997; Billington, *Guardian*, 6 November 1997; Nightingale, *The Times*, 7 November 1997.

66 Butler, *Independent on Sunday*, 9 November 1997.

67 Susannah Clapp, *Observer*, 9 November 1997.

68 Peter, *Sunday Times*, 9 November 1997.

69 Clapp, *Observer*, 9 November 1997.

70 Toni Morrison, *Playing in the Dark: Whiteness and the Literary Imagination* (Cambridge, Mass., 1992), p. 59.

71 Kenneth Branagh, *Hamlet, by William Shakespeare: Screenplay, Introduction and Film Diary* (London, 1996), pp. 1, 162. Branagh also requires Francisco to endure, in both scenes in which he appears, fear and gratuitous violence (pp. 2, 196).

72 Hélène Cixous and Catherine Clément, *The Newly-Born Woman*, trans. Betsy Wing (Minneapolis, 1986), p. 69.

73 On the O. J./Othello parallel, see Gary Taylor's provocative article, 'The Greatest Lie Ever Told', in the *Observer*, 9 October 1994.

CHAPTER 13

'Delicious traffick': racial and religious difference on early modern stages

Ania Loomba

> . . . we'll want no mistresses;
> Good swords, and good strong armours! [. . .]
> And fight till queens be in love with us, and run after us.
> (*The Knight of Malta*, 2.5)

For at least the last two hundred years, 'race' has functioned as one of the most powerful and yet most fragile markers of social difference. It is one of the great ironies of imperial history that ideologies of racial differences have hardened as a direct response to racial and cultural crossovers; conversely, colonial enterprises have facilitated contact and exchange between people of different ethnicities, religions and cultures. Notions of alterity or exchange thus derive their meaning from one another. Here I want to explore some aspects of this mirror-dance on the stages of Shakespeare's time – a time which can be characterized as either the last period in history where ethnic identities could be understood as fluid, or as the first moment of the emergence of modern notions of 'race'.

We are beginning to interrogate the crucial differences between twentieth-century and early modern ideologies of racial and cultural difference. Between the two stand four centuries of colonial relations which profoundly reshaped global relations. If, to use Stephen Greenblatt's words, Shakespeare's plays are letters we receive from the past, are we able to read and enjoy them only because there are powerful continuities and linkages between their vocabularies and our own? Or is it the case that these letters intimate alternate ways of being which denaturalize the dominant ideologies of our own age? The early modern period affords glimpses of other ways of being, some more flexible and generous, others more restrictive, than our own. Of course, precisely those aspects of the past which spell out a promise to some may signal danger to others. Our investment in interpreting these letters from the past, therefore, hinges upon our hopes and anxieties about the future.

Over the last two centuries, skin colour has dominated racist ideologies: races are common-sensically conceived of as

either 'black' or 'white' but never 'big-eared' and 'small-eared'. The fact that
only certain physical characteristics are signified to define 'races' in specific
circumstances indicates that we are investigating not a given, natural division
of the world's population, but the application of historically and culturally
specific meanings to the totality of human physiological variation.[1]

It follows that, in order to denaturalize modern concepts of race, it is
important to historicize the growth of colour consciousness. However,
I am struck by how many critics have recently claimed that colour
was *unimportant* in the racial imaginary of early modern England.
Such claims suppose that colour consciousness was generated through
colonial domination: since Africa was not colonized at the time that
Shakespeare wrote *Othello*, one critic argues, the hero's colour did not
necessarily connote bestiality or inferiority for its English audiences.[2]
Another suggestion is that notions of Englishness were honed in opposition to the Islamic world of Asia and North Africa and therefore blackness carried little negative charge in England. I believe that we cannot
historicize colour consciousness, or examine a time when it had not
acquired the virulent connotations of imperial times, by a down-
playing of the vocabulary of colour. It is more fruitful to see how such
a vocabulary is transformed during this period as it articulates itself
through other markers of difference such as religion and gender.

It is certainly true that dark skin was not a prerequisite for either
economic exploitation or cultural prejudice, as is evident from histories
of Irish, Jewish or Islamic peoples. It is also true that because early
modern scholarship has concentrated on the colonization of America,
these other histories have not been adequately considered. Because
imperialism was eventually to place natives of Asia, Africa and the
Americas in similar positions of inferiority *vis-à-vis* Europe, we tend to
assume that this was also the case during the sixteenth and early seventeenth centuries.[3] As Daniel Vitkus has remarked:

What has often been forgotten is that while Spanish, Portuguese, English, and
Dutch ships sailed to the New World and beyond, beginning the exploration
and conquest of foreign lands, the Ottoman Turks were rapidly colonizing
European territory. Thus, in the sixteenth and seventeenth centuries, the
Europeans were both colonizers and colonized, and even the English felt the
power of the Turkish threat to Christendom.[4]

How does this doubleness affect the English sense of global relations, and more specifically, its representation on the English stages of

the time? Elsewhere, I have suggested that Othello's difference from Caliban reminds us of the difference in perceptions of the Islamic East and the American West. Othello's mastery over language wins him Desdemona and charms the Venetian Senate; Caliban has to struggle to acquire and use Prospero's language. Othello serves the Venetian state as the captain of its army, Caliban's servitude is marked by punitive bondage. The differences between Othello and Caliban can be productively read against Hayden White's distinction between the Wild Man and the Barbarian in classical thought – the former (like Caliban) is imagined as outside civil society whereas the latter (like Othello) is regarded as living under an alien law.[5] Julia Reinhard Lupton uses a similar distinction to highlight the famous schism within Othello himself: a black Othello (whom Lupton reads as analogous to the uncivilized American or Caliban) is a barbaric figure outside all religion and therefore more easily convertible to Christianity, whereas a Muslim or Turkish Othello is less convertible because he already owes allegiance to a rival religion of the book.[6] Lupton argues that a scandal of 'monstrous miscegenation' inherited from the nineteenth-century racial imagery has (wrongly) come to govern *Othello*'s 'economy of differences'. In the Renaissance, a black Gentile could be legitimately placed within the narrative of an international romance, in a way that the Infidel Turk could not: 'whereas for the modern reader or viewer a black Othello is more subversive, "other", or dangerous, in the Renaissance scene a paler Othello more closely resembling the Turks whom he fights might actually challenge more deeply the integrity of the Christian paradigms set up in the play as a measure of humanity' (p. 74).

In this argument, Islam, and not blackness, was the spectre haunting early modern Europe.[7] Of course the Muslim, as Lupton rightly points out, is connected to the Jew mythically via the figure of Ishmael, and bodily through the mark of circumcision.[8] Judaism and Islam both provide Christianity with a frightening image of alterity. Lupton compares this early modern proto-racism to what Etienne Balibar calls the neo-racism of our own times, which also does not hinge on the question of colour, indeed 'does not have the pseudo-biological concept of race as its driving force'.[9] In this important reading, to de-link racism from colour consciousness is to trace connections, rather than disjunctures, between our own times and Shakespeare's. Connections between sixteenth-century and twentieth-century anti-Semitic and anti-Islamic discourses become clear, and religious as well as cultural factors in the construction of racism are highlighted. However, Lupton highlights religious difference by explicitly downgrading the significance of colour: 'in *Othello*', she remarks, 'religious difference is *more powerfully felt* than racial difference, which was only then beginning to surface in its virulent modern form'. In conclusion she quotes Lynda Boose's assessment that 'circumcision *rather than skin color* is the trait that Othello "invokes" as the final, inclusive sign of his radical Otherness' (p. 81; emphasis added).

'Valiant Othello' with his 'bombast circumstance / Horribly stuffed with epithets of war' (1.1.13–14), his 'sword of Spain' (5.2.260) and his violent jealousy certainly evokes a Renaissance stereotype of the 'malignant and turbaned Turk' (5.2.362) or Muslim. But I am unable to dismiss the forceful colour-coding of the play or the passionate repetition of explicitly colour-based image of monstrosity, too well known to require repetition here. How do we understand the images of monstrous coupling and animal imagery that kick-start the play's relentless exploration of love across the boundaries, or the repetitive harping on a black–white dichotomy, both by those opposed to the Othello–Desdemona marriage and by those sympathetic to it? Surely, these *images* have not been imported from the nineteenth century, reverberating as they do with hundreds of others evoked on Renaissance stages? Othello does not move from a glamorous black to a hated Turk: rather, we need to notice how both blacks and Turks can be glamorized as well as hated in contemporary representations, and how the two were interconnected, both in *Othello* and in the culture at large, via the Spanish discourse on Moorishness, via medieval stereotypes of black Turks, or Egyptians, and also by more recent developments in global relations.

Ranking somatic, religious or national differences *vis-à-vis* each other is to continue to think of them as discrete categories. If we assume that racial thinking had not developed in early modern Europe because colour was not the primary marker of difference, we are still working with a conceptual equation of race and colour. It is more useful to trace the complex articulation between skin colour, religion, ethnicity and nationality during this period and to see whether *each of them* was viewed as a feature that could be acquired, or as derived from a more unchanging quasi-biological essence. I use the word 'articulation' to describe not a simple coexistence but a relationship between different categories which transforms all of them.[10]

Consider the argument that colour prejudice was produced by colonial relations. It is indeed true that it is 'premature to characterize, as some critics have done, the early seventeenth century as a society "exhibiting" cultural hegemony' and driven by 'the economic imperatives of imperial trade'.[11] But racial ideologies do not automatically and crudely *reflect* economic relations, although the two are always interconnected. Well before the actual enslavement and colonial plunder of Africans began, an obsession with colour and nakedness was firmly in place. As has been fairly well documented by now, contemporary writers drew plentifully upon biblical, classical and medieval images of black monstrosity which were often located in Africa.[12] Medieval morality plays routinely linked devilry and blackness, a link that Emilia reiterates in her outburst against Othello: 'O, the more angel she, and you the blacker devil' (5.2.140). Blackness was a staple (although not static) ingredient in images of wildness, of evil, of class difference, and of female disorderliness.[13] In fact in several colonial situations these earlier stereotypes provided an ideological *justification* for different kinds of exploitation.[14]

I am not suggesting that blackness has the *same* negative charge over centuries, only that it becomes a highly mobile metaphor that can be reworked to establish a wide spectrum of differences. But what we also have to remember is that, despite England's tardiness, a larger European proto-colonialist discourse had been circulating awhile. African royalty provided occasional images of glamour: the fourteenth-century ruler of Mali, the King Mansa, captured the European imagination as equal in power and sophistication to any Christian prince. By the mid-fifteenth century, after the Portuguese penetration of Gambia, Mansa's heirs were depicted in terms of crude racial stereotypes 'with dangling simian sexual organs'.[15] Of course, these negative images cannot be equated with the full-blown ideology of species difference, which had to a certain extent been retarded by the Christian belief in monogenism. As Robert Bartlett points out, 'while the language of race – *gens, natio*, "blood", "stock" etc. – is biological, its medieval reality was almost entirely cultural'. In practice, races were defined more in social terms of customs, language and law. Since customs and language, and even religion, could be acquired, pre-modern forms of ethnic differentiation were more fluid than their modern counterparts: 'When we study race relations in medieval Europe we are analyzing the contact between various linguistic and cultural groups, not between breeding stocks.'[16]

However, the seeds for a biological understanding of race were sown when, following the expulsion of Jews and Moors in 1492 and 1502, the concept of purity of blood (*limpieza de sangre*) not only took ideological root in Spain but became the basis for discrimination in social and political and economic life. If racism is not just the belief that human beings are biologically different, but the translation of that belief into social inequalities, then sixteenth-century Spain certainly engendered modern racism.[17] Differences of faith now became signs of different interior essences:

Who can deny that in the descendants of the Jews there persists and endures the evil inclination of their ancient ingratitude and lack of understanding, just as in Negroes [there persists] the inseparability of their blackness? For if the latter should unite themselves a thousand times with white women, the children are born with the dark color of the father. Similarly, it is not enough for a Jew to be three parts aristocratic or Old Christian for one family-line [. . .] alone defiles and corrupts him.[18]

The important point about this passage is that a conflation of faith and genetic essence occurs *both* in the descriptions of Jews, where lack of colour differentiation becomes a source of anxiety, and in discussions about Moors, where colour is more obviously at stake. In fact, these overlaps are the basis for a comparison between Jews and Moors.

Balibar admits that 'bodily stigmata play a great role' in anti-Semitism, but suggests that 'they do so more as signs of a deep psychology, as signs of a spiritual inheritance rather than a biological heredity' (p. 24). I would argue, instead, that 'spiritual inheritance' and 'biological heredity' are intricately connected. Therefore, the signs of visible difference are always translated into moral, and even religious, alterity in the case of blacks. Thus Leo Africanus finds tawny or white Africans or 'Moors' who are Christians, but claims that in 'all the Negros Land' there are no Christians.[19] Colour here operates as a sharp dividing line between Christians and non-Christians. In the case of Jews and Muslims religious difference is expressed in moral and often in physical terms. While circumcision certainly is a crucial and recurrent sign, these discourses also construct more indelible marks of difference. Thus Jewish men are said to menstruate, smell, be capable of breast-feeding or have hooked noses; blackness, mis-shapenness and grotesque features, including swollen heads and hooked noses, are routinely attributed to many Muslims.[20] This is not to minimize the enormous anxiety produced by the physical similarities between Jews, Christians and Muslims, but to show that such anxiety results in a strenuous production of a discourse of difference.

The crucial question is: was England immune from colour prejudice, and especially prejudice against Moors? According to Eric Griffin, the strong anti-black discourse in *Othello* comments on Spanish, not English, attitudes to race and Moorishness, and Iago and Roderigo are portrayed as stereotypes of Spanish racists.[21] The play thus suggests an affinity between Othello the Moor and the English, an affinity that was evoked by several writers as Elizabethan England tried to establish trade with Barbary. Elizabeth herself claimed that both she and the Great Turk were enemies to idolaters.[22] Thus Griffin argues that Othello is a proto-Protestant Muslim who is attacked by Catholic racists, and whose own conversion to Catholicism pollutes him with the sin of idolatry.

Notice that Griffin and Lupton suggest absolutely divergent valencies for Islam in early modern England. For Griffin, Islam was viewed as an ally of Protestant England, Hispanic Roman Catholicism was the Other against whom an English identity was forged, and Othello's tragedy results from his conversion to Catholicism. Lupton argues that Islam and the Turks are the real adversary, and the tragedy is that Othello cannot fully convert from Islam. Griffin's argument, moreover, depends on an astute insistence on the double meaning of Moor – as black *and* as Muslim – whereas Lupton's derives from a divorce between the meaning of Moorishness and blackness. What interests me is that despite their completely different assessments of Islam and blackness, both Griffin and Lupton suggest that somehow anti-black prejudice did not animate the *English* during this period.[23] The English are seen as romancing either Islam or blackness, and *Othello* is therefore a play about a racism elsewhere.[24]

'Spain's national obsession with purity of blood', says Griffin, 'had met its ideological reverse in an English Protestant obsession with purity of faith' (p. 82). I want to suggest that, both in Spain and in England, purity of faith and purity of blood were necessarily yoked together, a yoking that is most clearly visible in contemporary discourses about conversion. Religious conversion, by signalling the possibility of crossovers, necessarily engenders several kinds of anxieties about authenticity.[25] If the faithful constitute a permeable and changeable body, then the purity of both the original body and those who are allowed to join it is always suspect. Worse, a permeable boundary can allow the faithful to both enter and leave: 'The institutionalized violence represented by the Inquisition was a product of the anxiety that this boundary of conversion might be transgressed in the wrong direction.'[26] Moreover, conversion was viewed as a perpetually unstable condition: converts to Christianity were suspected of covertly practising Judaism or Islam, or of interpreting Christianity in the light of their previous faiths.[27] The assimilation of Moriscoes (converted Moors) and

Marranos (converted Jews) within the Christian community was an affair strenuously policed by civic and ecclesiastic authorities. Moriscos, for example, were even forbidden from dancing and singing in their traditional way, for they were suspected of using words and gestures with double meanings which mocked Christianity.[28] Such anxieties were not confined to Spain: James Shapiro points out that in an England where even the official religion had changed so often, the question of genuine versus assumed faith had a specially sharp resonance: 'Faith was disguisable, religious identity a role one could assume or discard if one had sufficient improvisational skill' (p. 17).

But it is precisely when faith could be improvised that the question of authenticity became especially urgent. Fears that the exterior show did not match the inner faith were underlined by the fact that Jews, Moors and Christians were never simply religious categories, but variably articulated with nationality and ethnicity, and often colour. Categories such as 'A Christian Jew'[29] or 'a Turke, but a Cornish man borne'[30] attested to the fact that religion and nationality were affiliations which conversions could not entirely erase. The articulation of a religion which can be chosen and an ethnicity which cannot is particularly complex in the case of the category called 'Moors'. The Spanish derived the word 'moro' from the Latin word 'maurus' which in turn came from the Greek 'mavros' meaning black.[31] But they used it to designate their conquerors who were not black at all but a mixture of Arab and Berber Muslims.[32] Earlier I suggested ways in which religious difference provides a vocabulary for the expression of racial difference. Here we see an instance of how religion and ethnicity were expressed through a vocabulary of colour.

Travel writings and plays of the period, including English ones, regularly play with and between these two senses of the word 'Moor': Caesar Fredericke's *Voyage . . . into East India* clarifies that 'wheras I speak of Moores I mean Mahomets sect'.[33] But John Lok who brought five black men from Barbary to England in 1554 calls people of Ethiopia 'Moores, Morens, or Negroes, a people of beastly living, *without a God, lawe, religion, or common wealth . . .*' (emphasis added).[34] Here Moors are not Muslims who obey an alien God, but people outside of civil society and organized religion. According to Leo Africanus, Moors come in various colours, and a variety of religious affiliations: some Moors 'are Gentiles which worship Idols; others of the sect of Mahumet; some others Christians; and some Iewish in religion'. But, as mentioned earlier, he also claims that there are no Christian Negroes, so that

Moorishness, but not blackness, is compatible with Christianity.[35] *The Merchant of Venice* refers to the woman made pregnant by Launcelot as both a 'Moor' and a 'Negro' (3.5.37). In this sense Moorishness is something that cannot be either acquired or shed. Although Timon of Athens complains that gold can make 'Black white, foul fair, wrong right' (4.3.29), the black maid Zanche in Webster's *The White Devil* fails in her attempts to wash her colour by acquiring a large dowry.[36]

The word 'blackamoor' thus collapses religious and somatic vocabularies, which, despite knowledge about white Moors and non-Muslim blacks, could not be unknotted. In fact the same writer can make distinctions between the two and collapse them. Sexuality becomes a recurrent point of knotting Muslims and blacks: both are seen as promiscuous and desirous of white women, and this contributes to their being enmeshed in the 'common sense' of the period.[37] Evidence can of course be amassed to bolster up two completely divergent assessments about Renaissance ideologies of colour: one, that black skin was thought of as a 'natural infection'[38] and was therefore indelible, like the proverbial leopard's spots and that the 'blackness of the Parent's sperm or seede' would overpower whiteness if the two were coupled, and two, that blackness was seen as derived from geographical location, and as mutable. But crucially, proponents of both views concurred that *blackness* was dominant and could contaminate whiteness, rather than the other way around. For example, a 1562 Act of Elizabeth expressed the fear that earlier laws against foreigners would be unable to deal with a new problem regarding gypsies or 'that false and subtil company of vagabonds calling themselves Egyptians'. Now, it says, 'persons as being born within this realm of England' are joining 'the fellowship or company of the said vagabonds, by transforming or disguising themselves in their apparel, or in a certain counterfeit speech or behaviour'.[39] This fear of 'turning gypsy' was most often expressed in relation to English rogues and vagabonds: thus the boundaries of culture are also imagined in class terms.[40] The blurring of boundaries between English people and gypsies is conjured up via images of brown Englishmen rather than white gypsies. Thus blackness (both as a moral quality and as skin colour) can more readily contaminate whiteness rather than itself be washed into whiteness.

The tension between black skin and a Christian interiority, therefore, needs to be constantly negotiated, explained, addressed. The romance of a black Christian, perhaps like all romances, always contains within it the idea of its own impossibility. As a matter of fact, not only blacks but Moors and Turks were romantically treated in European literature. In Spain, 'the gap between the idealized picture of the noble Moor and the miserable circumstances of the Moriscos tended to confirm the belief of Old Christians that the maximum social distance, including expulsion, ought to be placed between the truly Spanish and . . . recent converts'.[41] Thus a literary tradition of the Noble Moor indicates cultural stress rather than cross-cultural indulgence or harmony.[42] In English theatre, the figure of the noble Moor, such as Joffer in Heywood's *Fair Maid of the West*, was usually the exception that proved the rule of Moorish incivility, or devolved into a tragic figure like Othello who illustrated the impossibility of sustaining a perpetual contradiction.

But the Moorish convert to Christianity also represented something far closer to home – the possibility of self-fashioning. Peter Berek astutely suggests that English theatrical obsession with self-fashioning is expressed most powerfully through the figure of the converted Jew who represents 'the idea that identity is not stable and can be represented by individuals themselves'. Figures such as Othello (or indeed even Aaron or Morocco) can be credibly located within such a framework. However, whereas Berek suggests that the cultural anxiety represented by the Marrano 'isn't about Marranism, or Jewishness, or even [. . .] about emerging ideas of race and nation, but about cultural change and a fluid sense of self that one could call "modern" ' (pp. 130, 158), I think the figure of the convert demonstrates precisely that emergent modernity or cultural change are inextricable from ideas of race and nation. All self-fashioning represents a transgression of boundaries that is both romantic and terrible, heroic and tragic. In the case of alien figures such crossings necessarily evoke anxieties about English, Christian or Protestant identity: the fluidity of the self is marked also by the changing boundaries of the faith or the nation. The romance and terror of self-fashioning becomes especially acute in the case of such figures: thus a Marrano or a Morisco cannot be a quintessential Renaissance man even though he may represent the essence of Renaissance self-fashioning.

More often than not, however, the converted Moor on the Renaissance stage is a woman. We have the recurrent spectacle of a fair maid of an alien faith and ethnicity romanced by a European, married to him, and converted to Christianity. Her story, unlike those of converted men, does not usually end in tragedy, nor does it focus on the tensions of cultural crossings. Whereas converted men must remain single or be destroyed, her religious turning is also a romantic turning to a Christian husband. Instead of a self-fashioning, hers is a re-fashioning by her Christian husband. Unlike the Moorish man, she does not represent a fearful alterity to Christendom but the possibility of a controlled exchange. Nevertheless, her fair skin confirms that colour is in fact crucial to narratives of conversion and assimilation. Such a figure thus profoundly shapes ideas of both alterity and exchange in early modern England.

In an important essay, Daniel Vitkus has drawn our attention to the sexual connotations of the drama of religious conversion. Conversion and perversion were both implied in the verb 'to turn'; the phrase 'to turn Turk' carried erotic connotations which drew upon ideas of Muslim hyper-sexuality as well as female immorality. Protestants viewed the conversion of Christians to Islam or Roman Catholicism as a sexual transgression or spiritual whoredom.[43] Turnings towards Christianity, I want to suggest, are also expressed through a sexualized vocabulary, but, when inscribed on the body of a 'fair' but 'alien' woman, this is a vocabulary of romance and marriage instead of whoredom.

Sexual intercourse between members of different groups was the kind of crossover that generated the greatest anxiety.[44] Since sperm was widely understood as man's purest blood, sexual activity was an exchange of blood, and a crossing of boundaries more profound than conversion. In the Christian, Muslim as well as Jewish communities, a double standard operated and punishments for female transgression were much harsher than those accorded to men: 'According to classic Islamic jurisprudence, Muslim men could marry Christian or Jewish women . . . but Muslim women could not marry non-Muslim men' without risking a death penalty.[45] European travellers and commentators claimed Turkish harems were filled with abducted Christian girls, and Turkish strongmen or Janizzaries were captured Christian men who were converted to Islam and sometimes castrated. Othello's alliance with Desdemona evokes the popular and oft-told tale of Irene the Greek maiden who was abducted, loved and murdered by a Turkish emperor.[46] In Philip Massinger's play *The Renegado* (1621), the fair Paulina has been sold to Asambeg, the Viceroy of Tunis and is, her brother Vitelli says, 'Mewde up in his Serraglio, and in danger / Not alone to loose her honour, but her soule' (1.1.129–30).[47]

The Turkish damsel Donusia, who falls in love with Paulina's brother Vitelli, rants against the double standard within Islam:

> Indulgent *Mahomet*, doe thy bloudy lawes
> Call my embraces with a Christian, death?
> [. . .] and yet want power to punish
> These that with scorne creak throgh thy Cobweb edicts
> [. . .] to tame their lusts,
> There's no religious bit; let her be fayre
> And pleasing to the eye, though Persian, Moore,
> Idolatresse, Turke, or Christian . . .
>
> > (4.2.128–36)

Donusia also draws attention to the difference between her fetters and the liberty enjoyed by Christian women:

> I have heard
> That *Christian* Ladies live with much more freedome
> Then such as are borne heere. Our jealous Turkes
> Never permit their faire wives to be seene
> But at the publique *Bannias*, or the Mosques
> And even then vaylde, and guarded
>
> > (1.2.16–21)

Her English-born eunuch Carazie responds by picturing Englishwomen as leading a carnivalesque existence – hunting, hawking, feasting, entertaining, wearing breeches, commanding their husbands and apprentices, and cuckolding men freely: 'women in England / For the most part live like Queenes' (1.2.27–8). Paulina is eventually rescued from Asambeg and Donusia also escapes the Turkish patriarchy by marrying Paulina's brother Vitelli and converting to Christianity.

In medieval Europe, the most common form of sexual transgression had in fact involved Christian men and Muslim women. In stories of Christians turning Turk that circulated in early modern times, Muslim women are temptresses who ensnare Christian men into a licentious faith. This spectre is repeatedly evoked in plays such as *The Renegado*, Robert Daborne's *A Christian Turn'd Turke* (1612) or Fletcher's *The Island Princess* (1620–1), in which Muslim women initiate sexual contact and ask the Christian hero to convert to Islam. But such fears are theatrically allayed by either the destruction of such women or their own conversions to Christianity and marriages to Christian men.

Fine race and colour distinctions always operated in the case of sanctioned interracial sex. Albuquerque 'invited his men to marry "the white and beautiful" widows and daughters of the defenders of Goa, making a distinction between them and the darker South Indian women whom he called "Negresses"'.[48] In English theatre, the desire of black people for those with fairer skins is usually lampooned, as in the case of the King and Queen of Fez in Heywood's *The Fair Maid of the West*. Such desire is either not reciprocated or clearly marked as foul lust, unredeemable by marriage or conversion. Black men, like Joffer in the same play, can be converted to Christianity and eulogized for their inherent nobility but only if they show no signs of a desire for white women.[49] The marginality of black women, on the other hand, is routinely expressed through the folly of their desire for white men. In play after play, black women, usually servants, are sexually but never romantically linked to white men. However, just as often we have an interracial romance featuring Muslim women, and such a romance is always also a story of religious conversion and marriage.

In a perceptive essay on Shakespeare's *The Merchant of Venice*, Mary Janell Metzger shows that Jessica's 'whiteness and femaleness make possible her reproduction as a Christian in the eyes of the "commonwealth"' and that her 'incorporation into Christian society is essential to defining her father's alien status' (pp. 57, 59). If circumcision was the major physical barrier to the idea of the converted Muslim (or Jew), then women, whose bodies did not bear this mark, could be more easily imagined as crossing the religious and racial divide. I have earlier remarked on the translation of circumcision into more indelible marks of difference. The uncircumcised body is imagined as literally fairer: thus, when Shylock claims a shared racial identity with Jessica, 'I say my daughter is my flesh and blood', he declares (3.1.34), Solanio tells him, 'There is more difference between thy flesh and hers than between jet and ivory, more between your bloods than there is between red wine and Rhenish' (3.1.35–37). Here gender difference produces a crucial difference *within* races.

A similar difference was suggested and amplified by an influential history of the Moluccan islands by Bartolemé Leonardo de Argensola, *Conquista de las islas Malucas* (1609), on which Fletcher's play *The Island Princess* was based.[50] Argensola claims that the 'Natives Differ from one another, as it were through a Miraculous Bounty of Nature, for it has made the Women Fair and Beautiful, and the Men, of a darker Colour than Quince'.[51] Fletcher's play reserves this somatic difference for the Moluccan Princess Quisara. Unlike Shakespeare's Cleopatra, who is 'with Phoebus's amorous pinches black', 'the very sun', the Portuguese soldier Christophero tells us, dares not dye Quisara 'Into his tawny livery' (1.2).[52] But his companion Piniero contends that this is less a matter of nature than one of nurture: the princess 'dares not see' the sun,

> But keeps herself at a distance from his kisses,
> And wears her complexion in a case: Let him but like it
> A week, or two, or three, she would look like a lion.
>
> (1.2)

He also suggests, taking a dig at the whole literary tradition of lovely princesses, that beauty is a matter of class power:

> She is a princess, and she must be fair,
> That's the prerogative of being royal;
> Let her want eyes and nose, she must be beauteous,
> And she must know it too, and the use of it,
> And people must believe it, they are damn'd else. . . .
>
> (1.2)

Nevertheless, like Jessica and the 'too fayre' Donusia in *The Renegado*, Quisara is converted and married to a Christian man. Thus perceptions of colour, class and female tractability shape one another.

In play after play, conversion and penetration are often literally the same process. Quisara's maid is told by Piniero: 'I'll get thee with Christian, / The best way to convert thee' (5.4). In Beaumont and Fletcher's *The Knight of Malta* the soldiers want sexual access to the Turkish prisoner Lucinda '. . . to make her a good Christian' (2.1).[53] The children of such liaisons might be 'ill Christians' in genetic terms, but, says her master Miranda, 'We'll mend them in the breeding.' Like Jessica's offspring, and unlike the offspring of the Moor impregnated by Launcelot, the children of Muslim women can be blanched of their inner stain. Thus the successful assimilation of Jessica and her ilk highlights the marginality, not only of men of their race, but also of darker women.

Lucinda's conversion is offset by the expulsion of the black maid, Zanthia, whose white lover is the evil Mountferrat. Zanthia is his 'black gib there, his Succuba, his devil's seed' and Mountferrat's villainous disposition is measured by his lust for her which, he confesses,

> . . . is not love, but strong libidinous will,
> That triumphs o'er me; and to satiate that,
> What difference 'twixt this Moor, and her fair dame?
> Night makes their hues so alike, their use is so;
> Whose hand's so subtle he can colours name,
> If he do wink and touch 'em? Lust being blind,
> Never in women did distinction find.
>
> (1.2)

If 'lust' makes no racial distinctions, 'love' rests on a finely calibrated sense of difference.[54]

There were significant differences in Christian attitudes towards sex with Muslims and Jews in medieval times. Muslim women were generally poorer, and risked enslavement by consorting with Christian men. Jews, on the other hand, 'were closely tied to the Crown and had a good deal of financial and political power that they could use to reinforce the sexual boundary around their community. A Jewish woman accused of miscegenation might be fined, tortured, mutilated, or even executed, but she could not become chattel.'[55] But on early modern English stages, the desirable Muslim and Jewish woman both promise wealth: as she elopes, Jessica pauses to 'gild myself / With some moe ducats' (2.6.49–50). Shylock's 'stones, his daughter and his ducats' are a package deal (2.7.22). In *The Island Princess* the fabled wealth of the Moluccas, 'The wealthy magazine of Nature' (1.2), is promised to Quisara's mate. In Massinger's *The Renegado*, Donusia woos her Christian lover Vitelli with 'bags stuft full of our imperiall coyne . . . These Iems for which the slavish Indian dives / To the bottom of the Maine' (2.4.83–114). The motif of the converted wealthy queen obviously harks back to the story of the black Queen of Sheba and to the black but comely bride in the Song of Songs. The blackness of these earlier figures is whitewashed in theatrical representations, with the exception of those of Cleopatra, although it finds readier expression in the royal masque, in mayoral pageants, in poetry and in paintings of the period.[56]

Daniel Vitkus has remarked that Othello's turn towards Christianity and assimilation into Venice is jeopardized by Desdemona's potential waywardness: she 'can turn and turn, and yet go on / And turn again' (4.1.254–5). But if the changeability of women, a theme pervasive in the drama of the period, provokes anxieties and threatens to disrupt social stability, it is also necessary for the cementing and remodelling of social structures. Quisara in Fletcher's *The Island Princess* also 'turns, for millions . . . For a ton of crowns she turns' but in the direction of Christianity, and her to-be-husband Armusia, and away from other men, including a Moorish priest who incites her to rebel against the Portuguese. Desdemona's fairness depends upon her fidelity: when suspected of being a whore, she is as 'begrimed' as Othello's face. Quisara's beauty depends upon her religious faith: when she asks Armusia to convert to her religion, she spirals down from goddess to whore – her perfect beauty 'looks ugly now methinks'. Of course, once she declares her intention to convert to Christianity, she recovers her status as a 'blessed lady'.[57]

The changeability of women is thus both a threat and a promise. Their ability to adopt alien cultures is crucial to their value as currency that secures patriarchal alliances, just as it threatens the security of cultural borders. Foreign queens were an integral part of European feudal courts and their trans-national alliances. They brought along a different culture and would, if not properly assimilated, breed 'alien heirs'. Hence they spelt 'the danger of cultural alienation'.[58] But at the same time, as Louise Fradenburg astutely points out,

> being liminal figures – such as the wild people also were – queens could be identified with 'land', 'people', 'nation', their liminality serving the very principle of identity – of the invulnerability rather than the vulnerability of the body of the realm. Queens themselves, then, are talismanic; they are a potential threat – a foreign body let in through open and even decorated gates, capable of causing internal torment – turned into an aegis of protection, a banner under which to ride against the enemy . . .[59]

The changeability, 'turnability' of the queen is thus central to her symbolic role. The ability to transform the queen from a foreign to a talismanic figure testifies to the power of the king, and assures 'the well-being of the whole body of the realm'. Fradenburg recalls the powerful connections between queen, wife and land encoded in James I's famous marriage metaphor ('I am the Husband, and all the whole Isle is my lawful Wife') and suggests that James's tournaments in Scotland featuring the black lady can thus be seen as representing the power of the sovereign to transform the land and his subjects.

However, rather than testify only to the power of the singular monarch, the romance of the foreign queen in English theatre also negotiates some of the wider national, religious, cultural and economic anxieties of the period. I have discussed how such gendered play underlines the power of colour differentiation while attempting to contain, and even invert, the meaning of Islamic or Jewish alterity. But the significance of female, especially queenly, conversion or assimilation is not limited to religious otherness. The exchange of women has always signalled the vulnerability of cultural borders. This exchange took on new urgent meanings in an early modern England which was simultaneously looking outward and consolidating its national culture in linguistic, religious and ethnic terms.

The disorderliness of figures such as Hippolyta, Tamora, Cleopatra and even Titania, and the necessity of their assimilation into the culture of their husbands, can be set against this pattern. In *The Two Noble Kinsmen*, Hippolyta's transformation from a fighting to a domesticated Amazon is described thus:

Most dreaded Amazonian, that hast slain
The scythe-tusked boar, that with thy arm, as strong
As it is white, wast near to make the male
To thy sex captive, but that this, thy lord –
[. . .] shrunk thee into
The bound thou wast o'erflowing, at once subduing
Thy force and thy affection

(1.1.78–85)

Unlike Hippolyta, Tamora, the Queen of the Goths in *Titus Andronicus*, and Cleopatra the Queen of Egypt resist such shrinking with varying degrees of success. Cleopatra's tawny skin as well as her political ambitions highlight a tension between her 'force' and her 'affection', whereas Tamora's liaison with the black Aaron problematizes her 'incorporation' in Rome. The convertible body of women is thus the 'delicious traffick' between cultures, religions and races.[60] On the stage, it provides a recurrent fantasy of exchange and mastery, while underlining the religious as well as somatic notions of alterity in the early modern period.

First published in *Shakespeare Survey 52*, 1999, with the title ' "Delicious Traffick": Alterity and Exchange on Early Modern Stages'.

NOTES

1 Robert Miles, *Racism* (London, 1989), p. 71.
2 Emily Bartels, '*Othello* and Africa: Postcolonialism Reconsidered', *The William and Mary Quarterly*, 3rd series, 54.1 (January 1997), 45–64. See also Lynda E. Boose, ' "The Getting of a Lawful Race": Racial Discourse in Early Modern England and the Unrepresentable Black Woman', in *Women, 'Race', and Writing in the Early Modern Period*, ed. Margo Hendricks and Patricia Parker (London and New York, 1994), pp. 35–54.
3 Ania Loomba, 'Shakespeare and Cultural Difference', in *Alternative Shakespeares 2*, ed. Terence Hawkes (London and New York, 1996), pp. 164–91.
4 Daniel J. Vitkus, 'Turning Turk in *Othello*: the Conversion and Damnation of the Moor', *Shakespeare Quarterly* 48 (1997), 145–76; p. 146. For other revisionist views of the Renaissance world picture see Shankar Raman, 'Looking East: "India" and the Renaissance', PhD thesis, Stanford University (1994); Julia Reinhard Lupton, '*Othello* Circumcised: Shakespeare and the Pauline Discourse of Nations', *Representations* 57 (1997), 73–89; Jerry Brotton, *Trading Territories, Mapping the Early Modern World* (London, 1997) and ' "This Tunis, Sir, Was Carthage": Contesting Colonialism in *The Tempest*' in *Postcolonial Shakespeares*, ed. Ania Loomba and Martin Orkin

(London and New York, 1998), pp. 23–42, and Jonathan Burton, '"A Most Wily Bird": Leo Africanus, *Othello* and the Trafficking in Difference' in the same volume, pp. 43–63.

5 Loomba, 'Shakespeare and Cultural Difference', pp. 176–7.

6 Lupton, '*Othello* Circumcised'.

7 Beerbohm Tree's assertion that 'Othello was an Oriental, not a Negro: a stately Arab of the best caste' makes it clear that some three centuries later it was the other way around. Quoted by Julie Hankey, ed., *Othello*, Plays in Performance Series (Bristol, 1987), p. 67.

8 Contemporary writers express this connection in a variety of ways: George Sandys claims that the Prophet Mohammed's 'father was a pagan, his mother a Jew both by birth and religion' (*A Relation of a Journey begun Anno Domini 1610*, third edition (London, 1627)), p. 52.

9 Etienne Balibar, 'Is There a Neo-racism?' in Etienne Balibar and Immanuel Wallerstein, *Race, Nation, Class: Ambiguous Identities* (London and New York, 1991), pp. 17–28, esp. p. 23.

10 My usage derives from but is not identical to Stuart Hall's deployment of the term 'articulation' to describe the coexistence of pre-capitalist and capitalist modes of production. Hall emphasizes the dominance of the capitalist mode in that interrelation whereas I want to emphasize greater equivalence between the concepts under discussion. However, like Hall, I want to draw attention to their mutually transformative power. Stuart Hall, 'Race, Articulation and Societies Structured in Dominance', in *Sociological Theories, Race and Colonialism* (Paris, 1980), pp. 305–45.

11 Vitkus, 'Turning Turk in *Othello*', p. 146, n. 4.

12 See, for example, Eldred Jones, *Othello's Countrymen: The African in English Renaissance Drama* (London, 1965) and *The Elizabethan Image of Africa* (Virginia, 1971); George K. Hunter, *Dramatic Identities and Cultural Tradition: Studies in Shakespeare and his Contemporaries* (Liverpool, 1978); Anthony Barthelemy, *Black Face, Maligned Race: The Representation of Blacks in English Drama from Shakespeare to Southerne* (Baton Rouge, 1987); Jack D'Amico, *The Moor in English Renaissance Drama* (Tampa, 1991); John Gillies, *Shakespeare and the Geography of Difference* (Cambridge, 1994) and Kim Hall, *Things of Darkness: Economies of Race and Gender in Early Modern England* (Ithaca, 1995).

13 Roger Bartra, *Wild Men in the Looking Glass: The Mythic Origins of European Otherness* (Ann Arbor, 1994); Richard Bernheimer, *Wild Men in the Middle Ages* (Cambridge, Mass., 1952); Louise Olga Fradenburg, *City, Marriage, Tournament: Arts of Rule in Medieval Scotland* (Madison, 1991).

14 Peter Fryer, *Staying Power* (London, 1984), 7; Miles, *Racism*, pp. 25, 27.

15 Felipe Fernández-Armesto, *Before Columbus: Exploration and Colonization from the Mediterranean to the Atlantic 1229–1492* (Basingstoke and London, 1987), pp. 146–7.

16 Robert Bartlett, *The Making of Europe: Conquest, Colonization and Cultural Change 950–1350* (Princeton, N.J., 1993), pp. 197–9.

17 In England John Foxe's *Actes and Monuments* (published in 1570) used the word 'race' in the context of royal lineage but, according to Ivan Hannaford,

such usage was not a starting-point for a biological understanding of the term because kings could enter and depart from Foxe's 'course' or 'race' depending on the nobility of their actions, and ordinary people could not enter it under any circumstances. It was Jean Bodin's influential treatise *Method for Easy Comprehension of History* (1565) which marked one of the early transitions from a culturalist to a biologist meaning of race by arguing that human characteristics are drawn from nature rather than from variable (and therefore unreliable) social institutions such as religion. Form of the body and colour are two criteria Bodin uses to distinguish between his major groups of human beings – Scythian, German, African and 'Middler' (Ivan Hannaford, *Race: The History of an Idea in the West* (Baltimore and London, 1996), pp. 155–7).

18 Fray Prudencio de Sandoval, *Historia de la vida y hechos del emperador Carlos V* (1604) quoted in Jerome Friedman, 'Jewish Conversion, the Spanish Pure Blood Laws and Reformation: a Revisionist View of Racial and Religious Antisemitism', *Sixteenth Century Journal* 18 (1987), 3–29; pp. 16–17. The same passage is also quoted by Mary Janell Metzger, 'Jessica, *The Merchant of Venice* and Early Modern English Identity', *PMLA* 113: 1 (1998), 52–63; p. 55.

19 John Leo Africanus, *Navigations, Voyages, and Land-Discoveries, with other Historicall Relations of Afrike*, translated by John Pory in Samuel Purchas, ed., *Hakluytus Posthumus or Purchas his Pilgrimes*, vol. v (Glasgow, 1905), p. 340.

20 James Shapiro, *Shakespeare and the Jews* (New York, 1996); Samuel Chew, *The Crescent and the Rose* (New York, 1937).

21 Eric Griffin, 'Un-sainting James: or, *Othello* and the "Spanish Spirits" of Shakespeare's Globe', *Representations* 62 (1998), 52–99.

22 Chew, *Crescent and the Rose*, p. 103.

23 Interestingly, Griffin's understanding of a larger international history of ideas where notions of race and religion travel across national borders directly contradicts Bartels's view where it would seem that the English had no access to the anti-black discourses of Iberia, but again the two arguments converge on the question of English prejudice against blacks.

24 It is true that if, on the one hand, the alterity between Christians and Jews/ Muslims increasingly animated the ideologies of difference in this period then, on the other, the Church itself had, from medieval times, become 'an arena of ethnic competition' (Bartlett, *Making of Europe*, p. 221). Later, the differences between Catholic and Protestant would be complexly mapped on to notions of ethnic, national and religious difference – thus Turks and Roman Catholics are viewed as equivalent by early modern writers such as Richard Knolles. But at the same time, the spectre of the Turk also serves, in a play such as Massinger's *The Renegado* (1621), to allow the differences between English and Italians, Protestant and Catholic, to be bridged and the notion of a composite European, Christian identity to be posited.

25 For early modern conversions see Chew, *Crescent and the Rose*; N. I. Matar, 'The Renegade in English Seventeenth-Century Imagination', *SEL* 33 (1993),

489–505. For thought-provoking discussions about conversion and Judaism in England, see Shapiro, *Shakespeare and the Jews*, and Peter Berek, 'The Jew as Renaissance Man', *Renaissance Quarterly* 51:1 (1998), 128–62.

26 David Nirenberg, *Communities of Violence: Persecution of Minorities in the Middle Ages* (Princeton, N.J., 1996), p. 128.

27 See Andre Hess, *The Forgotten Frontier: A History of the Sixteenth-century Ibero-African Frontier* (Chicago and London, 1978), pp. 151–2.

28 Hess, *Forgotten Frontier*, p. 151. In 1609, anxieties about converted Moors came to a head and Moriscoes were expelled from Spain.

29 John Foxe's *Actes and Monuments* speaks of how Turks killed a converted Jew: 'A Christian Jew'. This is discussed by Shapiro, *Shakespeare and the Jews*, p. 146.

30 Thomas Dallam, *The Diary of Master Thomas Dallam* (1599–1600), reprinted in *Early Voyages and Travels in the Levant*, ed. J. Theodore Bent (London, 1983), p. 79. Also cited by Vitkus, 'Turning Turk', p. 161, n. 62.

31 The word may in turn be connected to the Hindi word 'Amavas' meaning moonless night or dark. According to Martin Bernal, 40–50 per cent of Greek vocabulary comes from the Indo-European group of languages, and 20–25 per cent from Egyptian (*Black Athena: The Afroasiatic Roots of Classical Civilization*, vol. I (New Brunswick, 1987), p. xiv). See also Barthelemy's discussion of the term, *Black Face, Maligned Race*, pp. 7–17.

32 Albert Hourani, *A History of the Arab Peoples* (Cambridge, Mass., 1991), p. 41.

33 'The voyage and travell of M. Caesar Fredericke, Marchant of Venice into the East Indies' in Richard Hakluyt, *The Principal Navigations . . . of the English Nation*, vol. V (Glasgow, 1904), p. 411.

34 Hakluyt, *Principal Navigations*, vol. VI (Glasgow, 1904), p. 167.

35 John Leo, *Navigations, Voyages, and Land-Discoveries, with other Historicall Relations of Afrike*, in Purchas, *Hakluytus Posthumus*, v, 340.

36 Colour, then, is a marker of moral difference: in *A Midsummer Night's Dream*, Lysander spurns Hermia by calling her both an 'Ethiop' and a 'tawny Tartar' (3.2.257, 263). Tartars of course were not tawny at all, but, like the Turks, they acquired connotations of moral and sometimes literal darkness.

37 I am using 'common sense' in the Gramscian sense of combining both everyday life and also earlier ideologies which have sedimented into it. See Errol Lawrence, 'Just Plain Common Sense, the "Roots" of Racism', in Centre for Contemporary Cultural Studies, *The Empire Strikes Back: Race and Racism in 70s Britain* (London, 1982), pp. 47–94.

38 George Best described it thus in his *Discourse* (1578) reproduced in Hakluyt, *Principal Navigations*, VII, 262.

39 5 Eliz. c. 20, 'An act for the further punishment of vagabonds, calling themselves Egyptians', Danby Pickering, *The Statutes at Large*, vol. VI (Cambridge, 1763), pp. 211–12.

40 See A. L. Beir, *Masterless Men* (New York and London, 1985), p. 62.

41 Hess, *Forgotten Frontier*, p. 195.

42 As for the suggestion that the repeated English attempts to trade with Barbary resulted in a romancing of the Moor in England at the time when Shakespeare was writing *Othello*, we must remember that, despite official attempts to suggest commonality of interests between Muslims and Protestants, there was a far more widespread association of Muslims with Roman Catholics:

> If Mahomet, that prophet false,
> Eternetie doe gaine,
> Then shall the pope, and you his sainctes,
> In heaven be sure to raigne.

John Phillips, *A Friendly Larum, Select Poetry Chiefly Devotional of the Reign of Queen Elizabeth*, ed. Edward Farr (Cambridge, 1845), part 2, p. 528.

43 Vitkus, 'Turning Turk'.

44 I am indebted to Nirenberg, *Communities of Violence*, for rich connections between sexuality and conversion in the Middle Ages.

45 *Ibid.*, p. 136.

46 Mahomet the Great, according to Richard Knolles's *The Generall Historie of the Turkes* (second edition, London, 1610), p. 353, and William Painter's *The Palace of Pleasure*, ed. Joseph Jacob (London, 1980), pp. 190−7.

47 *The Plays and Poems of Philip Massinger*, ed. Philip Edwards and Colin Gibson, vol. ii (Oxford, 1976).

48 The Jesuit priest Francis Xavier drew the finest of colour lines while urging the *casados* to marry their local concubines, encouraging the men to abandon the dark ones and even offering to find fair substitutes for them. M. N. Pearson, *The New Cambridge History of India: The Portuguese in India* (Cambridge, 1987), p. 101.

49 The same logic governs, in my opinion, the casting of Denzel Washington as the Duke (Don Pedro) in Kenneth Branagh's film *Much Ado About Nothing*. Despite his high social status (or indeed because of it) the Duke is safe from romantic or sexual involvements; thus blackness is granted a nobility which does not threaten dominant sexual codes.

50 It is a matter of some controversy how Fletcher amalgamated his story from the sources. Gordon McMullan, *The Politics of Unease in the Plays of John Fletcher* (Amherst, 1994) argues that he relied on a French novel by Le Sr de Bellan, *L'Historie du Ruis Dias*, published in 1615, which was based on Argensola's history. Edward Wilson, 'Did John Fletcher read Spanish?', *Philological Quarterly* 27, 11 April 1948, suggests that Fletcher had enough knowledge of Spanish to use Argensola's text.

51 English translation of Argensola, *The Discovery and Conquest of the Molucco and Philippine Islands* (London, 1708), 4.

52 All references to *The Island Princess* are from *The Works of Beaumont and Fletcher*, vol. ii, ed. George Darley (London, 1866). This edition has no line numbers.

53 All references to *The Knight of Malta* are from *The Works of Beaumont and Fletcher*, vol. ii, ed. George Darley (London, 1866). This edition has no line numbers.

54 Since the play rests upon distinctions of women's colour and virtue, at the end of the play Mountferrat is expelled from 'our society, . . . as a rotten, / Corrupted and contagious member'. He is told that since he has 'a Barbary mare of your own; go leap her, and engender young devilings' (5.2). Thus the romance of conversion works more easily with Muslim than black women.

55 Nirenberg, *Communities of Violence*, p. 140.

56 For discussions of the poetry, artifacts and masques, see Kim Hall, *Things of Darkness*; for mayoral pageants, see Barthelemy, *Black Face, Maligned Race* and my Introduction to Middleton's 'The Triumphs of Honour and Virtue' in *The Collected Works of Thomas Middleton*, gen. ed. Gary Taylor (Oxford, forthcoming).

57 Fairness, blessedness and virtue are knotted in these scenarios of exchange. Unsanctioned sex blackens women, as in the Thornton manuscript of *Thomas of Erceldoune*, for example, when Thomas meets a 'lady bryghte' who turns black after he lies with her seven times (quoted in Fradenburg, *City, Marriage, Tournament*, p. 251). In *The Renegado*, Vitelli comments that Donusia has lost her blinding fairness after her sexual contact with him, and Oriana in *The Knight of Malta* claims that she is 'A fragrant flower cropt by another's hand, / My colour sullied, and my odour changed' (5.1).

58 Bartlett, *Making of Europe*, pp. 230–1.

59 Fradenburg, *City, Marriage, Tournament*, p. 252.

60 I am appropriating the phrase 'delicious traffick' from the records of the Grocers' Company where it is used to refer to the sweetmeats which were strewn on London streets during the Mayoral pageants sponsored by the Company. See Baron Heath, *Some Account of the Worshipful Company of Grocers of the City of London* (London, 1869).

Index

Page numbers for illustrations are given in *italics*.